I0626109

Poetry At Its Best

The Best of

Kermit R. Holt

Volume One

Poetry At Its Best

The Best of

Kermit R. Holt

Volume One

Copyright © 2002 by Kermit R. Holt

All Rights Reserved. No part of this book may be reproduced or transmitted in any form or by any means, electronic or mechanical, including photocopying, recording, or by any information storage and retrieval system without permission in writing from the publisher.

Books Academy LLC
112 SW H K Dodgen
Loop, Temple, Texas
76504 Hotline: (254)
800-1189

Ordering Information:
Quantity sales. Special discounts are available on quantity purchases by corporations, associations, and others. For details, contact the publisher at the address above.

Printed in the United States of America

ISBN # 0-8059-5850-9:

Paperback   978-1-964929-75-0

Ebook   978-1-964929-76-9

Library of Congress Control Number: 2024924585

Copyright ©2000 by Kermit R. Holt

All rights reserved. No part of this book may be reproduced in any form or by any electronic or mechanical means, including information storage and retrieval systems, without permission in writing from the author/publisher, except a reviewer who may quote brief passages in a review.

First edition Send
inquiries to;
Kermit R. Holt
121 6th JPV St.
Winter Haven, Florida 33880
or call 863-293-5089

Acknowledgements

I wish to thank all those who have encouraged me throughout the years. A little encouragement can do wonders to make one perform just as a few words of discouragement can kill one's spirit. For two years I wrote no poetry whatsoever due to discouraging comments by some who was very close to me. I wish to highlight the importance of an encouraging word as well as the destructiveness of a discouraging one.

I memorized several such as **Peter: The Big Fisherman** and **Jesus** Part I and presented them in various churches on a "love offering basis. After each presentation many said that they were extremely blessed by the program, however, I got very few opportunities to present other programs.

I know He didn't give me the gift so I could keep the poems in my head. Due to this I am having the book published.

I also have several hundred pages of Bible character autobiographical sketches which I hope to publish in the future.

About the author

The author is a retired Florida Master Teacher who received a BS degree from Florida State University, an MA from the University of South Florida, and an MRE from Southwestern Seminary in Fort Worth, Texas. He retired from teaching in March of 2000 after thirty-plus years of teaching science.

He took early retirement from the United States Department of Agriculture in 2016 as an inspector of fruits and vegetables. He held this job which he worked on a part-time basis for the last twenty-five years he taught.

He was nominated for Poet Laureate for the State of Florida in 1980 and was invited to attend a workshop and receive awards at Reno by Famouospoets.com in September of 2001.

He is published in a book called Teacher's Treasury and in anthologies by Famouspoets.com as well as Church and USDA Newsletters.

Table of Contents

Acknowledgments.............................. 1

Section A- Christian Poetry:

The Rich Man & Lazarus................ 10

Daily Prayer.....................................10

Loss of a Loved One........................11

Just an Ordinary Tree..................... 11

A Place to Come Back To................12

The Brother of the Prodigal Son.......14

A Christian's View of Death............15

Jonah...15

Blood...16

Death...17

Heaven's Scene................................17

The Real Santa................................ 17

Xmas...18

The Solution.....................................18

Hard To Say.....................................18

My Savior & Christmas...................19

Satan-Alive & Well.........................19

God's Unfailing Plan.......................19

Comfort Verse.................................19

Looking Forward to Death..............20

John the Baptist...............................20

The Christian...................................21

Prayer to keep Satan Away............ 21

God's Call.. 21

Peter's Testimony........................... 21

Proof of God.................................... 22

Death of a Christian........................ 22

Seeking Entrance to Heaven.......... 23

Man's Plan Foiled........................... 23

Discipleship.....................................24

Conversion......................................24

Church Attendance..........................24

Bus Ministry...................................25

Jesus' Love......................................25

The Great Commission.................. 26

The Christian Witness.....................26

Christ Knocks..................................26

Christian Service.............................28

Christian Pathway.......................... 29

Parnach..29

Christianity & Discouragement   29

The Devil's Tool............................. 30

When Things Go Wrong............... 30

When The Bubble Bursts...............30

Mountains to Valleys and Back   31

Why Worry......................................31

The Devil At Work......................... 31

The Clouds Of Life........................ 31

Treatment for Stress...................... 32

Rely on God's Word...................... 32

When Death Overtakes Me........... 32

Miracles... 32

The Big Fish.................................. 33

Peter: The Big Fisherman............. 34

Heart Be Troubled Not................. 39

Jesus.. 39

Abraham.. 46

The Innkeeper............................... 51

Dedication Prayer......................... 52

Prayer to Be Worthy..................... 52

My Best.. 52

Sorrow and Death......................... 52

If My People.................................. 53

Time for Everything- A................. 53

No Room at the Inn....................... 53

No God?... 53

Sorrow's Depth.............................. 54

Blessed are They........................... 54

The Good Samaritan Story............ 55

Pentecost....................................... 55

Face to Face with the Devil............ 55

Grief that Overwhelms.................. 56

Spiritual Leader............................. 56

Bi-vocational Pastor...................... 57

Dogging our Footsteps.................. 57

Salvation and Sharing................... 57

Plan of Salvation........................... 58

Temple of the Lord's..................... 59

Influence.. 60

Meeting Needs............................... 60

Improving Ourselves..................... 60

You Were There............................. 60

Let not Your Heart be Troubled. (also see:
"Troubled Heart-Be   Not)......... 61

Fellowship of Christian
Athletes... 61

Victory Over Sin........................... 62

Joy of Salvation............................. 62

He Never Said Life Would be Easy.
.... 63

Triumphal Entry............................ 63

His Will Ignored........................... 64

Easter Message-An........................ 64

Journey of the Wise Men.............. 64

A Proud American......................... 65

Loved One's Death-A 65

Fragile: Human Being................... 66

Unique Individuals........................ 66

Empty Tomb.................................. 66

Leaning On God............................ 67

Christian, Students........................ 67

Treatment of Jesus........................ 69

Paul... 68

A Sinner 81

A Special Tree.............................. 81

Total Commitment......................... 82

A Flock of Birds............................ 82

Cure.. 83

Purpose of Life.............................. 83

Jesus Came To Set Men Free.........84

Savior's Love................................. 84

Christmas Donkey.......................... 85

Angels Unaware............................. 85

Deep Sorrows................................. 85

Jesus Heals.................................... 85

Mission America............................ 87

Rainbow... 87

Resort Missions America............... 87

Home Missions.............................. 88

Jesus, The Promised One............... 90

No Use for Doctors........................ 90

How Much Love?........................... 91

Wise Men Watched........................ 91

Angelic Beings.............................. 92

A Manger....................................... 92

Teacher's Prayer............................. 93

Jonah's Decision............................ 93

Outlooks on Christmas................... 94

Jesus Tomb.................................... 94

The Stable...................................... 95

Star of Bethlehem......................... 95

A Candle....................................... 96

Sheep.. 96

Joseph and Mary........................... 96

Shepherds..................................... 97

Streets of Gold............................. 97

Prayer for Guidance...................... 97

I Love to Tell Christ's Story.......... 97

Take Us Home.............................. 98

Working For the Lord.................... 98

The Courage of Jesus..................... 98

A Wise Man.................................. 98

Why Me?....................................... 99

Rededication Prayer....................... 99

While I Was Yet a Sinner.............. 99

Our Samaria................................. 101

When You Feel Discouraged......... 101

Family and Friends....................... 101

Thy Boundless Love to Me........... 101

Starting a Bus Ministry................. 102

Unequally Yoked.......................... 102

Sin in Our Lives........................... 103

Sunday School.............................. 103

A Spot in the Cemetery................. 103

Atheism.. 104

What Would Jesus Do?................. 104

Treatment of Others...................... 104

The Serpent.....................................105

Nehemiah.......................................105

Troubled Waters............................107

Section B- Animals:

Toad or Frog; The Difference
Between...107

The Brown Pelican........................107

A Snake...107

The Alligator...................................107

The Turtle..107

The Gar..108

The Snowy Egret............................108

The Snail..108

The Sea Gull....................................108

The Greater Egret..........................108

The Pied Billed Grebe...................109

The Spoonbill..................................109

The Kangaroo..................................109

The Red Shouldered Hawk...........109

The Gallinule...................................109

The Black Skimmer........................109

The Swallow-Tailed Kite...............110

Crow - The......................................110

The Spider.......................................110

An Alligator.....................................110

The Anteater....................................110

A Grizzly..110

A Lion..110

Grizzly Bear....................................110

A Guppy...110

Grizzly Looking for a Meal............111

Ant...111

Mankind in the Web of Life...........111

Green Heron....................................111

Anhinga...111

Denning Bears.................................112

Spawning Salmon...........................112

Red Wolf..112

Monkey..112

Section C Environmental Poems:

The Bald Eagle...............................113

The Everglades: Piney Woods......113

The White Pelican..........................113

Christmas Tree...............................114

Everglades Endangered Land.........114

Everglades Story.............................114

God's Handiwork............................116

Step Poem- Grizzlies......................116

This Land Was Ruined by You and Me
....116

My Country is a Mess.....................116

Oh ugliness of Garbage Piles.........117

Everglades-Florida's Treasure.......117

Threat to Tiger Creek...................118

Wetland Heritage.........................119

Crawfish....................................119

Wetlands....................................120

Pothole Power.............................120

Kissimmee.................................120

Dangerous Wastes......................121

A Tree.......................................121

Everglades: Worth Protecting.......121

You're a Grand Old Earth.............122

Recycle......................................122

Section D- Miscellaneous Poetry:

Students....................................123

Hospital Remembrance................123

Santa and His Gifts......................123

Father's Day...............................123

Thanksgiving.............................124

Mother's Day..............................124

Attitudes...................................124

Sorrow......................................125

Evolution...................................125

A Writer's Life............................125

Requirements of a Writer.............126

Rudolph.....................................126

Leaves......................................127

The Storm..................................127

The Sun.....................................127

A Reefer....................................127

Summer and Winter.....................127

Santa..127

Wrong Dive................................127

Forest.......................................128

A Science Student........................128

Lab Student................................128

Handwriting...............................128

Teenager...................................128

Metamorphosis...........................128

Fish..128

Ferocity....................................128

Paperback..................................128

Embryo.....................................128

Molecules..................................129

Airplanes...................................129

Anger.......................................129

Loneliness.................................129

Snowflakes................................129

Moon And Sun............................129

Mountains..................................129

Teachers...................................129

Ocean's Edge..............................130

Thunderstorm.............................. 130
Gossip...................................... 130
Retirement................................. 130
The Decision.............................. 130
A New Baby............................... 131
Turkey Day................................ 131
Verse for a Wedding Card............ 131
Juice Lab................................... 131
Gifts for a Promotion................... 131
Thoughts About Getting Older......132
Fellowship.................................. 132
Snow Outside My Window.......... 133
The Tree in my Yard................... 133
Hungry Sparrow.......................... 133
Book... 133
A Falling Star............................. 134
Wind Through the Trees.............. 134
Time to Retire............................ 134
When You Look in the Mirror...... 134
Its a Girl.................................... 135
Nobody Special.......................... 135
Inspector................................... 135
Evaluation Day........................... 135
Halloween Night......................... 136
Tenth Anniversary...................... 136
Disappearing Pencil..................... 136
Rainbow Rope............................ 136

Lightning................................... 137
Promises.................................... 137
Dog.. 138
A Gossip................................... 138
An Unkind Word......................... 138
Rumor....................................... 138
Water.. 138
Retirement Activities................... 138
Life in the Lab............................ 139
Victim....................................... 139
Daughter.................................... 139
Friends and Family...................... 140
Inner Motivation......................... 140
A Snowman................................ 141
The Wreath................................ 141
Elves... 142
Straw.. 142
Santa Claus................................ 143
Reindeer.................................... 143
Santa Filling the Stockings........... 143
Mistletoe................................... 144
Dorothy..................................... 144
Three Bears................................ 144
A Drug...................................... 145
A Christmas Wish to the School.
.... 145
Student Success.......................... 145

Senior Citizens................................146

Land of Hershey............................146

Communication.............................146

A Notorious Liar............................147

Work...148

Gossiping.......................................148

Work Ethic.....................................148

The Adventures of Gaw.................148

Once I Was a Child........................149

Skunks..149

Work Ethic (Ideal)........................150

Fall Leaves....................................150

One Day Too Long.......................150

Friendship.....................................151

A Friend..151

Friend or Foe................................152

Seasonal Changes.........................152

Snow Showers...............................153

A Snowflake..................................153

Section E- The Bible:

Love I Corinthians 13...................153

Acts...153

Psalm 104.....................................155

The Book Of Matthew..................155

Matthew 26:1-51 (Alternate reading)

....193

Genesis 1-15(Alternate reading)....198

Matthew 3(Alternate reading)..........205

Philippians 4:4-9............................205

Philippians 4:8 (Two versions).........206

Philippians 4:9...............................206

John 1:1-2:24.................................206

Luke 19:2-10..................................210

Romans 1: 1-13.............................210

Romans 1: 10-2 13........................210

I Timothy 1:16:21..........................212

II Timothy 1-4...............................218

Miracles(John 2:1-10))...................222

Luke 1:1-55...................................222

Matthew 16:1-25:46......................224

Mark 1:1-4:29...............................241

Mark 4:1-14..................................247

Psalm 120.....................................248

The Rich Man & Lazarus

A rich man dressed in purple fared
sumptuously every day
While a beggar whose name was Lazarus at
his gate did lay.
He was covered with sores from the lack
of proper food. The crumbs from the rich
man's table would greatly improve his
mood. The crumbs, indeed, were many
but Lazarus was denied.
Dogs came to lick his wounds and finally
Lazarus died, Angels came and picked him
up and took him to Abraham While the
rich man continued to feast on bread, and
meat, and jam.
The rich man also died. His funeral was
rich and swell. The angels did not claim
him so he went instead to Hell.
He lifted his eyes and saw Lazarus with
Abraham so content. He was now the lowly
beggar instead of a pompous gent. He
prayed for a drop of water to cool his
tormented tongue. Abraham said, "You
reap what you sow. Your torment has just
begun." In your lifetime you had good
things while Lazarus went without.
Its fitting and proper he should receive while
you view him and shout.
You had your chance at compassion and
failed though you had much. So I will not
send Lazarus to you with a comforting
touch. I could not send him if I would. The
gulf between us is wide. He cannot come to
you and you can't come to our side. The
rich man said, "I pray thee, Send him to my
father's home To show my five brothers the
penalty if they don't cease to roam.
Abraham said, "No, my lad.

The prophets have shown the way. If your
brothers don't listen to them they, too, will
have to pay.

DAILY PRAYER

Dear Lord, We beg for mercy as we bow
our heads to pray. We ask you to be with
us throughout each passing day. We ask
forgiveness for the sins which we have
thus committed That we might, through
your mercy. from evil be remitted.
We ask that you might make a way to
witness through our deeds That others
might come to know you and let you fill
their needs. We ask that you will be with
us as we travel on our way. Give us
strength to do thy will as we struggle
through each day.
Dear Lord we need your guidance for every
move we make. We need guidance for our
footsteps through every step we take. We
ask that you will form our lips
for all the words they make. We need
guidance for our footsteps through every
step we take For we are known as
Christians and every wrong word used Is
a reason for the heathen from church to
be excused. They watch for every wrong
we do so they can point and say, "He's
supposed to be a Christian. He shouldn't
act that way."
Lord, Help us to be mindful of every gift
you bring. Help us to be so thankful that
your praises we might sing. We are quick
to take thy gifts and then to run away and
hide. Help us to be so grateful we put
away our pride;

10

To give thanks when we receive thy gifts,
when you supply our need. Help us to be
so thankful we put away our greed; For,
too often, after blessings, we have no
thanks to raise; But come with more
requests of thee and never offer praise.
Lord, Please forgive our sins for we are
very weak. Help us do better every day.
each year, each month, each week. Help us
to witness everywhere and tell others of thy
love. Keep us strong and make us ready for
thy service up above. Help us resist
temptation whenever it appears.
Convict us when we yield to it. Bring us to
our knees in tears. Now that I've poured out
my heart to you this very day Help me to
come more often to thy throne, and kneel,
and pray.

The Loss of a Loved One

To be absent from the body is to be
present with the Lord. When loved ones
die, however, we question God's accord.
We know the Christian who has passed is
better off than we For from sorrow, pain,
and worry he has been set free.
We sorrow not for him but for those he left
behind For we must try to find a way to
calm our troubled mind. When someone we
love is taken we should go to Jesus' word.
The comfort his word brings is worth all we
can afford.
God's word speaks to those in need and
tells them what to do. The assurance found
there brings comfort through and through.
Rest assured the dead in Christ are where
there is no sorrow. We also know, as
Christians, we'll join him on the morrow.

When we pass from this old world we
know that he'll be there. With open arms
he'll welcome us to the joys we'll all share.

Just an Ordinary Tree

I was just an ordinary nut. Just the same as
a million others. I fell to the ground and
sprouted and grew just like my brothers. I
was a fine, healthy specimen but nothing
real outstanding. When loggers came to
cut some trees. I wished them happy
landing. I stood beside the roadside. I grew
quite tall and strong. When men suggested
cutting me others said, "You're wrong!"
The people passing by all talked about a
stranger They said God's Son was born and
they placed him in a manger. Then I heard
about a plot to take the baby's life.
His father took the baby and passed me
with his wife. The years came and went. I
heard a lot of talk.
It seemed to me his teachings were founded
on the rock.
But then I heard the news they were to
crucify this man And though I'd never met
him I had become his fan. I was saddened
by the news and then the loggers came To
choose a very special tree.
I heard them call my name. They
pointed to my branches. I held my
arms out straight. They started
chopping at my trunk as they
discussed my fate. They said that I
would make a cross to hang the
stranger on.
They called him, "King of the Jews." He
said he was God's Son.

I knew which man they talked about. I felt real bad, "You see."
I wished that I could run away. yet I was but a tree.
They cut and carved on me. They shaped me like a cross. Some didn't want to do it, but they obeyed their boss.
When they were finally finished they brought this man to me. They placed him against Barabbas then set Barabbas free.
They put me on his shoulder. His touch was good and kind. I knew that he was sad but he never ever whined. He grew so weak and tired he fell beneath my load.
I wished that I was lighter as he stumbled down the road. A man called Simon came along. They made him bear my weight.
They put me in the ground. Their faces filled with hate. they hung God's Son upon me. I wished to hit the ground, But I could not manage it. My wood was strong and sound. After they removed him off to his tomb they started. They could not tell you how I felt, but I was broken hearted. I stood there on that hilltop. A pain shot through my heart. I had met the Son of God. In his death I had a part.
I watched the people come and go to the tomb where he was placed. Some came to mourn his passing as tears down faces raced. Soldiers guarded the entrance which was sealed with a stone. They watched it day and night so it never stood alone. After the Sabbath had passed, early the next day Two Mary's passed by me as they walked along their way. As they encountered the tomb they found an open door, An Angel seated on the stone who snow white garments wore.

The soldiers were badly shaken as they looked into the glare. The Mary's looked for Jesus but found he wasn't there. He had risen from the dead. The angel said they'd see. They went to his disciples and joyously passed by me.
I didn't feel quite so badly for the act which I had done
And I rejoiced with them and the victory of god's Son.
I saw it now as a part of God's own holy plan
To defeat the cunning devil and forgive the sins of man.
I didn't feel quite so badly for the act which I had done
For on this Easter morning redemption had begun.

A Place To Come Back To

I know you've all heard of the Prodigal Son; of the riches he had and the things he had done. How, one day to his father, he said. "I can't wait. This day I demand my part of the estate."
His father said, "Yes. You may have it, you know."So he packed his belongings and off he did go. Why! The places he went and the things he had done. All he did was throw parties and dance and have fun; But the day finally came when his money ran out. A famine had struck along with a drought. He was hired by a farmer to take food to the swine. The food looked so tasty he thought he might dine. Then his thought went to home where he knew there was food. The food of the hired man

would be good for his mood. So he went to his father and said, "I have sinned. The name of a fool on my robe should be pinned." But his father demanded they prepare a big feast. They brought the best robe and killed the best beast. The boy thought there should be something more he could do; but agreed that his home was a good place to come to. Now we are all like this prodigal boy for we like to be happy and filled with much joy. Perhaps our opportunities have not been so great. Our sin might be going and staying out late; but we know that we wander away from our God; from the teachings of Christ; from the path that he trod Then like the one known as the Prodigal Son we must humble ourselves and come on the run Back to our churches with only one plea "Dear God, I'm a sinner. Please forgive me.

The church is one family united in love which is the gift of God which is sent from above. They'll welcome you back with a wide open arm for they wish to help and never to harm. They long for all Christians to return to the fold. With Christ as our shepherd we can be bold For He's promised to keep us safe in His hand. He'll lead all who follow to the promised land.

If you've been offended for some reason or other its been done from outside and not by a brother For like the brother of the Prodigal Son there are some who will gossip just to have fun. If they belong to Christ, our Lord, they'll welcome you back with no unkind word.

People blame the church when they get offended. They claim that their church life has been ended. If the way they feel they'll analyze they'll probably find that they haven't been wise. They'll realize that the church. they have judged by a few who are stubborn and refuse to be budged Or perhaps they have said, "If they let him in I'll never return for he's done great sin." Who are they hurting with actions like this? They're hurting themselves for a blessing they'll miss. Christ came to earth to save people from sin. If we don't speak to sinners then who can we win?

We are all sinners. If this we denied we'd not be Christians. We'd say Christ lied. If you've left the church due to one or a few you'll find its a good place to come back to. If everyone in church was without wrong we wouldn't need the sermon or song. The church is a place we should all come. to strengthen each other, not to have fun. We have all sinned. That's why Christ came. He will redeem all who trust in his name.

If you're discouraged and far from the Lord come to church for strength from His word. Encourage each other, be much in prayer. Come back to church, find comfort there.

There may be some that the devil has sent. Pray for these people is what Jesus meant. Love your enemies, those who do wrong. Then leave later with a heart full of song."

Now if you have strayed away from the flock you must come back to God, the solid rock. You will discover there's much work to do.

Church is a good place to come back to. Angels will rejoice and friends will too. You'll be happier with a heart that is new.

You'll have a brand new family. Desires will change and become Heavenly. Because of what you have realized you'll follow up and be baptized; be so thankful for freedom from sin and tell all that you're changed within.

Your views will change for the better and you'll soon find out
its great to know that Heaven's in your future without doubt.

You'll rest easier and your family will too for they'll notice a change in what you do. You'll be a new creature, better than ever. All will be new. Old habits you'll sever.

The Brother of The Prodigal Son

The prodigal son is widely known, of his brother we seldom hear.

Though apparently obedient at home he's just as bad, we fear.

His temptations were different. He was very sly.
He stayed around his home waiting for dad to die.
He worked in the fields and helped to build wealth.
When younger brother returned he cared not for his health.
He heard the celebration. His slave told what it meant.
He said, "Your brother returned, now they make merriment.
Because he has arrived and he's safe and sound
They killed the fatted calf and now gather around." Older brother was angry and he wouldn't go in.
His father talked to him but he was filled with sin.
He answered saying, "Father, I've served thee many years.
I've done what you've asked though it sometimes caused tears.
All my life I've served you.. Your wish was my command.
You never let me have a goat or come to give a hand.
Now, for your wayward son who caused you much grief
You've killed the fatted calf.
This is beyond belief." His father said, "My son.
You've had pleasures wealth brings.
You've got keys to my doors.
You've enjoyed many things.
You have been around, but I thought he

14

was dead.
Now he has been found.
Don't let this go to your head. Don't sit
up here and brood.
Come and celebrate.
Your brother's come home. Don't
be filled with hate."
As far as we're told older
brother didn't heed.
His life was filled with misery and also with
greed.

A Christian's View of Death

I stand, gazing into the future staring
beyond the grave.
One should approach his coffin not
cowardly, but brave.
He is much like a caterpillar, spinning his
cocoon.
As he enters he appears dead but emerges
very soon.
He emerges not in his ugly form but as a
beautiful butterfly
And so it is with Christians as soon as they
shall die.
Their body rests in the grave.
Their soul gets heavenly garb. Oh
grave! Where is thy victory?
Death, where is thy barb?
Those behind might fear death, The
unsaved rightly so.
Christians should never worry for
they are prepared to go.
They'll travel from this sinful world in the
twinkling of an eye.
To the shore where Jesus is; to the Rapture
in the sky.

When you think of a reunion that will be
the best of all.
All the saved will gather round in the
great reunion hall.
Death is not an end of life, a climax to be
feared.
It's the beginning of a new life. To
Christians it's endeared.
When we die we enter
into a life with no more trouble.
We go to face eternal life where joys will
more than double.
When I die you can celebrate. I don't
want for you to sorrow.
Wear a happy face instead.
For I'll join you on the morrow.
I'm not dead and gone but really have
just been born.
I'll go when I hear the sound of
Gabriel's mighty horn.
The joys of Heaven can't be numbered
No sin is there to weight us down.
Each soul is unencumbered.
The street of gold are gorgeous.
The jasper walls are grand.
But the biggest joy I'll ever know is to
shake the Savior's hand.

Jonah

Jonah heard the call of God. The
command was very clear; But
Jonah fled to Tarshish.
Ninevah he'd not go near. He
boarded a boat in Joppa. He got
on and paid the fair.
If he left the country quickly he'd leave God
right there.
A storm tossed the ship. All

15

the sailors were afraid.
They tossed baggage overboard then
found where Jonah laid.
They asked, "How can you sleep?
Arise and call your God."
They cast lots to determine fault and Jonah
got the nod.
They asked, "Why did you run? What
should we do with thee?" Jonah said,
"Do what you must. Cast me into the
sea."
They didn't want to do it. They
tried to ride the storm.
When they found it useless they
dragged him from his dorm.
They lifted Jonah up and
threw him into the sea.
The storm abated instantly and
was as calm as it could be.
Now the Lord prepared a fish to
gobble Jonah up.
Three days and nights he was inside with
no breakfast, lunch, or sup Then Jonah
prayed to God
saying, "I tried to hide from thee.
Now I know I cannot find
a place where you won't be." He
was delivered on that day.
When he said, "Thy will be done." The
mighty fish coughed him up on dry land
with trees and sun.
Again the Lord said, "Jonah. Go! To
Ninevah and preach my word."
Jonah went there and preached the
message of the Lord.
He warned the people to repent or
prepare to meet their doom."
The people repented everywhere in
every street and room.

God saw that they repented turning from
their evil way.
He said they would be spared. This
was their greatest day.
Jonah was very angry because his
prejudice was great.
He wanted them destroyed for it should
be their fate.
"Lord, if you won't take them, kill me, I pray,
Instead.
"Doest thou well to be angry?" That
was all God said.
Jonah left the city
He sat down to watch it die.
He built a brushy shelter to hide the
brightness of the sky.
A vine grew up and shaded him and he was
very glad.
A worm bored through the stem making
Jonah very sad.
God said, "You've shown pity on the
vine with no soul
Yet you have judged my people. You'd
have them miss their goal. Your
priorities are wrong, Jonah, I'll not
destroy the city.
They've hearkened to my word.
Now I'll return them pity.

Blood

To some a fountain filled with blood
might seem a little gory.
To me it tells of Jesus' love. It tells the old,
old, story
for without the shedding of pure blood no
remission can be made.

Because my Savior shed his blood my
ransom has been paid.
The blood can't be ignored, you see.
It must never be left out. If
you forget this saving act Your
salvation is in doubt.

Death

We know this Christian loved one's death
will grieve us through and through; But
we also know he'd wish for us to do as
Christ would do.
He'd want us to proclaim to all the
message of God's love
for the only way he'll see us now is
for us to come above.
Though death can bring no comfort to
loved ones left behind
those who trust in Jesus will search His
Word and find some comfort from His
teachings; some joy in midst of sorrow; for
we know we'll be united in Heaven on the
morrow.
Though our souls still yearn for comfort
from this void left in our heart This comfort
comes from knowing that in Heaven we'll
never part.

Heaven's Scene

If we could gaze on Heaven's scene way
up in the sky
We'd be unhappy all day long wishing we
would die.
God was right to not let man see beyond the
gate
For if we could we'd want to go so bad we

couldn't wait.
He wanted us to live our lives and
witness to the lost
To put our trust in him, you see, for
he has paid the cost.
If we only knew what was in store for
those whom he did save
We'd want to pack and leave right now to
travel past the grave.

The Real Santa

Santa Claus comes on
Christmas Eve.
Nobody knows what he
has up his sleeve.
When they are finally all snug in their beds
with dreams of Santa
Claus filling their
heads
He comes and fills all
the stockings full
with toys you push and toys you pull;
With
mechanical toys and dogs and cats; with
purple fruit and
decorative hats;
And when he has filled all the stockings,
you see, he goes and puts presents in under
the tree. Now, maybe you feel he has
nothing for you because some people say
that Santa's not true.
If you'll stop and think about what God has
done; he sent us a Santa in the form of his
son.

17

XMAS

Some people would put Xmas
for our blessed Christmas day.
They'd take Christ out of Christmas.
For them we should all pray
why have the celebration
With all the pomp involved
And omit the central figure
for which it has revolved?
To do so would be foolish.
Yes. It would be absurd.
Like the buying of a birdcage
with no intent to get a bird.

The Solution

Ifmy people called by my name
shall humble themselves and
pray
And turn from their wieked
ways.
I'll not turn them away.
I will Answer all their prayers,
heal their sick and care for
them.
Ill guard them and protect them
like they were a precious gem.
If they do things as they should
T'll even heal their land.
Crops will grow and flourish
even in the poorest sand.
Those who listen and obey
will be blessed at every turn.
[They can't out give the Lord.
This lesson they will learn.

Hard to Say

Love is sometimes hard to say.
Often its never said.
Often when it does slip out
both parties turn bright red.
The meaning's sometimes misconstrued
by those with an evil mind.
Their rumors cannot be ignored
because they put you in a bind.
I am a little hesitant
to use that little word.
The word that some would like to hear
and others think absurd.
If I fail to say, "I love you."
I hope you'll understand.
Sometimes the words won't come
so I simply shake your hand.

My Savior and Christmas

Christmas is the time
of my Savior's birth
when God let his son
come down to earth.
He came down to earth
to set men free.
He came in the likeness
of you and me.
He lived on the earth
for thirty three years.
He died on the cross
in the midst of sneers.
He put up with punishment,
ridicule and scorn
and he rose on the third day,
just about morn.
Now he sits with his father way
up above
while he waits for the ones he
saved by his love.

Satan-Alive and Well

The devil is alive and well.
Over humans he has cast a spell.
The one who follow his behavior
will wish they had met the Savior

and Jesus they don't try to please.
If they die, believing never,
they must suffer and burn forever.
The choice is which road to take.
Eternity is what's at stake.
If they travel with the crowd
a flaming pit will be their shroud,
But if they choose the narrow road
Heaven will then be their abode.

They already know which road to take.
An attractive trap the devil will make.
He knows which sin they can't resist.
This temptation will head the list.
For once they put Christ aside
he'll double efforts to get their hide.

God's Unfailing Plan

They followed a great and distant star
guided by faith from lands afar.
They came expecting to see a king
so worthy presents they did bring.

As they approached they heard a plot
to kill the Savior whom they sought.
It was revealed to one in three
that they should pack their things and flee.
Sorrow awaited all who'd stay.

So, therefore, they should not delay. They
left the city that same night with the Holy
family as their light.
Herod had the young all killed and soon
the land was sorrow filled.
Man could not foil God's wondrous plan
To send his son to redeem man.

Comfort verse

(I Thessalonians 4:14-17 & I Peter 1:6-7)
These verses have
often helped me.
I hope they'll
help you too
For friends as good
and kind as
you are far
apart and few.
I pray that in
your sorrow
God will comfort
one and all.
If I can help
in any way
please feel free to call.

19

Looking Forward To Death

When my eyes shall close
and doctors pronounce me dead
that'll be the day I've waited for
not one that I dread.
It will mean I'll be at rest
with Jesus Christ, my Lord.
The joys of heaven will be mine
with the one I have adored.
Jesus gave his precious blood.
He paid the entire price.
No other being could do that
but his grace will suffice.
Do not mourn my passing
and do not weep or cry.
Live so you'll join me in heaven
when it comes your time to die.
You'll never see me here again.
Don't be distraught
It'll do no good to mourn.
If you want to see me
make sure that you have been born twice
You've all been born the first time. This
isn't what I mean
You must put your trust in Jesus
who can make you clean.
He'll take the fear from death
and the fear of its coming.
When your time approaches
you'll hear the angels humming. You'll
say, "Dear Lord, Come quickly for I
can't hardly wait.
I've grown a bit impatient
to get inside the gate.

John the Baptist

A wilderness voice proclaimed,
"The kingdom is at hand."
Repent of your sins, be baptized. The
Savior will be in our land. This
fulfilled Isaiah's prophecy
of the pleading wilderness voice
Saying, "Prepare God's way.
If you do you will rejoice."
The voice of John the Baptist.
He was dressed in camel's hair. His
food was locusts and honey but he
really didn't care.
Not concerned with how he looked or
with what he ate, you see
His message was of the Savior who
was sent for you and me. Preaching
in Jerusalem and Judea and in the
regions round about
He baptized in the Jordan.
Relief made them want to shout. The
Pharisees and Sadducees came the
baptism to receive.
John said, "You generation of vipers.
You can't till you believe."
He said, "If you are truly saved you'll
bear some worthy fruit
But trees which do not bear
will have the ax laid to the root.
They'll be cast out today
into the midst of the fire.
I baptize now with water.
There comes one who is higher.
There comes one greater than I. I'm
not worthy to lace his shoes. He'll
baptize with the Holy Ghost. With
him you'll never lose.
Then Jesus came from Galilee
to be baptized by Brother John.
John said, "You should baptize me
for I am but a pawn.
Jesus had this to say,

I need you to baptize me.
When John had baptized Jesus
he said, "God has set you free."
God's Spirit descended like a dove
saying, "Your mind will now be eased.
For this is my beloved Son
in whom I am well pleased."

The Christian

People gathered at the Church
as the message was proclaimed.
A silence fell and each one felt
that Christ had called his name.
The message rang out loud and clear
when our lives ran through the test
We found there was no person there who
could say, "I've done my best."
As each examined his own life
he soon was made to know
If he had done his very best
the room would overflow.
One person burning out for Christ would
draw crowds from far away.
We need this fire in all our lives
to be with us all to stay.

Prayer to Keep Satan Away

Dear Heavenly Father, Lord, we pray.
Help us be worthy of thee today.
Help us to keep away from sin
and to witness to those you'd have us win.
If we do not do thy will
Satan will move in for the kill.
He charges in when defense is down
to take you to the sinful side of town.
He'll get you down and keep you there.
He'll teach you to lie and also to swear.
The Devil's alive and doing quite well.

He'll drag you to the depths of Hell.
Satan can't stand the Living Word
or the voice of Jesus who is my Lord.

God's Call

As Christians we will hear God's call
We'll hear it and obey.
We'll listen carefully right now. We'll
hear his call today.
We will know what his will shall be.
We'll hear it loud and clear.
We'll know what he has for us to do.
We'll never have to fear.

Peter's Testimony

I denied my Savior three times
just like He said I would.
I told Him I'd never leave Him.
I'd be brave. I knew I could.
He said, "Before the cock shall crow ye
shall deny me thrice."
I said I'd follow Him to death
if that should be the price.
They came and took him away
and I was left behind.
I thought to follow him
for He was always kind.
Someone pointed to me and said,
"That man was with Him too."
I looked behind me quickly
and asked the question, "Who?"
They pointed in my direction
saying, "You were His fan."
I said, "I never knew Him.
I wasn't with that man.
"It got a little colder.
I crept nearer to the fire.

To get closer to Jesus was my goal. It
was my heart's desire.
One of them looked my way and said,
"He followed Him, I know."
I swore I'd never known Him
then I heard the rooster crow.
His words echoed back to me
as fear gripped my heart.
I said, "If you'll forgive me,
from you I'll never part."

Proof of God

People claim they don't know God.
They say he's passed away.
Other say that if he's there
he doesn't listen when we pray.
To prove their point they often say,
"If he is there at all
We should know his dimensions,
whether he is short or tall."
They say, "If we can't touch him
or see him. He's not there."
Many touch and see Him, though
while on their knees in prayer.
He is very real to us.
To us He means so much,
We know He's real and living because
we've felt His touch

Death of a Christian

When life on earth is over,
when eyes are closed in death,
This body will be useless.
It's taken its last breath.
For a Christian its a time
to rejoice and be with God,

The soul will go to its reward
before the head can nod.
Death is not a closing door
which should be greatly feared,
But the opening of a door instead
through which we've never peered. Its a
door through which the saved pass. It is
closed to every other.
When death shall come to us we'll join
our Christian sister and our brother. Its
not a time for sorrow
for those who enter in
But for loved ones left behind
there's no room for joy within.
We don't think of all the glories
in store for those of God.
We just see our loved ones lowered and
placed beneath the sod.
Our hearts are heavy as we think
of the void left in our lives.
Our hearts are pierced as if by
the sharpest of our knives.
We view the rocky road ahead without
this one we love.
We don't see God's love descending like
a gentle, peaceful dove.
These words our God has left with us,
"I'll not leave you comfortless.
If you'll put your trust in me
then I will give you success.
Success to overcome your sorrow,
to cheer you up indeed.
I'll be right here for you to call
whenever there's a need.
You can be assured that when you pray
I'll hear each word you utter.
I'll be here when you need me.
Your heart need never flutter.
So, put your trust in me.
Find a place of constant rest
For each day with me you'll find

that you'll be greatly blessed.

Seeking Entrance to Heaven

I approached slowly the gates of pearls.
My hair had lost all hint of curls.
As I got closer I heard someone sing.
"What rich treasure do you bring?"
I said, "I have no riches now.
I come unworthy and humbly bow."
Then said the voice, "What have you done?
To entitle you to see the Son?"
I said, "I have done nothing great.
I guess I shouldn't approach the gate."
But then the voice said, "Don't leave yet.
You have done some great thing, I bet."
I just said, "No." and shook my head.
"I'm at the wrong gate is what I dread."
The voice said, "What did you do on earth?"
I said, "I trusted in Jesus lowly birth.
I followed Him and did my best;
to win others to Him; to end their quest.
I guess those things were not enough
to enter in for the way is tough.
In my hand no price I bring
so I'm unworthy to see the king."
I turned and started to walk away
when I heard the voice behind me say,
"Well done my good and faithful lad.
Come in for you look very sad.
Riches won't help you to get in here.
You replied correctly through your fear.
I told you to follow at my call
forsaking all like John and Paul.
Come in for you have passed the test.
in my opinion you've done your best.
I walked through the gates now very bold. I
found the streets were made of gold.
The walls of jasper made quite a sight
and the lamb of God was the light.
No night existed in this land
and we all stood at His right hand.
There were no tears in people's eyes
for there never again will be goodbyes. No
heartaches were found in anyone. They
were all removed by God's Son.
All had been saved by his grace
and now we saw Him face to face.
All calenders were in the past
for time up here would last and last.
I talked with Peter, John, and Paul, Stephen
and Daniel, to one and all.
I had a mansion of my own
with no payments to make on a loan.
The most precious thing in this land was the
privilege to shake the Master's hand, To
sing His praises forevermore
and to listen to what He had in store.
We sang praises of what He did for us and
not one ever took time to fuss.
All here was joy forevermore
and none was ever known as poor.

Man's Plan Foiled

No room for Him was at the inn for
the one who could save mankind from sin.
The only place that could be found
was a stable with animals all around.
At His birth a brilliant star appeared
and angels came whom shepherds feared.
They said, "Fear not! We have good news,
A babe's been born whom God did choose."
I'll be here when you need me.
Your heart need never flutter.
So, put your trust in me.
Find a place of constant rest

For each day with me you'll find
that you'll be greatly blessed.

Wise men followed the star and found
a young child playing on the ground.
Rich gifts they offered for they were
wise. The king sought Jesus by disguise.
The wise men went another way instead
for they learned that he wanted Jesus
dead. Joseph and Mary to Egypt moved.
This was God's plan. It was later proved.
Herod had all the children killed
and all the land was terror filled
But all the efforts of mere man
could not foil God's unfailing plan.

Discipleship

Nobody ever promised you
a Christian's life would be easy.
It is clear to Christian people
that their paths aren't always breezy. When
troubles come our way
we often feel quite low;
But all things work together
to help a Christian grow.
Satan will try to use these things
to discourage and make us fall
Yet we know that Jesus Christ
will triumph over all.
We know that He is with us
over the rough and rocky road
And when times get too tough for us he'll
carry us and our load.
We know that we can come
whenever there's a care.
No problem is to large or small
to bring to Him in prayer.
We know He'll answer every one.

for the best, we can rely.
We may not know the reason.
We might be tempted to ask, "Why?" It
may be hard for us sometimes
to accept His answer now.
We know that in the long run
its for the best somehow.
Lay not up riches for yourself
where thieves break in and steal.
Lay your riches up in Heaven.
They alone are real.
When people taunt and tease you. When
they say, "Look what you'll miss." Their
eyes are on worldly things.
You can depend on this.
Your God above has so much more
to give His chosen ones.
He wants all people everywhere as his
daughters and His sons.

Conversion

Once I was a sinner
drifting in the world of sin.
Now I am a Christian
with God's peace within.

Church Attendance

When you miss church
do you ache inside?
Do you find something missing without
Christ as your guide?
Are you empty and hollow
until you've knelt and prayed?
Do you feel all unraveled
and worn out and frayed?

Do your problems stand out?
Do they overwhelm?
If so its time for you to put
Christ back at the helm.
He'll fill you with love
and give meaning to your life.
He'll bear all your heartaches,
envy, pain and strife.
He'll give purpose to life
and put a song in your heart.
You'll want to stick by him
and never depart.

Bus Ministry

We all will agree
our church needs to grow.
How can I be of service?
You might want to know?
People like to get visited.
Yes, From all of us.
We could bring in
more people with a bus.
For, although he says, "Great!"
and tells you how he feels;
he can't make it to church
without any wheels.
The walk may be too long
or his age may be such
that he's too young or old
or the strain is too much.
We must reach out and
preach to lands quite far away
but, for our neighbors, we also
find that we must pray.
We need to get started
without a big fuss
to bring people to church
in our Sunday School bus.
We say that we love
and we say that we care.

Do we really show love
when we leave them out there?
We'll step out on faith
with not a thing to fear
depending on God for
He's always quite near.
He won't let us down
while we're doing His will
but the devil will tell us
just to sit quite still.
He doesn't want us
to cross into his private domain
for buses would ruin him
and cause him much pain.
He'll cause all the members
to get in a big fuss
if that would prevent them
from getting a church bus.

Jesus' Love

Jesus came to set men free.
He suffered just for you and me
And though He didn't want to go
he went because He loved us so.
On His head was a thorny crown
while men beat Him and knocked him down.
He did not say an angry word
and complaints, from him, were never heard.
Even when the whip cut his back
he did not break. He did not crack.
The cross He carried down the road
until He fell beneath its load.
When, finally, it stood in its place
they plucked the whiskers from His face.
Then nailed Him to that cruel tree
where He bled and died for you and me.
The crowd said, "If you were God's Son
wouldn't the angels come on the run?
Wouldn't they save you for all to see
that you were the Savior of you and me?
Love held my Savior to the cross that day

for we owed a debt we could not pay.

The Great Commission

Christ told us to go preach to all nations and
he said to witness in all situations.
The Great Commission was given to all, the
fat, the slim, the short and the tall.
We must never forget these words of God
from deepest Africa to the tip of Cape Cod
God's people are spread over all the world so
let the Christian flag be unfurled.
Fly it proudly wherever you can.
Preach God's Word to every woman or man.
We must be more concerned for the lost. We
must witness to them at any cost. Worldly
wealth will do us no good
if we don't use it as we should.
Though our efforts seem very small
in hospitals we witness in every hall
And in our rush to other lands
let's not neglect our country's needy hands.
Christ gave the commission to begin at home.
To locate the lost we don't have to roam. We
must also remember our shut ins so dear. We
should visit the ones who cannot hear. The
ones in the hospital and ones who can't see
need attention from people like you and me.
Never forget the person next door.
He may never have heard of salvation before.
We don't have to look far to locate the lost.
We must never give up no matter the cost.
Part with your money without a big fuss.
Christ gave the commission to each of us.

Christ Knocks

When Christ starts tapping at your heart;
he wants to come in and have a new start

To the sin stained lives of earthly man.
He wants to give riches if he only can.
He'll bring you rewards in untold number
with eternal houses of gold not lumber.
Where moth and rust does not corrupt
and with lives that sin cannot disrupt.
When we get to heaven all sin's in the past,
where peace, love, and joy are all that'll last.

The Christian Witness

The Good Samaritan parable
is one Jesus told.
It classifies each person
whether he's young or old.
The thieves beat the man
and left him to die, you see.
They believed, "What you have
belongs actually to me."
The rabbi passed by and
did not even weep
but said, "What I have is mine
and only mine to keep."
Both of these groups
were selfish indeed.
These men will eventually
pay for their greed.
Then came the Samaritan,
despised by the rest.
They looked down on him
though he did his best.
He did not pass by
as the others had done
but cared for the stranger
as if he were his own son.
He spent of his time
and also of his wealth
to care for the stranger
and bring back his health.
His lifelong ambition
he went on to pursue

but told the man, "I'll be back
to take care of you."
This third type of person
is different, you see
for he said, "What I have,
I will give it to thee."
Are you of the type who will
take what is your brothers?
They earned what they have
and you somehow feel
If they have what you want
then its OK to steal.
Why should you have
what another has earned?Why
should you help yourself when
his back is turned
or hurt him or cause him
to suffer and cry

or, perhaps, to hurt him
so badly that he might die?
If
you fall in this category I'd
hate to be you
when your life is over
and comes up for review.
When the verdict is
given to depart into Hell
I think that you probably
won't feel very well. Perhaps
you will say,
"I'm not all that bad.
I earned what I had
and that's all that I had.
I've worked for my money and
kept it just for me
if others did likewise
they'd have some, you see.
When they are in need
I will just pass them right by.

I've earned what I have. They
could too if they'd try. Leave
me alone.
What I have I will keep.
Let them care for themselves.
What they sow they shall reap.
If this is your attitude
I pity you too.
For you don't have compassion
or know what you should do.
True joy is not found
in hoarding your pay.
You can't know real joy until
you give some away. Not just
of your money.
but talents and time.
A truly happy man
might not have a dime.
but he loses himself
in giving to another.
He has proven that he
really cares for his brother.
This parable encompasses
more than mere wealth.
It encompasses blessings which
aid your spiritual health.
Would you be the person you
know you should be
If you accepted salvation and
didn't share it with me?You'd
be like the person who kept
what he made.
The joy of your salvation
would soon, from you, fade.
The Lord gives us His talents
if we hide them we will find
these talents, we will lose
for the wise use of our time.
If we do not use

what he gives its a crime.
If a hungry person asks
for some bread
Would you turn him away
with a shake of your head?
Would you say you had none
and send him away
Or would you borrow from
your neighbor until the next day
And give it to the stranger
who has a real need
Or would you, perhaps,
add meat to his feed?
Christ taught us to help
those less fortunate than us,
To share what we had
and never to fuss
But we fail so often
to do all that we should.
We say we can't do
when really we should.

Christian Service

Its easy to promise Jesus
you'll serve all your life.
You promise your service
before mom, dad, and wife.
You step out in faith.
You step out with no fear.
You counsel with others
as you plan your career.
You look at the courses
and count years at school.
Each day you struggle
while friends sit by the pool.
Each summer you work
to save all that you earn

for matriculation fees
because you want to learn.
The days drag by like years
with never an end.
Discouragement comes and
your feeling's won't mend.
The devil whispers,
"Its not worth it, you know."
He'll undermine thinking
as he walks to and fro.
He'd like to cause
God's servant to quit;
to causing you
to give up and sit.
Don't let him win.
Jesus is preparing a crown.
Do you want Him to quit
and just put it down?
Remember when Jesus
took away your sin.
You wished all people
could this life begin.
You feel discouraged but,
in the faith you've begun
you must tell others
to trust in God's Son.

Christian Pathway

When the pathway's rugged
and progress painfully slow;
The end of the pathway so distant
you cannot even see its glow
At times worldly pleasures
have a fascinating appeal.
We wish to stray from God's purpose
but we know His promise is real.

At times when the course of study
seems extremely hard to bear;
At times when depression grips you
and you feel you don't really care;
He knows what is best for your
life. He has the answer to worry,
to depression, to envy, and strife

Parnach

My son Elizaphan
represented Zebulon.
He helped divide the land
which wasn't easily done.
Don't let depression get to you.
Don't let things keep you depressed.
Take time out to study God's word
for His ways are always best. When
money is in short supply
and its lack causes great stress.
Trust the Lord and He'll help you
to pull yourself out of the mess.
Trust Him in all you say and do.
Don't ever let the devil win.
Satan will try to deceive you
and cause you to fall into sin. They'll
be times when worry
will make you want to quit.
Stress and financial troubles
will team up and give you a fit.
In these times the Word of God
will shine like a lamp to your feet.
You'll find God's pathway is worthy.
You'll never give up and be beat. God
's Word is a lamp to your path.
It grows brighter with each new day.
It shows the best way for your steps
when you kneel by your bed and pray.
You'll love to talk with my Savior.

Christianity & Discouragement

You know that you're a Christian.
You've been saved by Jesus' grace
Yet everywhere you go,
it seems, that doors close in your face.
You've stepped out to follow Him,
leaving home and town and friends
Yet you have discouragement
and it seems the pathway ends.
You've prayed for many hours.
You're sure you're in God's will.
You've followed His commands
yet you can't climb up the hill.
It seems everything's gone wrong.
Every hit has been a foul.
You feel like going home
and throwing in the towel.
Keep up your faith dear brother.
Don't give up just yet.
When Peter's faith began to waver
he got a little wet.
Jesus came to him to give him a helping hand.
These trials are for your good.
You're not on sinking sand
Keep your chin up, my brother.
He'll be with you in the storm.
Troubles come to everyone.
Its no exception. It's the norm.
But with each trial that comes
there's a solution close at hand.
God won't leave us helpless
when we take a godly stand.

The Devil's Tool

Discouragement is very real.

It is the devil's tool.
Its used against Christians causing
them to forget God's rule.
Once your hand is on the plow
you must never turn around
To look at worldly pleasures
which are easy to be found.
Don't take your eyes off God
or mess with the devil's crowd.

Learn the Bible's truths.
In their defense speak loud.
Don't despair over money.
Your father made the world.
He'll supply all your needs
as Satan's darts are hurled.
Be faithful and be patient.
Continue always in God's way.
Trust the Lord in all you do.
He'll see you through each day.
He's promised not to heap on us
more than we can bear.
It often seems that we, like Job,
get more than our share.

When Things Go Wrong

When things seem to go wrong
and It seems you're bound to fail;
When your ship gets full of water
and you're without a bail;
God will not forsake you.
He has promised not to leave.
He won't leave you comfortless
if you continue to believe.
Sometimes things get difficult.
The way seems hard and tough.
God's goodness will be sweeter
when the pathway has been rough.
Don't throw in the towel yet.

It may seem easier to give in.
The lesson learned through patience will be
worth it when you win.

When Bubbles Burst

Its easy to trust the Lord
when things are going well;
When things flow easily
and everything is so well.
When the bubble bursts
and troubles pile up fast
Its hard to put Jesus first
while the troubles last.
No temptation will be ours
that is not common to man.
There is also a way of escape.
With faith we know we can.
Trials are mountains to climb,
but sometimes the way is rough.
It seems you just can't make it
across another bluff.
Keep you anchor in the Lord.
Be faithful all the time.
Tribulation helps us grow
though hills are hard to climb.

Mountains to Valleys
and back

Salvation puts you on a mountaintop.
You wish you could always stay there.
Troubles and doubts come your way
and the joy gives way to despair.
In these times the devil comes to you
as he came to our Lord to tempt him.
He casts doubts of your salvation.

Your enthusiasm grows quite dim.
His way seems too straight and narrow;
the sacrifice too great to bear.
This road, in the end, leads to heaven
and you find that you do really care.
The other pathway's wide and easy
and there are many traveling that way
But the moment death overtakes them
they'll wish they had listened that day.

The plan of salvation looks easy.
Of the roadway ahead that's not so.
They'll be barriers placed in the pathway.
You'll wonder if you can continue to go.
Each roadblock you face is a challenge.
Each hurdle you jump improves you.
Each one has a purpose in your life.
It'll be worth it when you get through.
Keep your chin up in your trials.
Each one is improving your lot.
When you approach Heaven's gates
there will be reserved for you a spot.

Why Worry

When worry comes to you
And you don't know what to do
Rebuke Satan. He won't stay.
God's word drives him away.
The victory will be yours
And you'll hear Satan's roars
For we bring Satan to defeat
When we sit at Jesus' feet...

The Devil At Work

The joy that was yours
when you got saved

Should be with you your whole life through
Jesus intended that it should be thus,
but it gets lost when
His will you don't do.
Soon the devil whispers in your ear,
I told you it would never last."
You begin to get discouraged.
Things slip back as in the past.
The devil will try to convince you
That God's ways are not what you want.
When you try to ignore his urgings
He begins to laugh and taunt.
Don't underestimate him.
He'll come in the things you like best.
He knows all about your weaknesses.
His cunning he'll put to the test.
He knows that if you'll yield to him
Discouragement will make you fall.
You'll quit trying to please your Savior.
You'll bobble and fumble the ball.
When discouraged turn to Jesus.
He'll welcome you back to the fold.
He'll forgive you if you'll ask him.
In Heaven there are blessings untold.
You must arm yourself with the gospel.
When confronted the devil will flee.
Jesus will cure all your sorrow
and fill your heart up with glee.
You will be filled with his love
and he will cause you to know
the footprints of life will prove
He carried you when you couldn't go.

The Clouds of Life

When a cloud of worry descends;
When you're depressed
and pining God's words will cheer you
and show the cloud's silver lining.

When monetary problems beset you;
When the pathway seems rough and old;
God's Word shines out like a rainbow
which points to a pot of gold.

Treatment for Stress

Many don't deal with stress.
Some seek relief in alcohol.
It seems to give help
While setting them up for the fall.
Some go into depression
withdrawing from the world of the real.
Others look for relief
behind an automobile steering wheel.
Some just blame others
And won't face what's true.
Some overdose on sleeping pills,
turning to drugs for the cue.
Relief from these things
Are temporary, at best.
The Lord is the only real answer
To this very unwelcome guest.
Because Jesus made the world
And He owns all that you see
He also made our bodies
and knows what's best for thee.

Rely on God's Word

When troubles come your way
and worry gets you down
God's word is all you need
to take away that frown.
He'll wipe away all tears
and make you want to shout.
You'll wear a smile each day.

You'll have no need to pout.
Discouragement will come
when your defense is low.
If you don't watch out then
you'll let Christ's message go.
Satan will deceive you
and cause you to stray
But keep your faith in God
who will provide a way.

When Death Overtakes Me

When death overtakes me
I don't want you to mourn.
I've just passed from this scene.
I've really just been born
into the Heavenly Kingdom.
I can see it's dawning now.
I can see the face of Jesus.
I can see his blessed brow.
He says, "Welcome to my Kingdom
where all sorrow's are in the past.
You've been liberated from the earth
to a place where peace will last."
My death should not be mourned
for my life is better now.
I'll be waiting here to greet you
when in death your head will bow.

Miracles

Jesus used His miracles to show
He was divine.
He healed the sick, raised the dead,
and turned water into wine.
At the wedding feast in Cana
the people's faith was tested

For the outcome of a miracle
quite often on faith rested.
He walked upon the water
and the raging storm He stilled.
He caused the lame to walk
and the hungry to be filled.
After multiplying loaves and fishes
for the people's nourishment
He said, "I am the Bread of Life
who was from Heaven sent.
So you see, Christ miracles
were powerful teaching tools.
To point to His divinity
for he suspended natures rules.

The Big Fish

I started as an egg
then hatched into a fry.
That's what little fish are called.
I cannot tell you why.
I learned quickly to hide.
I learned to avoid bigger fish.
If I didn't do this constantly.
I would be their next dish.
I grew and grew and grew.
I thought I was king.
Then I saw a mountain move.
It was a living thing.
I knew at once I must be
careful to hide away.
If I neglected to do it,
it might be my last day.
I continued to grow
until I outgrew a shark.
I knew that I had grown enough
to leave my mark.
I swam around sometimes in
plain sight for all to see.
I now had little to fear for
others fled from me.

At times I still hid
so fish would come near.
If they didn't know I was there
they'd soon lose their fear.
I knew there was a God.
He was with me every day.
He watched me on the hunt
and saw me while at play.
One day he spoke to me.
He told me to leave my home.
I was to leave my family
and just begin to roam.
He said that he'd direct
and Fame would follow me
He said he had a plan
and I would be the key.
He told me as long as people
lived on earth and believed
My story would be told
so I was quite relieved.
After I set out that day
he told me where to go.
He told me to follow a ship
and my mission I would know.
As I followed the ship.
The waters became quite choppy.
Lightning flashed all about.
Conditions were quite sloppy.
Above the storm I heard the
voices of several men.
The worried voices stopped
then I heard them again.
They pitched baggage overboard.
Nothing interested me.
What was my mission way
out here in the sea?
I heard the voices again.
God told me to get ready.
I followed closely now.
My nerves were quite unsteady.

They threw a man overboard.
I quickly swallowed the guy.
I took in a lot of air.
I wondered if I'd die.
God told me to turn around
and to go the other way.
For three days I swam then
I heard him say.
Your going to throw up now.
Do it on the shore.
I swam as close as I could then
I heaved with a roar.
I saw the man I swallowed
land upon dry land.
He began to move around.
I felt rather grand.
I knew I'd done God's will f
or this wayward one.
This was my purpose.
Now God's will had been done.
I saw God's hand on my life.
He had saved me many a day.
He guided and protected me
so I'd be there that day.
If God's hand is upon you
look for his will and do it.
Don't pout and say I can't or
you never will get to it.
Sometimes we're his chosen vessel
to do a certain task.
We need to move by faith and
not sit still and ask.
God will point out our mission
if we're faithful in what we do.
He might not reveal ahead of time
the events that will ensue.
If we missed God's purpose
it would be a shame.
His will might not get done
and we would be to blame.

Peter: The Big Fisherman

Hello Peter, my brother!
How are you today?
What are you doing with those nets
with the sea so far away?

Alternate reading: Hello Peter. How are
you? We hear somebody say.
What are you doing with those nets
when the sea's so far away?

These nets are old and decayed.
They are a reminder of the past.
I used them daily once
but that occupation didn't last.
Jesus walked along the shore.
He looked up at me then.
He said, Simon. Leave your nets
and I'll make you a fisher of men.
I left my nets that day
to follow Christ as Savior.
Everything about me changed;
including my rough behavior.
I knew what he said was true.
I knew I was a sinner.
I repented of my sins
and I became a winner.
I never regretted leaving my nets
to follow Christ as Lord.
I left them willingly
and I grew stronger in his word.
I was a master fisherman
in the Sea of Galilee.
Now I fish for men
as I seek to set them free.
I tell them they are sinners.
I lead them to Jesus then.
He gives them eternal life.
Their repentance tells him when.

I was a strong willed child
and a boisterous, impetuous man.
I didn't think there was room for me in
God's wondrous plan.
Jesus told us one day of things
that would come to be.
I rebuked him boldly.
He said, Satan! Get behind me.
He said if any would follow
he must deny himself for the cross.
If any would gain eternal life
he must give up being "Boss."
He asked, What it profited a man
if he gained the world as a whole
If he lost his eternal life
and condemned to Hell his soul?
Another time I was with him
when people all crowded about
When he asked, Who touched me?.
My mind filled with doubt.
How could he ask such a question
with so many people around?
He said that virtue had left him
and no longer did abound.
A woman fell down saying
from sickness she sought release.
He said, your faith has healed you.
Get up and go in peace.
A disciple is a learner
and I learned day by day
That nothing is impossible
if we have faith and pray.
Jesus asked us one day
who Men said he was
Then he asked us what we thought of him
and his Heavenly cause.
I said, You are The Christ, God's Son.
My answer came as a shock
He said, Your name will no longer be Simon
but Cephas which means,

"The rock."
My native language is Aramaic
Now I speak mostly greek.
Cephas means "rock"in aramic
It's Peter in the language I speak.
Whichever term you use it means
"Rock" if you care to search.
Jesus said upon this rock
I will build my Church.
That's why I keep this rock.
It reminds me of that day
When Jesus changed my name
and he had much more to say.
Jesus used my boat.
That's why I keep this oar.
He stood and preached from it
to multitudes along the shore.
He walked on the water once.
I asked him if I could come asunder.
I walked on the water too, then lack of
faith almost took me under.
One day we came in exhausted
for we had fished all night.
The eastern sky was glowing
with the morning light.
No fish were in the boat.
We hadn't caught a one.
The men were extremely tired
for the night was done.
Jesus hailed us from the shore.
Cast your nets on the other side.
Though we were all exhausted
to his will we did abide.
Why! We caught so many fish we
couldn't get them into the boat.
Another boat was called.
It's a wonder either stayed afloat.
I was so impressed that day as were
James, John and Andrew, too
That we left our nets for our
fishing days were through.
When we came to Capernaum they

asked if tribute was paid.
Jesus said not to offend.
Catch a fish and we'd have it made.
Open the fish's mouth
and locate the coin in there.
Give it to the man
for it would pay our fare.
This showed his authority over nature
and his ability to supply.
Accept the Lord's provision
and never question why.
My mother-in-law had a fever.
Word of her illness to Jesus was sent.
He came with James and John.
He healed her. She was content.
From that day on my home
headed his Lakeside ministry.
My boat was at his disposal.
Everything I have will always be.
The twelve disciples were chosen.
I was appointed head.
James, John and I were there
when Jesus raised the dead.
Jarius' daughter was raised to the
wonder of all three.
We witnessed his transfiguration
and, in the garden, his agony.
John and I prepared a meal in the upper
room one day.
Jesus said one at the table
would my Lord betray.
He said that he'd be put to death.
I said I'll follow too.
He said, Peter, You'll deny me thrice
before this night is through.
He said before the cock would crow these
things would happen for sure.
I said I'll never deny you and my
intent was pure.
When they came to arrest him I cut

off Malchus' ear.
Jesus rebuked me for it
and healed the one whom he should fear.
They lead him away.
I followed, but far away I stayed.
They became aggressive.
I grew a bit afraid.
All of the others had left him
fearing persecution or death.
I had promised never to leave
as long as I had breath.
I followed to the palace
and into the inner court.
I was accused of being his follower.
Never, was my retort.
I was accused again.
I've never been with him I lied.
I cursed and denied him.
When the rooster crowed I cried.
Jesus looked at me.
He knew what I would do.
He told me that I'd do it before
this night was through.
I repented of this act done in
confusion and fear.
How could I deny the one whom
I had held so dear.
I witnessed his suffering and their mocking
and their lies.
I heard not a word from Jesus.
Then I heard their ugly cries.
Crucify Him!
Crucify Him!
I heard them shout with glee.
I heard them choose Barabbas as the one
they wished to free.
I heard his sentence read.
They were to crucify God's Son.
I trembled like a coward for I had denied this
one. They crucified him and he said, Father

why forsakest thou me? They stuck a spear
into his side. I thought, How could this be?
John and I ran to the tomb after the Marys
had had their say.
We found it empty as they said. He
appeared to me that day.
Later by the Sea of Galilee John
recognized Jesus on shore.
I jumped out of the boat and swam to meet
him once more.
I shared breakfast with him cooked over the
coals of a fire.
He asked, Peter. Do you love me? I said,
Yes, You know my desire.
He said, Feed my lambs,
then asked the question once more.
He said, Feed my sheep., then repeated it as
before. He said shepherd my sheep. Why? I'd
grown no smarter.
He revealed to me on the shore that I'd die
as a martyr.
He changed my name to Peter. He told me to
shepherd his sheep.
He showed me my life's end and rewards that
I would reap.
On the day of Pentecost we were gathered in
one place
The sound of rushing wind was heard as it
increased its pace.
It settled as tongues of fire on the twelve of
us there.
We spoke in other languages to men from
everywhere.
The Holy Spirit filled us and spoke through
us that day.
Men from every nation heard the gospel in
his own way.
They marveled for the twelve of us were all
from Galilee.
We were unlearned men; yet each could

plainly see.
That God was using us.
Each heard the message fine.
Someone suggested we might be filled with
the new wine.
I stood up with the eleven and addressed
the group as a whole,
These men are not drunk,
but fulfill the words of Prophet Joel. He
said that in the last days God's spirit would
be poured out.
Young men would see visions.
The old their dreams would shout. God
said, I'll pour my spirit out on my servants
who have behaved.
Everyone who calls on me shall
immediately be saved.
This same Jesus whom ye crucified is
willing to set you free.
You must accept him as Savior and from
sinful ways must flee.
We know that all have sinned, but Jesus
will forgive.
He'll pardon in an instant and he will help
you live.
He'll give eternal life to those who come
unto him now. I know it seems amazing,
but he loves us somehow. With many other
words
I begged them to be saved.
Many accepted him
and said that was what they craved. Three
thousand accepted him and were baptized
on that day.
They continued daily with us and showed
they knew the way.
I healed a cripple who was present at the
temple gate.
I defended John and pronounced Ananias
and Sapphira's fate.

Herod had James killed just to
please the Jews.
Then he had me thrown in prison to please
them with the news.
Four quaternions of soldiers guarded me in
jail.
He'd call me forth at Easter for
their will to prevail.
Before that time came prayers for me were
made.
I slept between two soldiers Chains
determined where I laid. Soldiers
stood before the gate.
Security was thick.
An Angel awakened me and said, Get up
and make it quick.
The chains fell from my wrists.
He told me to get dressed.
He told me to follow him; before its too
late, he stressed.
I followed from from jail him but I thought
that I had dreamed.
I thought I'd had a vision for that's the way it
seemed.
When we came to the city gate it opened of
its own accord.
We stepped into the street he
disappeared without a word.
I knew he was an angel, sent by
God to set me free.
I went to Mark's mother's house where
they had prayed for me.
I knocked at the gate.
Rhoda answered then ran back inside.
Peter's at the gate, she said.
You're mad. They began to chide.
She insisted I was there. they said, An
angel it must be.
I continued to knock until

they came out to see.
I told them what God
and the angel he sent had done. I
told them to tell the others and I'd
be on the run.
I performed many other miracles.
Always in Jesus name.
John and I went to Samaria where the
Spirit came.
I healed Aeneas
and raised Dorcas up from death.
A vision came to me.
Preach while you have breath.
Cornelius accepted the Lord and his
whole family as well.
I spoke before the counsel.
Their support was swell.
I went to Antioch to preach to the Jewish
Christians there.
I went to Corinth as well.
To go to Rome I now prepare.
Its rumored that I'll be crucified in a
Roman town.
I'm unworthy to die as Jesus did so I'll
request
that it be done upside down. If
they should crucify me. Please
do not lose heart.
Don't quit or blame God for we must all
depart.
It means we'll be separated for a while but it
really won't be long
If you've been born again
and have joined the Heavenly throng.
In the future you'll die too for
everyone must go.
After that its judgment time.
To some it will be woe.
To those who are in Christ Jesus it

will be eternal bliss.
We'll be reunited once again and
we can thank God for this.
It'll make a world of difference to me if
you've been saved.
Don't let money, lust, or pride keep you
from what you've craved.
Admit that you're a sinner.
Turn from a life of sin
Come to Jesus as you are and you'll be
cleansed within.
Confess the Him as the Savior and tell
others what you've claimed.
If you do, on judgment day you'll face him
unashamed.
Your ransom has already been paid.
It won't cost you a cent.
Don't wait until you're 'good enough' or
you never will repent. The unrepentant
sinner
will have a place in Hell.
Because Jesus died for him too that won't
make him feel well.
Don't look up from Hell
like the rich man we're told about.
Reserve a place in Heaven where God's
praises we will shout…
We know that all have sinned. God's word
says that its true.
The wages of sin is death regardless of the
good we do.
So come to Him today. Before it
is too late.
He is the only way to escape that
awful fate.
Once you have accepted Him
you'll never be the same.
So come right now while there's still time
and confess His Holy name.

Heart Be Troubled Not

Let not your heart be troubled.
Ye believe in God and Me.
In my Father's house are mansions.
I go build one for thee.
If I go to build it for you I will come for you
to get.
For where I am you shall also be My
own I won't forget.
If loved ones have passed on Who
put their trust in me
They will also have a mansion which I
built for them, you see.

Jesus

The Heavenly Father, and I,
and the Holy Ghost are one.
Parts of a triune God.
We were there when the world was begun.
We created the flora and fauna and knew
that it was good.
We created man and the garden and gave
him the things that we should. We created
Eve to be with him and commanded them
to multiply.
We said if they ate from one certain tree
that very day they would die.
Satan tempted Eve and
lied to her that day.
Adam ate what she brought him so I sent
them away.
Death came to all mankind through Eve's
and Adam's deed;
They were spiritually dead but I
still loved their seed.
I planned a way of salvation but they

weren't ready yet.
In due time mankind would find that I
would pay his debt.
I was there when Abel came
face to face with the "Grim
Reaper"
I was also there when Cain asked, "Am I
my brother's keeper?"
I saw man's wickedness increase I told Noah
to build an ark.
I warned of coming judgment if they
continued to miss the mark.
I gathered the waters together and wiped
out their wickedness.
Almost before the waters dried man started
to digress.
I commanded Abram
to leave his family with due haste.
I blessed when he obeyed. When
not I laid to waste.
I promised him a blessing.
I changed his name to Abraham.
I warned of Sodom's destruction and Lot's
if he didn't scram.
I directed Esau and Jacob and protected
Joseph too.
I sent Moses to rescue my people and tell
Pharaoh what to do.
I gave the Ten Commandments to show the
error of man's ways.
I gave the sacrificial system which served
them many days.
I enabled David kill Goliath and to play his
harp for Saul.
I caused him to become the king and to win
the hearts of all.
David wanted to build the temple but he
had bloody hands.
I told him Solomon would do it and I'd give
wisdom, wealth and lands.
I was with Elijah in the drought and when
rains brought relief.
I was with Elisha also and I saw Naaman's
grief.
I witnessed the temple's rebuilding and the
testing Job received.
I blessed him for faithfulness when few
around believed.
Jeremiah recognized my leadership and of
my judgments he did tell.
He saw Jerusalem destroyed. He
wrote and spoke as well. Daniel
trusted and obeyed and faithfully
interpreted dreams.
Shadrach, Meshach, and Abednego defied
the king it seems.
They were cast into the furnace to
teach a lesson, you see,
The king learned God's awesome power
and of man's futility.
King Belshazzar saw my handwriting as it
appeared on the wall.
Daniel told him that it meant His
kingdom would soon fall.
Daniel's enemies convinced the new king
to declare that none could pray To anyone
except to him,
Daniel prayed to me that day.
Because of the law the king had Daniel
thrown into the lion's den.
He didn't sleep much that night for he'd
never see Dan again.
Daniel called to him In the morning
when he heard the king's low moan.
The accusers were thrown in. The
lions broke every bone.
Jonah called out to me from the belly of
the whale. He was at the point of despair

but found that my plans don't fail.
It is said a man and boy went out to rescue
some birds one night,
The birds avoided them
oblivious to their plight.
The boy asked, "Is there no way to show
that we mean no harm?"
"I'd have to become a bird myself so they
won't sound the alarm." That's how it is
with man and God.
Man will continue to go astray.
Unless God becomes a man and comes
down to show the way.
My plan from the beginning was to rescue
my special creation.
I would become a man and
explain the situation.
To do so I would be born to a human,
flesh and blood, mother.
My father would be God
so she must know no other. My mother was
betrothed to Joseph, a carpenter by trade.
She was found to be with child which by
the Holy Ghost was made.
Joseph was a just man,
unwilling to embarrass, of course.
He thought quietly to separate then
privately divorce.
While he thought on these things an
angel appeared in a dream Saying,
"Do not be afraid to marry her for things
aren't the way they seem.
Do not be afraid to marry her for we know
you love her most.
The child who is within her was
conceived by the Holy Ghost. She
shall have a male child.
Jesus will be his name.
He'll save people from their sins.

He'll take away their shame."
All of this has been done
to fulfill what the prophet told.
"Behold a virgin shall bear a son.
He'll be the Emmanuel of old.
His name shall mean 'God with us' " He
was prophesied long ago. Joseph arose
and said,
"Let this thing be so." He did as the angel
said,
He knew that it would please us.
He knew not his wife until she
had a child named Jesus.
Though I was born "King of the Jews" I
wasn't born in luxury
I was born in a Bethlehem stable and
placed in a manger, you see.
King Herod learned of my birth and
demanded to know where.
He said he wanted to worship me and to see
how I did fare.
He really wanted to discover where I had
taken my first breath
So he could send soldiers and assure
himself of my death.
I was delivered from this and taken to Egypt
instead.
Herod had all the children killed to make
sure that I was dead.
He hatched up this wicked plan which, to
him, seemed mighty fine
He didn't realize he could not foil a God
who is divine.
After King Herod had died to Israel I
was to be taken.
Joseph feared the new king. He
was quite badly shaken.
He took me to Nazareth instead for he
feared that I'd be killed.

It was prophesied I'd be a Nazarene.
So this prophecy was fulfilled.
When I was twelve years old to
Jerusalem we went.
My family was part way home when they
realized I was absent.
They returned to Jerusalem and searched
all around for me.
When found In the temple.
I said, "About my father's business I
must be.
Those who heard were astonished at the
understanding I had.
I taught as one with authority. My
teachings made them glad. I went
to John the Baptist to be baptized in
the Jordan there.
He had baptized many.
His clothes were of camel's hair.
At first he refused to do it
"Why do you come to me? I should not
baptize you.
I have need to be baptized of thee."
I told him it must be done to fulfill all
righteousness
So he baptized me in the Jordan with
utmost humbleness.
When He came up from the water, a dove
came down from above. My father
said, "This is my son in whom I
am pleased and love.
I was led into the wilderness.
It was the devil who tempted me. I'd
fasted for forty days and nights.
My hunger was plain to see.
The devil tempted me.
"If you are God's son," he said, "Look
at all these stones.
Command that they be bread." I

told him it was written,
"Man shall not live by bread alone, But
by every word of God; not by things
he'd not condone."
He took me to a large city:
on the pinnacle of the temple to sit, He
said "If you're the son of God cast
yourself down from it.
Angels will bear you up
so you won't dash your foot on a stone.
They'll catch you in their hands so you'll
never be alone.
I said again, "It is written Thy
God thou shall not tempt."
He lead me to a high mountain saying,
"Surely you are exempt."
He showed me all the worldly
Kingdoms and all the glory
there was to see.
He said, "All this I'll give to thee if
you'll fall down and worship me.
I said, "Get behind me Satan.
You've sure got a nerve.
It is written thou shalt worship God and
him only shalt thou serve."
Confronted with God's word
three times
the devil went away.
Angels came and ministered to
me on that very day.
I heard that John was in prison so I
went to Galilee.
I left Nazareth for Capernaum in Zebulon
and Napthtali.
This fulfilled Isaiah's prophecy that to
those who in darkness sat
A great light would come and they'd be glad
of that.
From that time on I began to preach

throughout the land
Repent of your sins and be baptized for
God's kingdom is at hand.

I walked by the Sea of Galilee.
Simon and Andrew were casting their
nets. I said, "I'll make you fishers of
men.
They followed without regrets.
I then saw James and John in the boat with
Zebedee.
They left him when called and
followed after me.
I taught in the synagogues. The
true gospel I preached..
I healed those who were sick. Many
with ailments were reached.
Word spread through all Syria.
They brought sick from everywhere.
Multitudes followed me
in every country where I'd share.
Multitudes followed me one day.
Seeing a need I sat down to teach.
My disciples came to me, but to
the multitudes
I did preach. "Blessed are the poor in spirit
for the kingdom of
heaven is theirs.
Blessed are those who mourn.
They'll be relieved of all of their cares.
Blessed are the meek
for they shall inherit the land and those
who hunger for righteousness will be
filled and will feel grand.
Blessed are those who show mercy for they
shall receive the same.
Blessed are the poor in heart.
They'll see God and receive a new name.
Blessed are the persecuted
when its for righteousness

For theirs is the kingdom of heaven.
In that day God will bless.
You are blessed when men revile and
persecute you
And, for my sake, say false evil against you
too.
Rejoice and be exceedingly glad.
You'll be rewarded one day.
They treated the prophets the same.
Of them they had much to say.
When they reject your message and slam
doors in your face
Remember you'll be rewarded one day and
they will reap disgrace.
You are the salt of the earth but if its
preserving power is lost it is
then good for nothing.
It's not even worth its cost.
It is fit only to be cast out and to be
walked on by man For if it has lost its
purpose. and can never be used again. You
are the light of the world.
A city on a hill can be seen.
You don't light a light then hide it but to
illuminate is what I mean.
Its light shines all around so
people can see throughout.
Let you good works be seen by men and
glorify me with a shout.
Don't think that I came to destroy the
prophets or law.
I did not come to destroy, but to
fulfill without flaw.
Listen! for I say to you
till heaven and earth shall pass The
law will not be changed until it is
fulfilled at last.
Whosoever breaks a commandment and
teaches others to do so

Shall be least in the kingdom of heaven.
Listen so you all will know.
Whosoever is faithful to teach them the
way they are written is great. He'll be
thus called in heaven when he's
rewarded on that date.
I tell you this thing right now.
Your righteousness must be greater Than
that of the scribes and Pharisees if you'll
enter heaven later.
You have often heard it said if you kill
you'll receive judgment.
I say if you're angry you're in
the same predicament.
Whoever calls his brother stupid shall
receive counsel to do well but if he calls
his brother a fool he's in danger of the
fires of hell.
So if you come with your tithe while
disagreeing with someone
First reconcile yourself with him then give
when you're done.
Quickly agree with a brother when you're
at odds with him or he might take you to
court where the punishment might be
grim.
All three parts of the triune God
want now to rescue you.
I knock at the door of your heart to see what
you will do.
Knocking and waiting now for
you to open the door.
I've knocked and waited often when you
heard before.
You need to be saved now and rescued from
eternal Hell.
You need to drink from the Word, the
everlasting well.
He who drinks from this well will hunger

and thirst no more
So respond to the knock at your heart and
open up the door.
There is no latch outside.
It must be opened from within.
Open your heart today and it
Will be cleansed from sin.
The free gift of salvation was costly to me
and should be highly prized
So open the door today.
Repent and be baptized.
Again you have heard it said, adultery, you
shall not commit.
I say not to lust
or you're also guilty of it.
This is because in your thoughts you
committed this act in your heart.
You have also missed the mark so, beware,
before you start.
If your right eye causes sin pluck it out and
throw it away.
This would be better for you than in hell for
your body to stay.
Likewise cut off your right hand if it can't
resist an evil desire.
It is better that this should happen than for
the whole body to burn in fire.
You have heard it said
if you'd break fellowship with a wife Give
her a writ of divorcement
and be separated for life.
I say to you today
do not in such have a part. Except for
fornication
don't think this matter to start.
You'll cause her to commit adultery and
he who marries her also.
This would be a grievous shame and would
cause both parties woe.

44

Again you have heard it of old, you
shouldn't swear except by God's
name.
I tell you not to swear at all
for God's throne you're not to profane.
Do not swear by heaven
or by earth which is God's footstool. Do
not swear by Jerusalem for the king's city
is but a tool.
Don't swear by your own head. You
can't make one hair black or white.
but just say "Yes." or "No." Always
say what's right.
It has been said, you've heard, an eye for
an eye, a tooth for a tooth
But I say to turn the other cheek.
Any less would be uncouth.
If a man sues you for your coat give
him your cloak as well.
If he compels you to walk a mile walk two
and you've done swell.
Give to him who asks.
To him who'd borrow lend.
Its been said, love your neighbor and hate
an enemy who'll offend.
I say love your enemies.
Bless them who curse you too. Do
good to them who hate.
Pray when they persecute you.
Do this so you'll be children of
your Heavenly Father
for he Makes sun to shine on good and bad
and sends rain on all, you see.
If you only love those who love you
what reward do you think you'll get?
The worst sinners do this also.
You don't want their reward, I'll bet. Strive
for perfection in all you do.
Continually try to improve.

God alone is perfect
but closer to it you can move.
Don't show off when you give or you'll
receive no other reward.
Don't announce that you are giving or
that'll be all you get from the Lord. The
hypocrites announce their giving by the
showiness of their oath.
They're praised by man, not God.
That's all. They can't have both.
When you give to the Lord don't let your
left hand be aware Of what your right
hand is doing.
There's no need for that to share.
What is given in secret
is only for the father, you see;
For he who sees in secret shall reward thee
openly.
When you offer prayer don't do as the
hypocrites do
For they love to be seen by men.
They'll be no other reward when
through.
When you pray, enter a closet and close the
door behind.
Pray to the Father in secret.
His reward will be open, you'll find. Don't
pray with vain repetitions as the heathen do
to be heard.
They think they'll be heard for that. He
knows needs without a word.
After this manner pray: Our
Father, who in heaven are.
Hallowed be thy name.
Thy kingdom come from afar. Thy
will be done on earth as, in heaven,
it is, we know.
Give us this day our daily bread.
Forgive all our debts also.

Forgive us as we forgive others.
Don't into temptation lead But
deliver us from evil
and from the temptation of greed.
Yours is the heavenly kingdom and the
power and glory too.
This shall be forever and ever.
Amen and Amen to you.
If you forgive men's trespasses your Father
will forgive you
But if you do not forgive others no
forgiveness to you will ensue.
When you fast for a season don't try to look
overly sad.
The hypocrites do this.
They disfigure faces to look bad. They try
to look like they fast.
They'll get no other reward than this For
many notice their fasting.
Their proper reward they'll miss.
I tell you when you fast
anoint your head and wash your face.
Don't let others know about it.
You'll be rewarded without disgrace. Lay
not up treasures on earth where moth and
rust does corrupt;
Where thieves break in and steal and your
peace of mind interrupt.
Lay up your treasures in heaven where
corruption will never be: Where no thieves
break in to steal and heartaches don't come,
you see.
Wherever your treasure is your
heart is there too.
If your treasure's laid up in heaven a
heavenly heart will be in view.

Abraham

God told me to leave the land I'd lived in
since I was a tot.
I left with Sarai, my wife, Terah
my father and nephew, Lot.
We moved to a city called Haran and there
we did abide.
It was a trading city
where we stayed until Terah died. God
commanded me to move to the land
that he'd show unto me.
He told me that from my loins a great
nation would come to be.
We traveled to Shechem
and I built an altar there.
God appeared to me at Bethel. Another
was built with care.
The Lord said he'd give the land to my
descendants one day.
We continued on with our flocks, but a
famine came our way.
Egypt was known for its grain. We
went there to get filled.
I said Sarai was my sister so I would not
be killed.
She was beautiful.
I was afraid they'd kill for her.
Reports of her beauty reached
Pharaoh and he began to stir.
He took her into his house
and gave me servants and livestock.
The Lord sent plagues his way and
people began to talk.
He sent Sarai back to me and
urged us to leave the land.
We left for the hills with herds and
flocks so many that it was grand. Strife

46

developed over grazing rights between
my people and those of Lot.
We agreed to leave peaceably when others
would have fought.
Between the Jordan and the plains I let Lot
have his choice.
He chose the Jordan with Sodom and
Gomorrah and he did rejoice.
I took my herds and flocks
and headed toward Hebron to
the west.
The land was barren and not as good but I
would do my best.
God renewed his promise there and said
my descendants would be Like the dust
of the earth so no man could number
them, you see.
The kings joined forces and against
Sodom and Gomorrah fought. They
defeated them and took captives,
one of which was Lot.
I gathered my men and gave chase and soon
had the victory.
I brought back Lot and the goods
because the Lord was with me...
Sodom's king asked for the people and told
me to take the stuff.
I wouldn't take a sandal thong.
What my men ate would be enough. God's
word came to me saying that my reward
would be great.
I said, My Lord what will you give? I'm
childless with my mate.
God said, Do not worry!
From your body shall come an heir. He
took me outside and told me to look at
the stars up there.
So shall your descendants be; more
numerous than you can count..

They'll be as the sands on the shore and
proportionate in amount.
God promised that my descendants would
one day possess the land.
They'd be captive four hundred years but
their return would be grand.
In the fourth generation they shall
return right here.
I make this covenant with you and I hold
my covenants dear.
Sarai who bore me no children had a
handmaid named Hagar.
Sarai said God closed my womb. Her
child might take you far.
She hated Sarai more and more after she
bore me a boy.
Sarai blamed me because Hagar had taken
away her joy.
I said she is yours, do as you like.
Please do not blame me
She treated Hagar harshly until Hagar
wished to flee.
An angel told her to return to Sarai and
submit.
He told her he'd multiply her seed until
their was no end to it.
You'll have a child, Ishmael.
He'll be wild and live to the east.
Everyone will be against him for he'll be
like a beast.
I was eighty six when Ishmael was born
and grew up wild.
At ninety-nine God promised me that
Sarai would soon bear my child.
The Lord appeared to me and
identified himself as "I am."
He changed my name to "the father of
many nations", Abraham.
God said I'd be fruitful and nations and kings

would come from me too.
God promised Canaan's land and that
blessings would not be few.
God promised also that Sarai would no
longer be the same.
He said from that day forth Sarah
would be her name.
I laughed when God promised Sarah and
me a son.
I said, I'm a hundred; Sarah is ninety.
Will we really have one?
My covenant will be with Isaac whom
Sarah who is old will bear.
Ishmael will also be blessed for twelve
princes will be in his care.
I was sitting at my tent
when three men appeared in the door.
I ran and bowed to them and said
please don't pass me once more. Let
me wash your feet and you can rest
beneath this tree.
I'll bring you bread.
You'll be refreshed. Stay and visit with me.
After you have visited me you can go on
if you see fit.
They said we'll wait as you say. Go.
Get on with it.
I hurried and asked Sarah to make
three cakes of wheat.
I ran and chose a calf
to be quickly prepared to eat.
I took the calf and curds and milk so the
men could be fed.
I stood under the tree with them when
together they said,
Sarah will have a son
a year from now when we return.
Sarah listened from the tent to
discover what she could learn. She

laughed to herself saying. why I am
way to old.
She said my lord is old also. The
very idea is too bold.
He asked why Sarah laughed about what
had been done.
He said I'll return next year and she will
have a son.
Sarah denied laughing, but he said she
laughed indeed.
They walked on toward Sodom. I
followed with deliberate speed.
The Lord said, Shall I hide from him
what I'm about to do?
He'll become a great nation and a
blessing to all men too.
I chose him and he'll teach others to keep
to the Lord's way.
Sodom's outcry and their sins are
exceedingly great today
I'll go and see if they have done all their
outcry declared to me.
They went toward Sodom and left me with
the Lord to plea.
I said, Will thou sweep away the righteous
and the wicked too? If there are fifty
righteous
then what will you do?
The Lord said, If I find fifty righteous I will
spare the entire city.
What if there are but forty five? Their
destruction would be a pity.
The Lord said, If there are but forty five I
will the city spare.
Abraham said, Do not be angry, but what if
only thirty are there?
He said, For the sake of thirty I'll still leave
the city around.
I spoke again saying.

Suppose only twenty can be found. He
said, If there are twenty I'll still show
them that I care
I said, Do not be mad,
but what if only ten are there?
Before the Lord departed, he said.
For ten I'll still show grace.
I was satisfied with that and returned to my
place.
The angels went to Sodom and Lot stood to
meet them there.
They told him that they intended to spend
the night in the square.
He urged them to come with him.
He cooked and they ate.
The wicked men came to his house and
tried to make a date.
Lot went outside and said, Do not do this
wicked act. He said, Take my daughters.
They are beautiful in fact.
They intended to run over Lot and break
apart the door,
The angels grabbed Lot before they could
do any more.
The men were struck with blindness and
couldn't find there way.
They tired of looking for the door so the
went away.
The angels rescued Lot, his daughters and
wife as well.
Lot spoke to his sons-in law but they
thought things were swell.
The angels told them to flee
and not to look back or halt.
Lot's wife looked back in spite of it and
turned to a pillar of salt.
I arose early and went to where the Lord
and I spoke.
I looked toward the cities and saw only

ascending smoke.
I journeyed toward the Negev then to
Gerar I came.
I said Sarah was my sister. This
added to my shame.
King Abimelech took Sarah but the
Lord sent him a dream.
This is a married woman. Things
aren't as they seem.
He had not come near her and this fact he
did stress.
He said, Will thou slay a nation when it is
quite blameless?
He said she is my sister and she said it too.
I innocently took her in because the truth I
thought I knew.
God said, You acted in integrity then your
emotions began to stir.
I kept you from evil because I didn't let
you touch her.
Restore this prophet's wife and he will pray
for you. If you don't return her you and
yours will all die too.
Abimelech called me and said, What
is this you did to me?
Why did you do this evil which
should never have come to be.
I said that I thought there was no fear of
God in this place.
They will kill me because of my wife and
bring me to disgrace.
She's actually my half sister.
She's my father's child.
I told her to say I was her brother.
My mind was running wild.
Abimelech took rich gifts and gave me all
of these Then said,
My land is before you.
Settle wherever you please.

The Lord had closed all the wombs in
Abimelech's household.
I prayed and God answered so they had
children who were bold.
Sarah bore to me a son
just as the Lord had said she would.
I was a hundred when she did. Who
would believe she could?
Sarah said, God has made me laugh.
We both burst with pride.
When he was weaned I made a feast for
God's peace did abide.
Sarah told me to drive off Hagar's
son so he wouldn't be heir.
God said, I'll make him a nation too so do it
without despair.
I arose early in the morning and told them
they couldn't stay.
I gave them bread and water and then sent
them away.
God called to me and I said, God, I
am here, you know.
He said take Isaac, your only son, to the
land which to you I'll show.
Take your beloved son to Moriah as a burnt
offering to me.
I will show you which mountain.
Take your wood with thee. Early the
next morning I went with two men
and Isaac too.
We split wood for a burnt offering for what
we had to do.
We went as God directed and on the third
day I spied the place in the distance where
my faith was to be tried.
I said to the young man,
Stay here with the donkey, you two.
I and the lad will go worship and
then return to you.

I took the wood and laid it on Isaac,
my only son
I took the fire and knife.
Our journey was thus begun. Isaac
called my name and I said, Here am
I, my son.
He said we have what we need, but
with no lamb it can't be done.
I said with a broken heart, God
will provide the sacrifice
So the two walked on together without any
more advice.
We arrived and built an altar, and
placed on it the wood.
I bound Isaac, my son,
as the Lord said that I should.
I held forth the knife when a voice called
out, Abraham.
I stopped my hand in mid air and
answered, Here I am.
He said do not harm the lad.
Do nothing to this one.
I know you fear the Lord for you have not
withheld your son.
I had told Isaac that the Lord would
provide a lamb.
I raised my eyes and in the thicket I
saw a tangled ram.
He was caught by his horns so I
offered up this one.
God provided because I had not withheld
my son.
A message came from the Lord,
Your family will I bless.
I will multiply your seed and their enemies
will they possess.
Through your family I will
bless all people of the earth
For in your line someday there will be a

holy birth.
This birth will be a Holy birth.
The Messiah he will be.
At his name kingdoms will shake and the
Devil will also flee.
He'll give man a second chance to gain
eternal life
lost when God's order was disobeyed by
Adam and his wife.
He'll bear the sins of all who
confess his name to men.
Those who die before they confess won't
get the chance again.
The wages of sin is death and separation
from God forever.
Those who accept him now will be
separated never.
Accept Christ as Savior now while you still
have opportunity.
You may never have another and may be
lost for eternity.

The Innkeeper

I am the Innkeeper. I
serve the public too.
I provide lodging for them.
That is what I do.
On one very special night;
When the census was being taken A couple
came to me.
The woman was badly shaken. She was
great with child.
It would be born this very night.
They'd searched for lodging everywhere.
I sympathized with their plight. I
searched my mind for a place.
I wanted to give the best.
I saw God's hand was on them and this was
my greatest test.
All the rooms were filled.
There was no room at the inn.
It looked like they'd struck out. I wanted
them to win.
All I had was a stable.
I could give them clean hay. It
was shelter from the rain.
What more could I say? I
offered them the stable.
The manger would hold a child. The
animals wouldn't mind. The
weather was quite mild.
They accepted the offer for the woman was
getting faint.
They were glad to have a place and went
without complaint.
Soon afterward music filled the air. It
was the sweetest I'd ever heard.
The sky was filled with angels. Each
hovered like a bird. They proclaimed,
"Fear not. A savior was born tonight.
You played a key part as
God sent the world his light.
The cattle joined the chorus. The sheep
joined in as well. The donkey brayed in
tenor.
The camel rang the bell.
Soprano was supplied by the rooster.
Alto was sung by the hen.
Bass was supplied by the bull as he joined
in now and then.
I had given what I had.
It was accepted by the most high.
I'll treasure this night forever; even to the
day I die.

Dedication Prayer

Dear Lord, we invite you to come and be
Our Savior and Lord for all to see. A
change that cannot be explained. One that
is real, that can't be feigned.
We are sinners and want to be
Servants working just for thee.
We know that you'll be on our side And a
lasting peace will still abide. Though we
can't be perfect yet.
Your forgiveness we will get.
We'll try our best to serve thee good And
do the things we know we should.

Prayer to be Worthy

Dear Heavenly Father, Lord we pray Help
us to be worthy of thee today. Help us to
keep away from sin and witness to those
we should win
For if we don't try to do thy will Satan will
move in for the kill.
He charges when defenses are down. He'll
take you to sinful parts of town. He'll get
you down and keep you there and teach
you to lie and also swear.
For he's alive and doing quite well.
He'll drag you down to the depths of Hell.
But Satan can't stand the Living Word. The
Voice of Jesus who is our Lord.

My Best

The people gathered at the Church. as
the message was proclaimed
A silence fell and each one felt that he

alone was named.
The message rang out loud and clear When
our lives run through the test
that no person in the crowd could say, "I've
done my best."
As each examined his own life he soon was
made to know if he had done his very best
the building would overflow.
One person burning out for Christ would
draw crowds from far away. We need this
fire in all our lives to be with us all to
stay.

Sorrow And Death

Why must men and women die Leaving
ones behind to cry? Though he's a Christian
I'll weep Though I know his is a pleasant
sleep. His suffering is over at last.
All tears and sorrow are in the past. He gone
above to begin new life with no more toil or
stress or strife' where he'll walk along on
streets of gold.
He'll never be hot and never cold. He'll
have a mansion made just for him, and his
private pool in which to swim. He'll no
longer sin and feel ashamed. To God's Holy
Choir he will be named.
He'll walk right up and shake God's hand.
He might play first part in the angel band. I
know he's better off up there where men
don't ever drink or swear. Even knowing
this I'm filled with sorrow for I'll have to
wake up and face tomorrow and I'll have to
live without him here. My sorrow is
selfishness it is quite clear. I don't feel bad
for him, you see. My sorrow is for myself.
It is for me.

If My People

If my people which are called by my
name Shall humble themselves and pray
and turn away from their wickedness I'll
never turn them away.
I will answer all their prayers; Heal their
sick and care for them. I'll guard them and
protect them Like I would a precious gem.
If they do things the way they should I'll
even heal their land. Crops will grow and
flourish even in the poorest sand. Those
who listen and obey will be blessed at
every turn. They'll find they can't out give
the Lord. THIS lesson they will learn.

A Time for Everything

Man's rights include a time for birth' and a
time and place to die; a time to rejoice and
be happy and also time to cry: a time to
labor hard all day and to do his very best;
a time for retirement and also
a time for rest.
In God's plan are many things which we
don't understand.
We'll know and comprehend it all when we
hear the heavenly band.
Although our hearts are saddened we must
accept God's will.
We know that all He does is good. Our
cups he'll overfill.
Many have been blessed here by the
kindness of this one; By his gentle
understanding and the kind things that he's
done. God's people's words speak highly
of this man called by God who was

required to leave his tools to walk were
Jesus trod.

No Room at the Inn

There was no room that day at the inn for
one who could save mankind from sin.
The only place that could be found was a
stable with animals all around. At his birth
a brilliant star appeared and angels came
whom shepherds feared. They said, Fear
not! We bring good news. a baby's born
whom God did choose. Wise men
followed the star and found A young child
playing on the ground. Rich gifts they
offered for they were wise. The King
sought Jesus by disguise. They returned a
different way instead. They learned the
king wanted Jesus dead. Joseph and Mary
to Egypt moved. This was God's plan it
was later proved. Herod had all the
children killed and all the land was terror
filled. All the efforts, however, of mere
man could not foil God's unfailing plan.

No God?

Some people claim they don't know God.
They say he's passed away. Others say if
he's there He's not listening when we
pray.
To prove their point they often say, 'If
He's there at all,
We should know His dimensions; Whether
he is short or tall."
They say if they can't touch him or see Him
He's not there
But many touch and see him While on their
knees in prayer.

Not only do we speak to Him To us He
means so much.
We know He's real and living because
we've felt His touch.

Sorrow's Depth

Sorrow is never deeper than when a loved
one dies.
In these times of sorrow
The soul for comfort cries. It cries out long
and loud.
The sorrow is very real.
Only God can comfort then the sorrow that
we feel.
He said He'll never leave us. We found He
told the truth.
For us to have doubts in Him Would
be a bit uncouth.

Blessed are They

Jesus saw the crowds and went
upon a hill.
As the disciples gathered around.
He taught them, "Blessed are the poor.
For in my kingdom they'll abound.
Blessed are those who mourn For
God will comfort one and all.
Blessed are the meek.
Their reward will not be small.
Their patience is well known.
It is recognized by all.
Blessed are those who
wish to please God. They
shall be satisfied.
Blessed are the merciful.
God's mercy shall be applied.
Blessed are the pure in heart For they'll see
God in Heaven. Blessed are the
peacemakers. Their peace shall rise like

leaven. Blessed are those who do God's will
and are persecuted for it.

The Kingdom belongs to them.
They'll probably adore it.
Blessed are ye when men revile you
and falsely gossip about you.
Your reward will be in Heaven for
everything you do.

Troubled Waters

When waters of life are smooth we feel close
to the Lord. Its easy to trust Him
then and to believe His word.
When a ripple disturbs the water we take
the trial in stride.
We can lick our problems with Jesus on
our side.
When the tempest starts to howl and the
surface is really choppy
Our faith might start to waver, church
attendance might get sloppy.
When the water really gets rough and the
winds begin to howl
We feel like giving up on life, like
throwing in the towel. Jesus can calm the
storm.
He has the world in His palm.
The placid waters will return.
Once again they will be calm.
When we return to the Lord again
we'll know and feel His grace.
We'll feel better back with Him.
Everything will take its place.

The Good Samaritan Story

The Good Samaritan Story Is
one we all know well.
The man who helped the injured in the
ditch right where he fell and though the
races of the two kept their people far apart
this man used his own money to give a
brand new start.

Pentecost

They returned to the city.
To the upper room they went.
All again joined in prayer For
the Spirit to be sent.
When the day had come they were all of
one accord.
Suddenly there was a noise
A rushing wind was heard. It filled the
entire house.
Cloven tongues of fire came. They
sat on each of the twelve. They
came in god's Holy name. All filled
with the Holy Ghost. Each spoke
with other tongues.

The Spirit told them what to say. He
filled with power their lungs. Men from
every nation their native language
heard.
Each heard his own dialect. They
understood each word.
They marveled at this miracle but some
were quick to say the men were drunk, not
sober so early in the day.
Peter delivered a sermon.

He said, These men are not drunk.
Their fast is still in progress.
They had consumed no junk. If they were
drunk as claimed it was not from food or
drink but was of the
Holy Spirit and each was
made to think.
After graphically showing Jesus describing
miracles and signs.
He said, You murdered Him then claim
these are drunk with wine.
God raised Him from the dead Having
loosed the pains of death;
Showing Jesus as Messiah by
giving back His breath.
Now know ye this same Jesus whom
you sent to the cross stands waiting to
forgive you though you tried to cause
Him loss.
When they heard Peter's message they
asked what shall we do?
He said, Repent. Be baptized every one of
you.
Be baptized now in Jesus name..
You shall His gifts receive.
Three thousand souls came forward Saying,
We believe.

Face to face with the Devil

Face to face with him, the devil.
Face to face what will it be?
He has promised this world's riches.
Satan, he who tempted me.
Face to face he had beheld him with the
promise of the world.
Face to face the devil's power he had at
my Savior hurled.
Face to face with him, the devil. Satan

said, Come worship me!
I will give you all your wishes but you can
bet it is not free.
Face to face he had beheld him with the
promise of the world.
Face to face the devil's power he had at
my Savior hurled.
Though the devil tempted Jesus o'er
and o'er again that day.
Jesus never yielded to him or from God,
his father, strayed.
Face to face he had beheld him with the
promise of the world.
Face to face the devil's power he had at
my Savior hurled.
What rejoicing with my Savior who has
banished sin and death.
What a blessed day is coming.
I shall praise him with each breath. Face
to face I will meet him and thank him for
what he's done.
Face to face I shall meet him and thank him
for the victory won..

Grief that Overwhelms

Sometimes grief grips our hearts and We
don't know what to do or say.
Sometimes we feel inadequate so
we sit at home and pray.
We know that our great God Holds the
future in His hand.
Sometimes He lays us low.
Sometimes we feel just grand.
Words often don't come easy With grief,
uncertainty and woe.
Add to this a busy schedule and we feel
we just can't go.
Inwardly we trust in God who knows
what's best for all.
We feel what we can do or say might be
inadequate and small.
Be assured that you are loved and that we
also share your sorrow.
Our prayers are with you always for a
healthier tomorrow.
God is the Great Physician. He
knows us, one and all.
We thank him for each ray of light and
every gain though it be small.

Spiritual Leader

God made man the stronger vessel.
It was for a purpose too.
He also made him spiritual leader that His
work a man should do.
How many men have delegated this
responsibility to their wives and shirked
their spiritual duties in order to live their
worldly lives.
Shame on all who do not take the spiritual
leader's place.
The shirking of this family duty will lead
them to reap disgrace.
If you have been one who has been a little
slack
it's not too late to take the reins and to bring
your family back.
Set up a family altar;
in Bible study take the lead.
Set the example of a Christian in word, in
act, and deed.
Your manliness won't be weakened it'll be
made strong instead.
Your family will look up to you. You'll
become its rightful head.

Bi-vocational Pastor

The bi-vocational Pastor
called by his dear Lord must
do a secular job
While proclaiming God's Holy Word.
He is often ridiculed
by some who do not rightly know the
things that he goes through to cause others
to Spiritually grow.
He must work very hard his family will to
this attest. His family must also sacrifice as
he gives God his very best.
He often does Church planting to reach the
ones who are without. The converts are not
many but are saved without a doubt. Each
soul is precious to God.
Angels rejoice when one is saved Many are
reached because
a working man has thus behaved. He heard
God's call and went to proclaim God's
Word to all.
He preached the Word of God to some
considered to be small.
Some have prison ministries. Some
witness to the poor proclaiming God's Holy
Word because Jesus is the only door. Treat
your pastor very well
bi-vocational or not
for God has called them both.
With his blood they were bought.

Dogging our Footsteps

Sometimes as a Christian like
Brother Job I feel.

The devil is dogging my footsteps.
His presence is very real. He's
tested my commitment.
He's been at me all the while with doubts,
frustrations and worries he works in his
devilish style.
I've still got problems but I'm on the right
track for I've got the devil worried or he
wouldn't be on my back.
The Lord will get the victory. I
know this thing he'll do.
I'll rob from Satan's kingdom taking many
before I'm through.
I'll be dogging his footsteps like he has
been dogging mine.
When his children are born again I'll say,
"That's mighty fine."
I know he won't leave me alone.
I'm prepared to fight till I die for death will
be gain for me.
Till then to win souls I will try.

Salvation and Sharing

To be saved we must repent of sins which
we have done.
We must invite Christ in to continue what
He's begun.
He said, "Behold I stand at your heart and
knock.
If you will unbolt the door and
release the lock
I will come in and sup with you and I
will save your soul.
If you let me take over
I'll make you completely whole.
After you invite me in make your
decision known.
My command is to baptized.

I'll proclaim that you're my own. Baptism is merely a symbol to tell others what's been done.
It symbolizes death to sin and the burial given to the Son.
It symbolizes the resurrection to a new and glorious life.
It won't be the end of worry, depression, sadness or strife.
Though these will be yours God promised you won't bear more than you can carry.
He will your burden share. With burdens that come
He'll provide a way out for you. You'll grow because of them.
Your faith will grow stronger too. These things might come to help you later give aid.
They might help you identify with mistakes others have made.
In this way you can help them to overcome problems of theirs.
This help is a steppingstone as they give Him their cares.
To Christians it is important to point others to Christ as well for missions is God's purpose to save
from the devil's Hell.
We are the tools of Jesus to reach those in need, to show they need a savior by action and in deed.
Where would we be now if nobody showed the way?
We'd be as lost as they are so let us share Christ today.

Plan of Salvation

God made the plan of salvation so simple a child can know beyond the shadow of a doubt
That to Heaven he'll later go Yet many people get hung up feeling it must have cost.
Because there is no charge they remain among the lost.
All of us have sinned says Romans 3:23.
The wages of sin is death and it will always be.
This death talked about means from God a separation and from Jesus Christ too which is a bad situation.
Salvation is a free gift but though the gift is there we must reach out and take it or the penalty we'll bear.
As in the work we do someone must get the wages.
Of the wages of sin that's true as seen in the Bible's pages

We know the wages of sin is to be cast into Hell.
Those wages must be paid.
Jesus paid them very well. He died on the cross to earn salvation for us.
Its a gift he gives by grace so why do many fuss?
Like Naaman in the Bible when told to dip in the river he got so angry then that he began to quiver.
His servant said to him if he required

great price for healing your
leprosy you'd gladly pay him twice so go
do as he says.
Have faith and believe.
Naaman did as told.
His leprosy was relieved.
If we were charged a price for
salvation
the rich would pay
but many would be excluded from
being saved that way.
It was provided free though. Many
refuse due to pride.
there's nobody without the price so they
won't be denied.
Some things we did earlier we
won't do any more.
We won't want to be the same as we
have been before.
That is not a cost of salvation.
Its a result of it instead for
we who were lost
are alive and once were dead.
Each thing we must give up is replaced by
something better.
We're no longer in bondage to sin.
We're not to it a debtor.
We need to repent of sin and ask for
forgiveness too.
Having realized the wages this isn't too
much to do.
Each must accept Christ and invite
Him into his heart.
The Bible says all who believe will be give
a brand new start.
God's gift is eternal life.
To heaven with Him we'll go.
We'll no longer face Hell. We'll
no longer suffer woe.

God demonstrated his love while
we were yet sinners Christ died
on the cross for us so we'd,
through Him, be winners.
If we confess with our mouth as Romans
10:9 said
and believe Jesus is Lord and God raised
Him from the dead.
We shall be saved completely as the Bible
does declare.
All who come unto Jesus will, with Him,
His glory share.
Whoever calls on His name shall
immediately be saved.
He'll give us all good things for which our
hearts have craved.
Won't you accept Him now;
There, right where you are?
He is always near you. He's
never away very far.
He stands at your heart waiting to be
invited in.
If you'll open up the door He'll save man
from sin.
Tell Him you know you've sinned and
death is the wages you owe.
You want to take Him as Savior and more of
His will to know.

Temple of the Lord's

My body's a temple of the Lord's.
The Bible tells me that.
I need to be careful what gets in or my
temple will get fat.
I need to remember this thing. You
should remember it too.
I can't honor Him with what I say if I

don't in what I do.
If my body's out of shape and I
don't really care
I'm not honoring God.
I need some time in prayer. A
few sins can be hidden This one
can never be.
It shouts of weakness. Its out
there for all to see. We can't
blame it on others.
The problem is our very own.
It rests squarely on our shoulders.
Ours and ours alone.
If we show by eating habits we
can't our wills subdue then we
can't be used by God As He
would like us to do.
concern for other's cares.
As they crucified Him on the cross he
wished to give them life anew.
He cried, "Father forgive them For
they know not what they do."
They pierced His side with a spear and
gave Him vinegar to drink.
He asked God to forgive them. His
words caused some to think.
They removed Him from the cross. and
placed Him in the ground.
He arose and walked the earth. God's
miracles did all abound.

Meeting Needs

God is so good to us though
unworthy are we He will meet
our needs wherever we may
be.
He sometimes lets us go Until we
feel left out

to see if we react with worry,
stress or doubt, He sends his
saints to us when we're in need.
He works through people in word,
thought and deed.
His loves us although we're
unworthy to be His own.
We are just babes in him striving to be
full grown.

Improving Ourselves

Everyone has good points and
everyone has bad. At times
each is happy.
At other times they're sad.
There are things about us which we point
to with pride.
Other things we see
we wish that we could hide.
Some things we can change.
Others we cannot.
We should try to change the bad
whenever these we spot.
We don't change the good unless we can
improve it.
If something's in good's way we
should work to remove it.
Nobody is so good
he shouldn't want to change.
Each person can improve and their image
rearrange.

You Were There

Were you there when Christ was
placed in a manger that day?
Were you there when wise men came to

60

worship and pray?
Were you there when
when Herod
said children should be slain?
Were you there then?
What did he hope to gain?
Were you there when Jesus grew and
worked in the carpenter's shop or when
He rebuked people saying their evil
should stop?
Were you there in the upper room When
He revealed his death or when He
prayed in the garden
with agony in each breath?
Were you there at the trial of Jesus?
Did you shout, "Crucify Him?" Did
you scream, "Release Barabbas?"
It was done on a whim. Were
you there when they scourged
Jesus.
The treatment was cruel indeed.
Were you there while He
carried the cross.
Did you stand and watch Him bleed?
Were you there when He fell too
weak to carry the load?
Were you there when He fell again on that
hot and dusty road.
Were you there when they nailed His
hands to the cross piece of the tree? Were
you there mocking him and watching His
agony?
Were you there when He cried,
"Father, forgive for they don't know
what they do."
Were you there when they removed
Him when His last breath was through?
Did you hear the centurion utter, "This
truly was God's Son."

Were you there when the tomb opened
and redemption was begun. You were
there because your sins helped to nail
Him to the cross.
He died to save you and others.
This is what your sin cost. You were
there all this time.
Did you turn to Him in prayer?
When the Book of Life is opened will
your name be written there?

Let not You Heart be Troubled

Let not your heart be troubled Jesus says to
you and me.
I go to prepare a mansion and I'll
make one for thee.
If I go to prepare you one I will
come back for you.
I'll carry you in my arms to a place
where all is new.
These promises are to Christians who are
born again.
These promises are a comfort to those
otherwise in pain due to the
loss of a loved one who will be
greatly missed.
In the Book of Life of
Will your name will be on the list.

Fellowship of Christian Athletes

FCA is interdenominational. We
meet for Christian fun.
Christians have fun too and we

learn how its done.
We have respect for all beginning with a
word of prayer.
We try to make each one really welcomed
there.
We learn to let Christ shine in each person's
daily life and how we can lean on Him in
good times and in strife. We
use various methods to
illustrate His Word.
We want to make sure in all that Jesus
is our Lord.
We reach out to those in need and
cheer up those in sorrow.
We don't know what tomorrow holds but we
know who holds tomorrow.

Victory Over Sin

Our human life is empty.
Its completely void within. Human power is
not enough
to give victory over sin.
Some have tried drugs. the
emptiness remained.
When they did this they were
greatly pained.
Others felt that money and success were
the key.
The rich found life as empty as
any life could be.
There's no answer from riches.
They were at a loss until they knelt to
pray at the foot of the cross.
The cross is the method that God chose to
use to forgive people's sins.
We must not, this way, refuse.
It'll puts meaning into life. Spiritual

fruits it brings filling life with love
and joy.
peace grows and life sings, long
suffering, goodness and faith,
temperance and meekness too.
Refuse these brings emptiness which is
felt through and through.

Joy of Salvation

The joy present when you got saved
Should be yours your
whole life through.
Jesus intended it should be thus. Its
lost when His will you don't do. The
Devil whispers in your ear,
"I told you it would never last." You
begin to get discouraged. Things slip
back as in the past.
The devil will try to convince you that
God's ways are not what you want. When
you try to ignore his urgings he begins to
laugh and taunt.
You can't afford to underestimate him.
He'll come in the thing you like best. He
knows about your weaknesses.
His cunning will put you to the test. He
knows that if you'll yield to him
discouragement will cause you to fall.
You'll quit trying to please the Savior.
You'll return to the worldly ball. When
discouraged turn to Jesus. He'll
welcome you back to the fold. He'll
forgive you if you'll only ask. In Heaven
there are blessings untold.
You must arm yourself with the
Gospel. From it the devil will flee.
Jesus will cure all your sorrow and
He'll fill your heart with glee.

He Never Said Life Would be Easy

He never said life would be easy. He
said He came to bring a sword.
Many a family has been divided when one
accepted His Word.
We know these things are true yet as
Christians we must go on.
He said, "Preach My word."
If He sends us we must be gone.

In the past and in other countries Service
meant persecution or death. We have the
freedom to preach yet many think it a
waste of breath.
Consider the wanderings of Paul and our
efforts seem small and weak.
We often sit silently watching when we
should stand up and speak.
We hear His Word profaned by some
destined for Hell.
If we cared for them as we ought we'd step
in and God's story tell.
We fail our Savior, quite often yet His love
for us is great
He forgives us when we ask Him. He
forgives us without debate. His
service may not be easy.
It's the best way to live, I know.
If it wasn't for the love of my Savior to Hell
is where we'd go.

Triumphal Entry

His entry was one of triumph.
His followers cheered all the way.
Hasannah! Hosannah! They shouted.
This is a most glorious day.
They might not have shouted laying palm
branches on the path if they knew his
destination and the result of people's wrath.
Inside was darkness and turmoil. His
grief had turned to despair.
If possible let this cup pass for this cross
is hard to bear.
His sweat turned to blood as He
prayed while His disciples laid
down and slept. He prayed, "Let
this cup pass from me. Yet, Thy
will be done, He wept.
He knew that His mission as Savior would
lead Him down this road.
He knew that nobody was able to help with
His heavy load.
He woke His disciples and told them my
hour is almost at hand.
The people are coming to get me.
They are here on this piece of land.
Judas came saying, Master." He
betrayed Him to all with a kiss.
Jesus asked, "Why come with an army? for
you know I will not resist.
They led Him away as a captive. They
went to a sham of trial.
They teased and mocked Him and made
fun of Him all the while.
They made a rough wooden cross.
making Him carry it through the street.
They placed a crown of thorns on His
head and put nails through his hands and
feet.
They still mocked and teased Him while
He hung on the cross in disgrace.
They offered vinegar when thirsty.
They even spit in His face.
They made fun of God's only Son. They

repeated His name asking,
"Who?" He begged God to forgive them
saying. "They no not what they do." He
shouted to God, "It is finished," the
moment He gave up the ghost.
Darkness came, people wondered if, in
this, they could really boast.
Some knew then that Jesus Was God's only
Son, as He said.
They found the truth of the Savior
When because of them He was dead.

His Will Ignored

A child lay in a manger.
There was no room at the Inn.
Savior of the world was He. He'd
take away man's sin.
No room was found for Him. He
was born in a cattle stall.
Mankind had no room either though He
came to save them all.
In the ages since that day
Things haven't changed a lot.
People still have no room for Him.
They don't do what they ought. They
won't find a place for Him in their lives
or in their heart.
Pay as little attention to Him as they did
right from the start they do things their
own way.
They do the things they want.
They don't obey God's laws. His
will they often flaunt.

An Easter Message

Other religions serve men Who are
dead and in the ground or they have
remains they worship.
Their idols can be found.
My Savior conquered death when He
from the grave arose.
I serve a living Savior separating
Christianity from those.
How do you know He's living, some
might be tempted to say?
I know it for a fact because I
talked with Him today. Its not a one-
way conversation.
He also answers me.
He gives guidance for my life.
He'll do the same for thee.
If He is not your Savior and he's not
your Master too Repent of your sins
today.
He's waiting now for you.
Repent and be baptized is His
command right now.
Don't wait until you're worthy just come to
Him and bow.
He is a Living Savior and a
sovereign God as well.
Come to Him right now and
escape the devil's Hell.

Journey of Wise Men

Some take our journey lightly: Not
considering what was involved.
They act like it was just a stroll with no
problems to be solved.
We were members of the Magi as such, we
were prepared.
For centuries men had waited and at the
heavens stared.
They expected to see a sign announcing

the Messiah's birth but their lives came
and went and
He came not to earth.
Although we hoped to see him we
also had to live.
We had jobs to do and
we had a lot to give.
When we saw the star appear we had to
leave our homes.
Leaving our wives and kids and the
temple with its domes.
Our journey took years. It
was not just overnight.
Much of the time was spent on guard and
filled with fright.
With the presents that we had for
the one to be our king many
would come to rob us for a much less
worthy thing.
When we found the young child we had
used up all our wealth.
We were lucky though that each of us still
had his health.

A Proud American

I'm proud to be an American.
I'm sure that you are too.
The beauties of this land will
soon be in your view.
God showed His handiwork with man a
majestic peak;
Sometimes a giant waterfall shows where
a lake has sprung a leak.;
Huge caverns beneath the
surface are decorated with
fancy forms.
Lightning flashing through the clouds
which accompany many storms.

The Grand Canyon,
deepest of them all;
or Bryce and Zion Canyons, more
beautiful, but small.
The peaks of Mount Ranier or the graceful
running deer.
God entrusted us with treasure and
blessings without measure; awesome is
Meteor Crater;
or the powerful jaws of a gator; animals
like the lordly moose in a land where elk
run loose.
Some don't depend on their speed but on
the beauty of their breed.
Snowy Egrets called Golden Slippers or
hummingbirds
with their long sippers.
All show God's handiwork very
well so as an American with pride I
swell.

A Loved One's Death

We cannot know God's reasons For
taking those we love.
We must trust Him for strength; this strength
comes from above.
He promised he won't heap on us More
than we can bear Though it seems
that we,
like Job get more than our fair share. We
look through the window darkly.
We do not know His will
and though in sorrow we remain we know
He loves us still.

65

Fragile: Human Being

Fragile: Do not bend, Staple, Or
mutilate.
I am a human being. I think. A
man bearing this message
Caused all he met to think. His
life had lost its meaning. He was
wallering is despair.
An Australian wore this sign as raw
sheepskin he did wear.
He. met a woman on a plane.
She witnessed to this man telling him God
loved him.
He should be in God's plan. He
listened as she talked.
He now travels for the Lord winning others
to Jesus Christ.
He is a preacher of the Word. Many
are lost in despair; feeling lonely,
down and blue.
It happens to all age groups as they search
for things to do.
To Christ we're all important.
We're valuable at any age, as
temples of the Lord's.
Our worth we cannot gauge by the years
we've lived or the
gray hairs on our head.
We're still important in God's sight for the
lost need to be fed.
The fragile need rescuing.
All are fragile in some way so reach out to
one who's hurting.
Point him to Jesus today.

Unique Individuals

A human by physical description has
two arms, two legs, two feet.
He has two eyes, two ears, one nose two
hands, one chin, one seat.
He has ten toes and fingers. ten
knuckles and two heels,
two elbows and two shoulders and two
knees on which to kneel.
We could continue on and on and list
similarities for a week.
We don't just want these only but to know
why he's unique.
After making all creatures God
made man just like Him.
We're not told whether Adam
was tall, short, fat, or slim.
We're told that man is the apex of all that
God created. He is a free moral agent and
can choose what is loved or hated.
Because he was unhappy God took a limb
from man.
He made a helper, woman.
She's a unique individual but when the two
shall marry they become one flesh who
Together burdens carry.

Empty Tomb

One morning two women came To
anoint Jesus after his death.
They discussed the stone.
Shock took away their breath.
They saw an empty tomb and an angel sitting
there who said to them,
"Fear Not." Don't have worry or care.
Ye seek Jesus of Nazareth. Go
because He's not here.
Tell His disciples now That

they are not to fear.
They went quickly out and fled and
didn't tell anyone.
He came to Mary Magdalene showing he
was God's Son.
She told this to his disciples but they
believed her not.
He appeared and others told but against
belief they fought.
He appeared to the eleven Scolding them
for unbelief and hardness of their hearts
but
He came to bring relief. Go
tell others everywhere.
Tell them of my Love.
Believers won't be condemned.
They'll live with Me above.

Leaning On God

We share your sorrow with you.
We pray for quick recovery.
God is the Great Physician and will
answer every plea.
In times like these we need to
lean on Him in prayer.
Be assured your Christian friends are in
prayer because we care.

Christian Students

Christian students
everywhere Should show
others that they care.
They should show respect for
all people at school; be
courteous and kind. and obey
every rule.

They should study hard and
must never cheat.
They must pass each test never admitting
defeat.
They must realize being educated is cool
for nobody wishes
to be called a fool.
If each does his best then he'll
graduate. find a worthwhile job; and
feel really great.
He'll get the best job having what it takes; be
successful in life;
learn from mistakes.
He is the one
we honor today for he has achieved and
has much to say.
He studied lessons, behaving at school.
We're proud of him. We
think he is cool.
Achievement is his.
He learned from each test.
His challenge ahead is to
give it his best.

Treatment of Jesus

Jesus was treated in a
bad way.
They mocked and teased
Him in His day.
He, like the God that He was proved
He was the best.
As God's sacrificial lamb He
passed every test.

Paul

I was born into a land where many
gods were known.
Only Jews worshipped one God
who, alone, was on His throne.
I was a freeborn Roman.
In Tarsus is where we stayed.
I studied under Gamaliel as
Hellenism decayed.
Flax and Cilician goats were raised for
making linen, tents, and sails.
Fortunes were made from these and
philosophers brought tales.

Most in Tarsus worshipped
Hercules and Persius, it seems.
Miracle workers and astrologers came and
interpreters of dreams.
I studied rituals and piousness
which were of Jewish law.
I was a Pharisee of Pharisees. I
performed without a flaw.
We believe in one God. The
Messiah we awaited. He'd be
king of Israel;
a political ruler as stated. The
Romans hated Judeans and
turned to Sadducees.
If the King of the Jews appeared
Roman soldiers would him seize.
Augustus followed
Herodians sending a
procurator to rule.
A carpenter appeared. and He
knew every tool. Zealots
watched carefully. As they
awaited a sign.
Many said he was Messiah. from

the Davidic line.
His kingdom wasn't of this world yet
messiahship He claimed.
Pontius Pilate asked him If the
messiah he was named.
A sign on the cross said King of the Jews
was He.
They thought by killing Him they would
block destiny.
Grieving seized His followers. They
knew not what to say. Jesus was
resurrected as
He said,on the third day.
Would He restore the kingdom?
He told them to wait.
He said a comforter would come if they'd
stay until that date.
Peter healed a lame man.
Word spread through the town. Religious
ferver struck them Turning it upside
down.
They stoned Stephen laying,
clothes at my feet.
His face showed no regret nor would he
admit defeat.
I was a Hebrew of Hebrews In
Pharisaical Law, the same.
I defended Judaism.
In righteousness without blame.

I caught many Christians and
had them put to death. I vowed
to track them down if it took my
last breath.
I got letters from the Priest;
These Nazarenes to seize. I
would go to Damascus.
My mission would be a breeze. We
moved across mountains to capture

all we did seek.
Ahead was Mount Hermon.
Galilee was past its peak.
We'd pass mountains of Moab for in
Damascus they'd be.
We'd wipe out this heresy
before any could flee.
I fell to the ground.
Filled with much fright.
I'd been blinded as I fell by a dazzling
bright light.
A voice called asking.
Why persecutest thou me?
I heard the voice of Jesus and
wanted then to flee.
I could not flee, however;
to the left nor to the right for the light
blinded me.
Extinguishing my sight.
The voice said, "I am Jesus." I
asked, What should I do? He
said, go into the city and it will
be shown to you.
A man took my hand; To
my camel he led me. He
took me to Judas.
On a straight street lived he.
He was compassionate. I
didn't eat for three days.
In these days of fasting
I promised to mend my ways. I
envisioned a man with God.
Ananias was his name.
He came with affection though he
knew why I came.
Stephen said as he died, Lay
not this to their charge. He
prayed for his killers who
released a barrage.

When Jesus died he said, forgive, they
know not what the do."
I lay helpless and was told.
"Christians will care for you."

Ananias protested when told to find me and
restore my sight.
He said, I'd done evil. coming
to do what's not right. When he
entered the house
All watched where he trod.
He placed his hands on me saying,
"Sight comes from God."
He was told when he came a chosen
vessel was I.
I'd preach Christ to kings.
praising God who is on high.
Ananias was a believer who from my
wrath had fled.
Now he was humble and I knew he was
Spirit led.
He took me to Nazarenes; who
were tending their cuts. They
welcomed the enemy.
This took a lot of guts. I
was, to them a traitor;
To Nazarenes, unproved. I
knew that I was Christian. By
his power I was moved.
They praised God for the change.
My sword Christ put aside.
God had changed me, and
with them I'd abide.
I was charged by God's call on the
shores of Galilee.
I had seen God's blazing truth.
It caused a change in me.
I went to the desert to think to find what
God had in store.

God showed me love there. Of
this love I wanted more. He said
to go into the world; and preach
to every man.
Heal the sick and raise the dead.
I said, "I will if I can.
He told me, I couldn't do it. "All
things are possible with Me."
I said, "I'll do what you ask. For your way
will my way be.
I went to the Synagogues.
My reason was different indeed.
I didn't go now to take captives but to meet
and have met a need.
Jesus gave me a new chance. He
gave me a brand new start;
a new tongue and message and He gave me
a new heart.

I talked of mistakes I had made and
changes Christ had done.
I told of His graciousness and of the victory
I had won.
I knew danger lay ahead. Five
times lashes I received.
I knew what to expect.
I'd caused others to be grieved.
Damascus was a violent city. The
world's oldest, you see.
Soothsayers, merchants and priests might
be spying for their country.
Aretes' men came after me seeking to put
me in a casket.
My friends let me down the wall, through a
window in a basket.
I walked back to Jerusalem over the road I
had ridden before.
I knew of the dangers awaiting. God
was sufficient once more. In the

outer courts I preached for I had
much to say.
I preached also in the streets to my enemies
dismay.
Barnabas, a Cypriot and a Jewish man of
might spoke and judged me and took me
to Peter one night.
I spent fifteen days with Peter. Firsthand
knowledge I gained.
Peter's relationship with Jesus was what
God ordained.
I met James, the brother of Jesus who also
taught me much.
Jesus was the center of life for they had felt
His touch.
I was the intellectual man
unfamiliar with tenderness. They
knew this side of Jesus and they
did my soul bless.
I went to Galatia
and Syria and Cilicia also.
While in the temple
I was warned from Jerusalem I
must go.
Get out of here quite rapidly. They
won't receive your word.
I will send you far away.
This Word came from the Lord.
I went to Tarsus for a number of years.
A time for sowing and reaping to
all who had ears.

Two major trade routes
joined east of that town.
One road lead to the city where education
was renown.
I was beaten five times.
One time I was stoned and three times

70

shipwrecked to perils of my own.
Robbers were a threat; My
countrymen were also. The
heathen threatened me.
There were perils wherever I'd go.
I traveled much to preach
Wherever God sent, you see.
A traveler without a permit from robbers
would need mercy.
I assessed Jesus ministry.
My message was on love and freedom
revealed by Christ.
which lead to Heaven above.
Persecution spread the gospel for
others were like me.
Wherever they went they preached before
they had to flee.
In Antioch the Jews reached out. The
professing Greek group grew.
Barnabas, sent from Jerusalem came to see
if this was true..
Barnabas went to Tarsus and
returned to them with me.
Some had suffered at my hand before I was
filled with glee.
My experience was needed As
were my tireless skills.
Here I learned the value of collective
minds and wills.
Later I was to write that the
body's not one, but many.
If feet quit because they weren't hands of
feet there wouldn't be any.
If the ear quit because it wasn't an eye how
would the body hear.
All the parts are essential for
the body to appear.
I became part of the community: preaching
and being wise.

When one suffered we all did, if
one rose we'd all rise.
We went out as one body; self
supporting and dignified. We
witnessed to others around
hoping they'd join Christ's side.

This was a city of pleasure.
Sounds of these would ring.
I said, Grave, Where is the victory?
Death, where is thy sting?
All around were superstitions and mystery
Cults of Greece.
Their acts rivaled Christianity; but
they brought no peace.
Nazarenes preached of hope with a live
God as the way.
He was the God of the living and there was
no fee to pay.
Tears flowed at the message.. of
forgiveness of sin.
Each could choose the way and help others
salvation to win.
Gentiles, slave or free, Each
had to answer on his own. Nobody
was too poor to enter.
It couldn't be bought with a throne.
For a Jew to eat with a gentile was
not a natural act.
It violated code and proved the change was a
matter of fact.
How can members of one body
separate themselves at the table?
It was a measure of their love to show that
they were unable.
It was also in Antioch where the name
"Christian" was first used.
We were way seekers and saints. The
names were never abused. Peace in

Judea was elusive with Caligula and
Herod too.
Many brought their agendas each threatening
all to undo.
Agrippa came as king wishing his patriotic
duty to have filled.
He set eyes on the Nazarenes. Having
James, the disciple, killed. When Herod
saw the pleasure and ratings which did
ensue he had Peter imprisoned so he
could kill him too.
Peter chained in prison.
Many soldiers watched the cell.
After Passover Herod planned to have him
killed as well.
Supplication and prayer for him were offered
to God, on high.
They prayed for a miracle not dictating when
or why.
His chained form sleeping
between soldiers was a sight.
His way was illuminated by a
brightly shining light.
An angel awakened him and
freed him from the chain.
He followed him to the street
where he was alone again.
He went to the house of Mary, the
mother of John Mark.
He knocked at the door.
The streets were still quite dark. The
maidservant saw him and left him
standing there.
She ran and told the people God
had answered prayer. He was
left there pounding.
They were too shocked to believe. They
finally went to the door and did the
miracle receive.

Herod had the guards killed then
dawned his royal robe.
He spoke as a god.
They began to mock and probe.
Herod had heard all his life that an
owl would spell his doom.
He looked out and saw an owl then terror
filled his room.
He cried with stomach pains like
flames as brilliant red.
He lived for five days then he
was pronounced dead.
Agrippa's son was too young to be
expected to rule.
Judea came under a procurator. He
was used as Claudius' tool. Christians
loved their freedom.
It offered all men hope.
They must be wise as serpents if they'd
be able to cope.
They must be harmless as doves in order
to survive.
To follow the Great Commission; for
this they would strive.
I told them we must be true to our
calling without doubt.
Barnabas, Mark, and I must leave so for
Cyprus we set out.
Cyprus, an island, colored by
mountains of copper was a
Phoenician colony till
Rome set out to top her.
Barnabas, John Mark and I
Crossed the sea and
preached in the Synagogue of Salamis
when that area was reached.
Aphrodite held power there of a
fearful barbaric force.
Her cultic worship flourished. We

went steadily on our course.
Our destination was Paphos. We
met a magician there.
Bar-jesus was his name. Sergius
Paulus was quite fair.
He was moved by the message.
Bar-jesus became alarmed.
I said he'd be blind for a season
otherwise he was unharmed. From that
time on to this day
I ceased to be called Saul.
I quit using my Hebrew name my
Roman surname was Paul.
We went to Perga in Pamphylia without
hesitation we went.
Malarial seizures came.
My sickness was quite intent. John Mark
refused to stay so he went home by ship. We
went to Pisidia-Phrygia, a very dangerous
trip.
We came to the Phrygian plain four
thousand feet above the sea.
Beyond the range of snowy hills
Pisidia Antioch awaited me.
Galatia, a wild, majestic country
was lost in antiquity. Pisidians,
mountain people had mythical gods,
you see.
Pisidian Antioch was a colony: a
small piece of Rome.
Galatia was not colonized.
Many Jews called Galatia home.
We went to the synagogue; were
given honorable seats alright.
I said neither Jew nor Greek were in
God's sight.
I gave them the key
to end their lives of strife.
I taught them grace not works would
lead to eternal life.
These stirred up trouble for
many reasons there.
They rubbed them the wrong way.
There was controversy everywhere.
Some questioned why we preached
to non Jews by birth.
God sent us as light to the Gentiles
bringing salvation to earth.
Legal action was taken claiming we
disturbed the peace; forbidding us
to speak.
Our talks they wished to cease. We
shook dust from our feet;
were prevented from sharing our load.
It was a gesture of irony as
we started down the road.
We went East toward Iconium some
eighty miles away.
Hitite gods and inscriptions were there as
in Abraham's day.
We went straight to the synagogue.
Many believers to us flocked.
Those who didn't believe
at the message were quite shocked.
We stayed a long time
leaving many with a faith quite strong.
When opposition mounted we
thought we'd be getting along.
We went south to Lystra;
some six hours away.
There were few Jews here. It
was a safe place to stay.
They worshipped ancient gods;
Hercules, Hermies and Zeus. They
were open to Christianity.
They'd called a religious truce.
We talked plainly to them and their
superstitions dispelled.

A lame man heard my message and was
immediately made well.
I spoke no terrifying words and
demanded no sacrifice.
They thought we were gods. We
told them to think twice. They
started to sacrifice to us. We tore
our clothes in protest.
We said we're just men like them and
sacrifices we did detest.
Enemies from afar came to mix up their
heads. stones were thrown until
I fell then I was left for dead.
We went back to the city.
They said I disturbed the peace.
They beat me and sent me away so all my
preaching would cease.
We set out for Derbe
on the south eastern edge of the plain.
The hills were old volcanoes; shaped
by gravity, wind, and rain.
On these volcanic rocks men
had carved their gods.
They worshipped these idols unaware that
they were frauds.
There was a country synagogue made up
of sinful men.
They responded to the message and wanted
us back again.
We planted much fruit there and watched it
mature and grow.
When we left we left in peace back to the
cities we'd go.
We urged those to received our
message and to stay in the faith
they had.
we told them not to be dismayed by
persecution which was quite bad. They
should gather together so the strong
could bear the weak;
to speak as the spirit moved.
Words of love to speak.
When we came to Pisidian Antioch we
found those who held on
Strongly rooted and growing for the Greek
Jews had gone.
They returned to traditionalism. They
had left their old beliefs.
We left the mountains.
The Silician trip was a relief.
Great was the welcome home to the church
in Antioch.
A door no man could shut and certainly
could never lock.
God had opened the door to let the Gentiles
in.
His mercy extended to them and they were
saved from sin.
Jerusalem Christians came with
conditions for Gentiles to meet.
I had escaped this rigidness and would
challenge this deceit.
It would topple salvation by grace which we
had always taught.
We must never compromise and must teach
what Jesus taught.
Legalists must be resisted until
misunderstandings go away.
Compromise must never be for there is no
other way.
Christ broke down the middle wall;
partitioning Jews from Greeks.
I took Titus, a true witness
with me so he could speak.
We were upright in faith in Christ not by
doing what law commands.
A man is defiled by his thinking not by a
legalist's demands.

Peter arose and supported me; God
gave Gentiles the Holy Spirit
Making no distinction
between the two.
No work can earn His merit.
James' followers came to Jerusalem;
seeing the Jews and Gentiles eat.
They raised such a fuss in town for this
didn't their rules meet.
Barnabas agreed with them. Peter agreed
with them too.
I could not and would not retreat.
Grace saves; not what you do.
Peter refused to eat with them driving a
wedge between their trust.
I disagreed to his face.
Salvation by grace was a must.
If you add works to grace then Jesus died
in vain.
Their position saddened my heart.
Disagreement causes pain.
I asked Barnabas to go to Galatia to see how
the brethren did fare.
He asked if John Mark could go and we
separated there.
Silas joined me for the trip.
We headed north together.
I couldn't compromise God's work. This
storm we'd have to weather. The
Mediterranean was an area in which I
had preached;
before Barnabas came to me many
had been reached.
We went to the Cilician gates Then to
Derbe and Lystra also.
Timothy joined us there.
To the synagogues we did go.
We traveled then to Phrygia where false
gods did abound.

We headed to Asia and Ephesus
preaching a message that was sound.
Then I had a vision.
In Asia I was not to preach. No
seed had been sown there.
There were people for us to reach. I did
not question the vision but through
dangers did go.
We were going to Bithynia.
Once again the Spirit said, "No." We
went west across the highlands then
were drawn by the sea.
Troas, a Roman Seaport was known as Troy
to you and me.
A Macedonian came saying, "Come
and help us there."
We were joined by a friend to make a long
journey to nowhere.
They had no synagogues but we heard of a
praying place.
All were women there. Lydia
was saved by grace. I baptized
her when asked.
She insisted with her we'd stay.
Her household all accepted Christ and we
started a church that day.
A slave girl followed us in the city. a
cultic fortune teller was she.
She said we were God's servants to bring
salvation to thee.
Her voice blocked my message.
My words were just a blur.
In Christ's name I commanded the
demon to leave her.
Her madness left immediately. Her
identity was reclaimed.
She could prophesy no more and I was the
one they blamed.
They whipped and imprisoned us

tightly chaining us to a wall.
They told the guard to watch us until they
came to call.
An earthquake freed us.
The guard thought we'd fled.
He started to kill himself but we called to
him instead.
When he heard us call and saw that we'd
behaved he dropped to
his knees asking, How
can I be saved?
He took us to his house, washed our wounds
then we ate.
He had us talk to his household.
All were saved on that date.
Rulers knocked at his door saying we'd
leave or he'd be harmed.
Earthquakes were quite common but the
city became alarmed.
I tired of their harassment. I said, We
are citizens of Rome.
The magistrates were afraid because
Rome was our home.
They begged Silas and I to leave lest
there be a riot in the end.
We did not agree
until we'd seen every friend. We
spoke to Lydia's household;
comforting and encouraging all.
We went down the mountain for we had
answered Jesus' call.
The Roman road to Amphipolis paved
with marble was a sight.
The sea was on our left with mountains on
the right.
We went to the synagogue when to
Thessalonica we arrived.
Religious toleration was growing thin.
In Judea many had not survived. In

Syria eighteen were beheaded.
In Egypt Jews caused trouble. Asian
Jews were barred quelling uprisings
on the double.
I was watched constantly.
Spies listened to me speak.
I spoke of the Messiah, the Christ; saying
he's the one they should seek.
I told them to redeem the time and
the inward man renew
In His kingdom there's no bond or free and
neither Greek nor Jew
I preached to the Thessalonians. They
had to change their way.
From many gods to one and with one wife
they learned to stay.
We guided the converts with prudence
and diligence.
As we stayed in this place and from that
day ever since.
At Philippi I'd built a community
which held together under stress.
I wanted the same thing here because
Romans caused duress.
The prejudiced paid troublemakers to
create an angry mob.
They looked for Silas and me as
others began to sob.
That night Christians took me with Silas
and Timothy to another city. I worried
about new converts.
I had, for them, much pity.
We were welcomed in the synagogue.
They searched scripture and
heard me.
How did the Thessolonicans fare? Maybe
Timothy would return to see.
Some troublemakers followed.
They sent me far away.

I'd await God's Word in Athens for others
didn't come this way.
Silas would go to Philippi; To
Thessolinica Timothy went.
If the interdiction was lifted word to me
would be sent.
I spoke in the synagogues. I
debated in the street.
I debated in the marketplace where
people came to meet.
I headed for the town of Corinth.
The city lay on a plain.
It was dedicated to making money. With
pleasure they were insane.
People spoke of Corinth for
its evil and its vice.
Idolatry there was vicious. The
people were not nice.
In the worship of Aphrodite naked
prostitutes stood in streets.
Gods of every description
were there for all to meet.
Search for pleasure ran rampant. Many
hungered for spiritual fare.
They had gods around who
symbolized love and care.
These gods made fertile ground for
Christian seeds to grow.
God chose the base to bring good and
Christian seeds we'd sow.
The weak and foolish here could sink no
further down.
I spoke to them as fellow slaves.
They sullenly wore a frown.
I taught them moral order showing that
bodies need respect.
They welcomed the gospel message.
Their openness was direct.
Aquila and Priscilla were Christians.

They made leather goods and tents. They
welcomed me to their home.
Our friendship was intense.
Wealthy Greeks came also.
I turned no one away.
Shopkeepers and bronze workers came to
learn what I would say.
When I came to Corinth to
Thessolinica I wanted to go.
Timothy and Silas brought word. I
must help the Corinthians grow.
Thessolonican Christians mostly had
remained true and loved me.
Enemies to others there were
deceitful and I had to flee.
Someone told me to write a letter to
Thessolinicans whom I loved.
God nudges you toward faith while to others
he gives a shove.
His tenderness reaches out. Be
patient toward all men. In
everything give thanks. Do this
again and again.
May the God of peace sanctify.
You are children of the light.
You're children of the day; not
of darkness nor of night.
The synagogue split because of me.
They said I did blaspheme when I
said a man hanged on a tree was
Messiah and able to redeem.
I received thirty nine lashes. My
garments I did shake.
Your blood's on your own heads.
Tracks I began to make.
Many Jews followed me.
I baptized one called Crispus.
Next door to the synagogue they
welcomed all of us. Jesus, the disciples

and I all stressed brotherhood.
We broke bread together daily and
knew that it was good.
In their ungodly worship meals were eaten in
revelry accompanied by hysteria;
drunkenness and ecstasy. Christians of all
economic levels sat down in love together.
Equal in God's sight they
celebrated their tether.
They sang and pledged anew to
avoid a wicked end;
not to steal or commit adultery;
deny a trust or God's Word bend.
After eating anyone could speak whenever
the Spirit led.
God's not a god of confusion but by order so
all could be fed.
If any spoke is tongues
an interpreter must translate.
I'd rather speak five meaningful words than
five thousand in confused state.
Share with those in need.
Let fellowship be your guide. Be
courteous one to another.
Let prayer always abide.
Since a veil was dignified with
power and honor too.
Let a woman's head be covered.
Its the proper thing to do.
Corinth, my most gentle church also caused
the most despair.
How could you demand purity when
evil is everywhere?
I stayed a year and a half patiently building
stone on stone
The church vitality was exemplary.
Purity was a hard concept to hone. The
dangers we faced were many.
Cults tempted men to stray.

An impeccable purity of doctrine Must
distinguish the Church of the day.
The arrival of proconsul Gallio gave the
synagogue a chance to say;
that men were to worship God in
an unusual unlawful way.
Gallio saw through their ploy defining law
as a Jew would.
I can't judge your religious law.
Do with him what you think is good.
I saw what Galleo had done.
He had stated freedom of speech.
I could use his decision in Rome as I, to
others, extended my reach.
Aquila would to go to Ephesus where
luxurious tents were in style.
I decided to go there also.
I'd been considering it for a while.
Ephesians could scatter the Word for
it was commercially great; a
banking center of the world; its importance I
can't overstate.
I prepared to go to Jerusalem for the
Passover then I'd return.
I spoke in the synagogue where they begged
me to stay so they'd learn.
I left saying if God willed I
would return one day
The tending of first fruits would be
Aquila's while I was away.
Caesarean journey was a danger for tempests
could arise in your face.
In Galatia they added works;
circumcision added to grace. I
turned aside to visit them.
I thought their churches dear.
In the end, however, Galatian
churches would disappear.
Cults flourished in Ephesis.

Some who heard John were there. They
believed in Jesus and baptism. That would
keep them from the snare.
Priscilla and Aquila found Apollos
preaching gnostic twists of the Word.
His was allegorical and illusive, but
he gave credit to Christ the Lord.
They explained the Word to him. His
desire to learn was evident. He wanted
to go to Greece,
but to the Corinthians he was sent. I
preached there for three months, but
they argued and took time away.
so I rented a hall from Tyrannus teaching
from eleven to four each day. Pantheism
invaded the message in the Laodicean city.
Angels and spirits were worshipped.
For those people I had pity.
I was thrown into prison again. The cults
had their own way.
I wrote to the Colossians, Philippians and
Philemon while in my stay.
I needed to encourage some; to wean them
from milk to meat.
Others needed a tongue lashing tempered
with words that were sweet.
Though I speak as angels If I don't show
any love.
I might as well be silent. It
won't help me get above.
If prophetic powers I have and
understanding without measure; If
there's no love with it
I won't receive Heavenly treasure.
Love does not envy or boast. It
is kind and patient too. It's not
puffed up or proud or resentful
of what you do.
It isn't pleased with wrong.

Its pleased only with what's right. When
someone does wrong its not happy with
their plight.
Tongues, prophesies and knowledge will
be gone some day.
Love alone will be there.
Listen to what I say.
I answered the questions asked about
eating sacrificial meat which was sold
in public markets for prices that can't
be beat.
Others asked if they should take other
people to court;
how women should dress in Church; What
clothing was too short.
I said that I had received thirty nine lashes
five days.
Three times I was beaten with rods.
I was stoned and left in a daze.
Three times I was shipwrecked with all the
dangers at sea.
I was often endangered by rivers which
raged on all sides of me.
Robbers endangered my life as
did my own people often.
Always there were dangers which would
never soften.
The heaviest pressures of all came from
Churches I had started.
The weak, the frail, the wayward who fell
when I departed.
I agonized over them all.
From God's love, can any separate? Can
tribulation, persecution, distress?
None of these! I state.
Through Jesus who loves us we're
conquerors and more for one day we'll be
together to live forevermore.
Demetrius, the silversmith, said I was

taking his wealth.
He cared more for possessions than people's
spiritual health.
Those who heard were alarmed.
Mobs formed in the street.
Everyone heard their cries and
all were on their feet.
Gaius and Aristarchus of Macedonia were
seized and dragged away.
The town clerk quieted the crowd saying,
Do not riot today.
The two captives were set free.
I met with them that night.
I said Christians must stand fast.
We must carry the light.
I went up the coast to Troas to join with
Titus there.
Titus did not come.
My spirit was in despair. I
went to Macedonia and
Brother Timothy I met.
The churches he reported on stood fast
without regret.
Macedonian churches were poor but that
was nothing new.
They were rich in the Spirit. Their
liberality shined through.
They gave all they had for
Jerusalem, at my request.
Five years they had supported me. On
my journeys I was their guest.
Titus finally reached me with
reassuring news.
To the Corinthians I wrote,
with Christ we'll never lose.
I said, we are very bold; but
not like Moses indeed who
covered his face with a veil; but
we have seen his seed. Christ

removed the veil.
He was the seed of Abraham. He
was also preexistent God Who is
the great "I am."
God commanded light to shine into human
hearts today to show the glory of God and
for Christ to show the way.
If any man be in Christ he is a brand
new creature.
The old has passed away.
Newness is his best feature.
He sent Titus and two others to finish
collecting from all.
There was a symbolic meaning.
Generosity knit one and all.
The garment woven by generosity from
one church to another given as
Macedonia and encourage reconciliation
with a brother.
I made the trip to Corinth in
the winter of '56.
I came by boat because snow
would put me in a fix.
Sitting in the sun of Corinth I
dreamed of going to Rome
where Christians from Peter's flock were
there and called it home.
I wrote to the church in Rome to link all
Christians in loves bond.
I gave thanks for them of
whom I was quite fond.
Let love be the genuine thing. Hate
evil but hold onto good.
Be aglow with the Spirit.
Serve the Lord as men should.
Rejoice in your eternal hope. Be
patient in tribulation too.
Be constantly in prayer.
Bless those who persecute you.

Bless and don't curse them. Rejoice
with them who rejoice. Weep with
those who weep.
Living harmoniously is your choice.
Repay none evil for evil. Think
noble thoughts of all.
Never avenge yourself,
leave it to God who is always on call.
Do not be overcome by evil.
Overcome it with good.
Owe nothing to any man
Love one another as you should.
Tolerance is the measure of love.
Have respect for authority.
I'd like to come visit you now but
other places I must be.
We left one ship for another.
We'd go to Macedonia up the coast.
We had Passover at Philippi.
Jerusalem was the intended host. We
crossed the Sea of Troas to a church
which Eutychus led.
He was the young man who
God raised from the dead.
When we landed at Miletus
I sent a messenger to Ephesus to bring the
elders of the church
to me without a fuss.
Three days later they were back. I
told them of plots on my life:
a result of political turmoil; of fire,
sudden death, and strife.
They should shepherd the church and stand
firm on Christ,
the rock for after my departure
wolves would enter the flock.
We sailed on to Tyre.
For seven days we stayed. I
found the Christians there.

We joined with brothers and prayed.
They begged me not to enter
Jerusalem where bloody battles had
been fought.
Hundreds had been crucified. It
was not a vacation spot.
At Ptolemais on the way we again found
Christians there.
It was a encouraging to know such groups
were everywhere.
Philip lived in Caesarea. We
stayed at his house.
We were warned about warfare.
Felix was a monster not a mouse.
They begged me not to go.
I said don't weep and break my heart?
I'm ready to be bound and die.
I am willing from this world to part. I
delivered the gift to Jerusalem for
reconciliation of all indeed.
They tried to kill me as a traitor.
This time I think they might succeed.
(Henrietta Buckmaster,**Paul:**
A Man Who Change the World.
McGraw Hill Book Company:

A Sinner

Once I was a sinner drifting
in a world of sin.
Now I am a Christian with
God's peace within

A Special Tree

I was just a little nut. I
grew into a tree.
I heard about a Savior Who
came to earth, you see.
It was decided by men to
take His life one day. They

cut me like a cross and
carried me away.
They hung God's Son on me then took
Him and departed.
They didn't know the way I felt But I
was broken hearted.

Total Commitment

Total Commitment is what God demands of
all who do believe.
We must invite Him to enter the heart.
We must this way receive; after
receiving Him into the heart
we can't sit and not serve.
[1] Henrietta Buckmaster, Paul: A Man Who
Changed The World. McGraw Hill Book
Company: New York, Toronto, London;
1965

Total commitment is what He
demands.
From it we must not swerve.
Total commitment is what He
requires.
Its what we all must give.
We have to give up some worldly pleasures
if, for Christ, we will live.
We don't give them up without reward for
He will give us peace.
The world won't understand why but His joy
will not cease.
Chorus:
We must serve Him with all the heart the
mind, body and soul.
We must share His love with others so He
can make them whole.

A Flock of Birds

A pastor's boy,
while very young climbed up the mountain
slopes to invite a
Hermit to the Christmas Story but the
Hermit crushed his hopes.
The way was long and a storm came.
The boy could hardly go.
He fell in the snow and couldn't rise. He
called out for help, you know.
The Hermit heard and helped him and asked
the boy his name.
He asked how he got way up there and why
in the world he came.
The boy was the pastor's son and invited
him to the Christmas Story. The Hermit
said he wouldn't go for Jesus would not
have left glory.
The disappointed boy got dressed but a
storm was on the way.
The Hermit suggested he spend the night.
The boy decided to stay.
He was awakened in the night.
The Hermit beckoned to him. A flock of
birds were in the snow.
Survival's chance was slim.
The boy and man went outside and tried to
save each bird.
They couldn't catch them though and the
boy's voice was heard.
Isn't there something we can do? The
Hermit sadly shook his head. I'd have
to become a bird myself so these birds
could be safely led.
The boy went back to bed.
The Hermit sat before the fire.
He contemplated what happened and the
boys earnest desire.

Then his words struck him and
the picture became clear.
He'd have to be a bird himself to make the
others come near.
God had to become a man for man to
understand the way.
So he descended the mountain to
attend the Christmas play.
The boy was happy to see it but only the
Hermit knew how a flock of snow
blinded birds changed
his point of view.

Cure

There's a cure for every ailment but I
wouldn't hold my breath.
The ultimate cure for everything is the
event we call death.
But it is just a beginning of forever which is
eternity.
If you didn't accept Jesus it'll be torment,
you see.
Death wouldn't be the cure but the start
of something worse.
There is a way to blessing. Its
provided free, of course. If you
accept Jesus Christ before
death you will live
in a splendid world of Heaven for its what
Christ came to give.

Purpose of Life

No person who has ever lived; who
has set foot on this earth;
was consulted for his approval or for
permission for his birth.
Birth and life was a gift for which
nobody asked but each of us has
purpose and a very special task.
Each of us has worth.
We might wonder how much. Each
is priceless in God's sight. He wants
us to feel His touch. He loves us
each so much that He sent His only
Son
So we could have eternal life and from
Satan's grip be won.
His love for us was so great that God's Son
suffered death.
and loved the ones who did it with
forgiveness in His breath.

Father, forgive them, he said for
they know not what they do.
Help them to seek Thy face
so they'll join us when life's through.
Though we didn't have a choice about
coming on the scene we must choose the
second birth to
make our record clean.
When we choose Christ as Savior He
adopts us into the flock. because we're
founded on his will which is the solid
rock.
No greater gift can we receive than
eternal life with Him.
Those who do not choose it have a future
that is grim.
As recipients of God's love the
decision is ours now.
As to whether we receive it for He
has shown us how.
Christ provided the victory over
death and life.

He can end depression and give victory
over strife.
No matter what our age or condition we are
in Jesus Christ alone can give victory over
sin.
He alone can give purpose. In
Him we can find rest.
He is the source of life and the source of
happiness.

Jesus Came To Set Men Free

Jesus came to set men free. He suffered for
you and me And though he didn't want to
go He went because He loved us so. On His
head He wore a
thorny crown. Men beat Him and knocked
Him down but He didn't say an angry
word and complaints were never heard.
Even when the whip was on His back He
did not break. He did not crack. The cross
He carried down the road till He fell
beneath its heavy load. When finally it
stood in its place they pulled his whiskers
from his face.
They nailed Him to that cruel tree where
He bled and died for you and me. The
crowd said if He were God's son angels
would come on the run and take Him
down so all would see He was the Savior
for you and me. They tossed dice to
divide His clothes.
When He called for water they all rose.
They gave him vinegar for His thirst.
saying, If He's God He'll come down first.
He cried, Father seeing more than a few,
Forgive them. They know not what the do.

Savior's Love

The Great Commission says that we
must preach to all the world but it
also says to begin at home where
Satan's darts are hurled. If we can't
win those at home our faith needs
to be stronger then we must pray
until we can and try a little longer.
After we witness to those at home we must
lose all our pride.
We must go to Samaria and preach for its
here our faith is tried.
The Samaritans are a people of a
completely different race.
For a Jewish person, to talk to them was
really a disgrace.
This is the reason that Jesus put them second
on the list.
Their prejudice was a cancer that grew on
them like a cyst.
If this barrier they could overcome God
could, their talents, use.
They could witness everywhere and they
would never lose.
They'd be rewarded ten times o'er for giving
up their pride.
This is why Christ came to earth; suffered,
bled and died.
This message was good for them and it still
holds today.
Our Samaria might be the ghetto which is
not far away:
but until we can forget ourselves and show
these people love.
We cannot really serve our Lord who is
waiting up above.
Let us show our neighbors that we love as
Christ showed us.

Let us love our neighbors so much we'll
never fuss.
Let us reach out to our Samaria wherever it
might be
for we wish to conquer prejudice and
become much more like thee.
When we break these bonds that
make us act this way
we're ready to broaden horizons without
further delay.
When we reach out to the world with the
message plain and clear.
We'll witness for our Savior, whose
love for us is dear.

Christmas Donkey

I was just a weary donkey and I
had a weary task.
I took people around the country
whenever they came and asked. One
day I made a journey with a couple on
their way.
I heard them mention a census and how
they'd like to stay.
She was great with child but they said they
had no choice.
I was chosen for the journey. I
loved her soothing voice.
The going was rough and hard.
Often the pace was slow.
I heard them mention being late. I
went as fast as they'd let me go. At
town I started through the gate.
I heard the young man say, I
hope we're not too late.
I hope we find a place to stay.
The woman answered.
All is well; in a voice calm as could be.

We went from inn to inn and the problem I
could see.
Each innkeeper said quite kindly.
I'm sorry. We have no room.
Each time I saw the kind young man sink
deeper into gloom.
At the last inn the city had he thought they
would be able but was
told there was no room except the
animal's stable.
They soon settled there then a little child
was born.
Angels sang from the sky of this blessed
Christmas morn.
Glory to God in the highest. A
Savior has come to earth.
He'll save men from their sin in spite of
His lowly birth.

Shepherds came to adore Him
singing, Peace! Good will to men.
I felt proud to have carried Him and
rejoiced again and again.
They said He was God's Son who came His
own to save.
They said God made the sacrifice and His
dear Son He gave.
Sacrificial animals would soon be
unnecessary, you see because
God's unblemished lamb came down to
set men free.

Angels Unaware

An angel descended one day and
caused a hurrying man delay. The
man was angry and sad and he felt
really bad
till a train lay derailed in the way.

He asked himself that day if, on
time he had gotten away.
Where would he be?
In his mind's eye he'd see.
Under the train he would lay.

He was now happy in every way.
His anger had faded that day.
He said, God, I thank thee for
the delay you sent me. Help me
more often to pray.

Deep Sorrows

Sometimes it seems our sorrows are
more than we can bear.
It seems, at times, that we, like Job, get
more than our fair share.
We share with you your sadness.
Our prayers are with you too.
In the darkest hours there's Jesus.
He will see you through.

Jesus Heals

Jesus grew tired while teaching. He
preached and healed the sick.
As He left the Capernaum synagogue a
man's hand was healed real quick.
As He walked toward the sea A
crowd toward Him came.
The sick sought healing then for they'd
heard of His name.
He boarded a boat to keep from
being pushed into the sea.
The next day he went to a mountain where
to God he made a plea.
He called His followers together.

He had chosen twelve,
He said, to be His special helpers; to
heal sick and raise the dead. His
helpers were Simon Peter,
His brother Andrew and also James. James
brother John and Bartholomew, who was
called by two names.
He was also known as Nathaniel. He
chose Matthew and Thomas too. and
James, the son of Alphaeus;
as the list of helpers grew.
He also chose Simon, the Zealot and
Thaddaeus, son of James;
and finally He chose Judas Iscariot
who'd betray His holy name.
He taught them how to minister. To
Israel's people they were sent. He told
them to heal the sick and cleanse
lepers as they went.
He said not to take any money for their
power they didn't pay.
He told them to leave all baggage; all
extra clothing should stay.
Don't even take a walking stick for the
people will care for you.
Enter a city and choose a home and stay
there till you are through.
If you're not welcome
choose another place..
Jesus knew what was in store and
hardships they would face.
Remember, Jesus said,
the Father knows what you do.
He knows all that happens and He'll take
care of you.
The Father knows each sparrow that to the
ground does fall.
You're more valuable than they. He'll
hear you when you call.

He knows you better than you do.
He's numbered every hair.
He knows what you have need of and, you know,
He will take care.

Mission America

A is for abundance, the bountiful supply.
Fields are white with wheat, corn and rye.
Field are white, for bringing to God's fold.
The laborers are few and hearts are cold.
M is for Home Missions, a very worthy task. Why must we begin at home you might ask.Acts 1:8 says, begin where we are. Missions begins at home, not always afar.
E is for the energy which God gives today.
Energy to witness and energy to pray.
Remember all we have's from God. Use this energy to walk where Jesus trod.
R is for righteousness all need to show.
None is righteous but Christ declares us so. We must tell others of their eternal fate For when death comes then its a little late.
I is for the increase by the faithful few.
Increase by the few who leave the pew.
They go into the world to tell about His love giving others birth from Jesus up above.
C is for Christianity, a Christ who died for us. He paid the sacrifice with very little fuss. He gave His life and commanded us to tell others about Him to save souls from Hell.
A is for America, a wide open mission field with many called but very few who yield.
Home Missions offers a chance to serve the Lord.
Full or part time if we work with one accord.

Rainbow

A rainbow, a beautiful sight many have often seen.
Has many colors like red, orange, yellow and green blue, indigo and violet too,
all created by God especially for me and you,
God left them to remind us whether short, fat, thin, or tall;
He'll never again destroy all life by a flood which covers all.

Resort Missions America

This is a wide vast land we have from mountain peaks to seas;
from hills which seem impassable to giant mammoth trees;
from the peak of Sunset Crater to Crater Lake, so blue;
from the colors of Bryce Canyon to the alligator in the slough;
from the glaciers of Mount Ranier to the cliffs of Wisconsin Dells;
from the hand-made Indian ruins to natural

spring-fed wells.
Our land is very diverse and
communities separated.
The individual cultures can be appreciated.

They must be witnessed to for Christ
knocks at every door.
We can't neglect to witness
because a group is poor.
We must witness one to one to people
everywhere and there's a vast mission field
of which we are unaware.
People of every nation visit
from port to port.
They make up a mission field and must get
our support.
Foreign immigrants come here for
freedoms which they seek.
They must receive the Gospel whether
Spanish, French or Greek
Many communities in our land
suffer from lack of bread
and cannot concentrate on God until they
have been fed.
Many inhabitants in the slums have no
guiding light, you see.
They might only need attention to fill their
lives with glee.
They'll be receptive to the Lord because
they'll see we care.
We'll be their picture of the Lord and with
them we can share.
Puppets provide an avenue to present God's
Word to some.
Resort Missions provides a services to
entertain with more to come.
Along with the entertainment show them
all Christian love;
tell them about our Savior who comes to

them in love.
Isolated groups are here.
They are, for us, a mission field.
Home Missions can reach many as
spiritual lives are healed.
They cannot do it alone.
They need all our support, our prayer and
our finances or their task might come up
short.

Home Missions

God's handiwork is everywhere as in the
mountain peak;
but churches remind us all that we are very
weak.
The cities with many people remind us that
God came to brighten up the lives of all
who'd take His name.

Craters show God's power; of
His energy they tell.
The bubbling mud pots testify to the
temperatures of Hell.
The early ruins tell of failures of a
mission to aid all.
The broad Grand Canyon Remind us that
we're small.
The wide expansive spaces speak of the
vastness of this land.
The hills were carved by God with a mere
wave of His hand.
The river's ice cold waters are refreshing
from the heat.
The colors in Bryce Canyon are a sight
which can't be beat.
Formations show God's
handiwork in so many ways.
A fence shows the work of man and points

to where he stays.
The wagons of bygone years show man's
willingness to labor.
The viewers of a waterfall show us who is
our neighbor.
We see crowds viewing a tree. We
can't tell which are saved. We see
man's shelter in a log and pleasures
for which he craved.
Man's accomplishments are nothing.
We view the bridge he made.
Jesus was our bridge to God.
His love will never fade.
Simple reflections testify of the
grandeur in our land.
The shearing off of Half Dome shows the
power of God's hand.
Beauty is all around us; Here
or in Crater Lake.
On the Pacific's rugged shore we see what
God can make.
As we look into Canada from a mountain in
the states
we see the vast land we have and why
God's message cannot wait.
The slopes and glaciers of Mount Ranier;
Its reflection in a pool,
The bubbling mud pots at Yellowstone
which isn't quite so cool.
Old Faithful, the famous geyser shoots
into the air.
The canyon's running water shows us a
land so fair.
The majestic mountain peaks in a
place called Jackson Hole all show
God's handiwork.
God alone can make us whole.
The lake behind the dam
provides for recreation.

The dam itself gives power for the cities of
our nation.
Formations point to God who has power to
set men free.
The task of witnessing falls to
you and me.
Man leaves a mark on civilization by
painting on a wall.
A mine shaft shows where he's been but
accomplishments are small.
Wisconsin offers boat rides through the
Dells, a tourist spot.
The river ride is nice. We
might like it a lot.
Rock formations show ages gone telling of
God's patience with man for man built
worldly comforts
and forgot God's Holy plan.
Though man's creations help us in this
world of ours.
We constantly build more and forget God's
awesome powers.
Man parcels off the land
which he claims as his own and forgets to
witness to others
who we know are all alone.
He forgets that every building represents
those for whom Christ died
while he throngs to attractions which take
him for a ride.
Each person who is present is a
mission field indeed for missions
begins at home and goes
where there's a need.
In rural areas we find the
population very small;
but they need witnesses too for God loves
one and all.
Each monument testifies of God given

ability for God gave us the talent to build
the things you see. Each farm's a mission
field itself
for each of us knows well
the laborers are few who go to the world
to tell.
The monuments of mankind are
insignificant, I say.
The lighthouse points to a safe route but
Christ is the only way.
A man's face on the mountain carved by
nature's hand views a ripened mission
field in a very thirsty land. Witnessing
takes on many forms.
Puppets can be used.
They can often make a point but
sometimes are abused.
His Word will not return void if we are
faithful to tell.
The silver lining to the cloud is that
people will be saved from Hell.
We needn't wait for a rocket ship to blast
us to the moon
but we must become a lighthouse for
Home Missions very soon.

Jesus, The Promised One

A babe, promised so long ago; born
in Bethlehem as prophesied;
placed in a manger for a bed at the inn,
they'd been denied.
If people knew who He was it seems
they'd have made room.
Two thousand years later He's
still ignored and many thus
face doom.
He left a home in glory
to be despised and rejected by man.

He died to pay for man's sins. He
alone could fulfill God's plan. Man
blew it from the beginning. He sinned
in the garden with Eve.
He blamed her.
She blamed the snake.
and said he did deceive.
This is true but she chose to eat and
Adam likewise that day.
If we listen to others then sin we
will still have to pay.
God was unwilling for us to perish so
He sent His only Son.
He was born to die
so salvation could be won.
Because of Jesus' obedience all can be
saved from sin if we repent, turn to God
and invite the dear Savior in.
He'll not only give peace now and
joy in our hearts today.
He'll prepare a mansion above so He
can welcome us home to stay. Oh
death. Where is thy victory?
Oh grave, Where is thy sting?
With Jesus we have no fears for death will
happiness bring.

No Use for Doctors

A man seemed really healthy. If
sick he'd not hear a word. Go to
the doctor?, he said.
Why! I'll just trust the Lord.
Some said God used doctors to heal the sick
and the lame.
It's no less miraculous though to a doctor
one came.
God uses ordinary people to do
what he has to do.

He'll continue using them until the
age is through.
A man experienced a flood. The
water covered his shoes.
The National Guard came by bearing
evacuation news.
This man stood his ground. His
voice was plainly heard.
I'm not leaving here. I'm
trusting in the Lord.
The water continued rising until
it rose to his chest.
Everything was wet even
though he did his best.
A boat appeared at the door to
evacuate the man.
He said, I'll trust the Lord.
Help others if you can.
The water got so deep upon the roof he got
then up on the chimney.
The rising water he fought. A
helicopter hovered, saying, We
came to rescue you.
He said, I'll trust the Lord.
That's what I need to do.
The water kept on rising.
He stopped smiling and frowned. A
little more water came and this
Christian drowned.
He got to Heaven and asked,
Lord Jesus, I trusted you.
Why did you let me drown and not bring
me through?

You said with each temptation you'd
provide a way.
Why didn't you meet my needs in the flood
today? God said,
I sent the Guard, a boat and helicopter too.

What more could you want?
What did you want me to do?
Sometimes we must come Jesus'
way or none.
His way may not appeal to us its the way
it must be done.

How Much Love?

Jesus, Jesus, Jesus; The
name above all names.
Jesus, Jesus, Jesus; through all the world
proclaims.
Come thou unto Me.
Hear Me very clearly.
I'll adopt you all
because I love you
dearly. How much do
you love us? We hear
the question now.
Come, my child and see the scars upon my
brow; the nails in my feet and hands; the
wound in my side;
the scars from scourgings, but
the deepest are inside.
The heartbreak that I feel
to see so many lost can't be shown to you
but its not without its cost.
He said, I loved you enough to go down
to the grave now I sit with God on high
awaiting those I came to save.

Wise Men Watched

Wise men studied the Heavens.
They saw a new bright star.
They quickly made ready to
travel and search afar.

They knew the promised Messiah had
been born that very night.
They prayed and watched daily hoping to
see that sight.
The rest of the world was unaware.
Many remain so today,
but others are ready to follow and Christ
shows us the way;
the way to everlasting life; the
only way to God.
All other ways lead to Hell when
placed beneath the sod.
Jesus made the way so simple that a child
can understand
and it's free to all.
With Jesus all can stand. Many, however,
will choose
Hell because of their love for sin.
They'll continue in their ways until
they've entered in.
They like the rich man of old will beg God
for a chance but it
will be too late then.
On earth they took their stance.
You who are alive today: those
who still have breath,
can choose Heaven for your home.
You must do it before death.
Come to Jesus today.
Ask Him into your heart. Ask
Him for daily strength.
Don't worry. He'll do His part.

Peace, good will to men.
They knew it came from God and was good
as it had always been.
God set man in the garden. All
that He gave was good.
He gave him all good things to eat but of
one tree he never should.
The devil tempted Eve. She
ate and Adam too. Both
disobeyed their God.
Which isn't good to do.
No man could get to Heaven for
every one had sinned.
When Satan tempted Eve and Adam ate,
He grinned.
God had another plan that was beyond
belief.
He'd let His Son be crucified which would
cause Satan grief.
With this sinless sacrifice man's
ransom was fully paid.
Man, now, could go to Heaven though
he couldn't make the grade.

God's Son had to be born which
is what the angels saw.
It'd bring God glory.
Man wouldn't be under law.
Grace would save men; grace
through faith, you see.
My Savior, born that day would live and
die for me.

Angelic Beings

Angelic being gathered in the sky. In
awe they watched the earth. They
couldn't comprehend it all. They
witnessed the Savior's birth. They
shouted, Glory in the Highest!

A Manger

I stood still for quite some time.
Each day men filled me with hay.
I felt satisfied with my life.
A wonderful thing happened one day.

The animals usually came and ate the
hay I had held for them,
but at the close of this special day I
held more value than a gem.
A couple came to me that night,
Joseph and Mary, they said.
They had a boy at my feet and I
served as His bed.
They laid Him in my hay.
They called Him God's Son.
Wrapped in swaddling clothes. I
held him as life was begun.
Shepherds worshipped Him. They
talked of an angel band. They
called Him the Savior of
everyone in the land.
Some might call it vanity.
Others say I've gone wild but I feel like a
blessed manger to have held the Christ
Child.

Teacher's Prayer

Lord, We know some here are
academically behind.
Others do their best
to develop and use their minds.
Some strive for excellence but
many are satisfied; Content to
be labeled, "Slow" so they have
never tried.
Help us Lord to give each a
gentle little nudge.
Help us to know how hard to push to get
them to budge.
Not so hard we make them quit but that
they want more;
so they find learning rewarding and not an
endless bore.

Help each to be determined
to let the teachers teach and not to stir up
trouble putting
learning out of reach.
Help each teacher to see each
student as precious ore which
needs a little refining: a little
polishing and no more.
Some might be great poets; others
mechanics or engineers.
Some might be laborers,
doctors or citrus overseers.
Whatever they become may they give it
their best and see education as a tool And
do their very best
to reach their full potential and to become
really "cool."
May they go on from here to continue
their lifelong quest never satisfied to be
"slow"
but striving to be their best.

Amen.

Jonah's Decision

God said; Go to Ninevah.
Jonah didn't want to go. He
hopped aboard a ship. The
winds began to blow. A major
storm raged on. The men
became afraid.
They threw baggage overboard with all
they had to trade.
They lightened the ship. The
storm kept on raging. They tried to
find its cause. Jonah, they started
paging. They found him in the

hold. They asked about the storm.
He admitted responsibility. His
actions were not the norm.
He said things would be right and calm seas
they'd see if they threw him overboard into
the raging sea.
They threw him overboard. A
whale took him inside.
With one big gulp the whale gave Jonah
an elevator ride.
Jonah cried out to God from the belly of
the whale.
He promised if he lived he'd go to
Ninevah without fail.

The whale took him near the
nearest shore at hand then he
spit Jonah out.
Jonah walked on dry land.
He went to Ninevah.
God's message he proclaimed.
Men obeyed his warnings and among God's
people were named.
Jonah cried out to the Lord.
I knew you'd change your mind.
I predicted they'd not be doomed and pardon
they would find.

Outlooks on Christmas

At Christmas many think only of the
things they will get.
Some renew acquaintances with people
they have met.
Some use My Savior's birthday as an excuse
to have a drink.
They say that it won't hurt them.
That is what they think!
Stores exploit Jesus' birthday.

Commercialism is regretful. They
begin earlier each year. Their
tactics are disrespectful.
Some use it for one long party in which to
ignore God's Word.
Others remember the message which only
the shepherds heard;
Rejoice and be Exceedingly glad for your
Savior has been born.
Cheer up and be happy. Don't
be fearful or forlorn.
Jesus, himself, taught later it's better to
give than to get.
Greed for wealth on this earth will put one
in spiritual debt.
What shall it profit a man to get rich
from what he'll sell or to gain the entire
world if his soul winds up in Hell? The
true meaning of Christmas.
It's when we honor Jesus birth.
Without this glorious day there'd be
no hope on earth.

Jesus Tomb

I was a cave dug into the rock. I
was dug for a rich man's tomb. Like
many around me I thought.
I'd watch a rich man's doom. They
took the poor carpenter; wrapped him
and brought him in.

Some said He was the Son of God who
came to take man's sin.
I had my doubts about this for He
was crucified.
They brought His body here. God's
Son would not have died.

94

After He was safely inside a stone was
rolled in front of me.
This was my "eye to the world." I
could no longer see.
Three days passed and I heard the guards
changing twice a day.
Then I felt the body move and I
heard this man say, Open up!
Let Me out!
The stone rolled at His voice. He
walked out into daylight.
Angels did rejoice.
If rocks could talk I'd say
this was the Son of God.
My life's been changed because on my floor
the Savior trod.

The Stable

I was an out-of-the-way stable. For
animals, a place to stay. I'd had
this job for so long
I forgot any other way.
My life had been so normal. People I
saw swore a lot.
They griped about the odor or the price of
this spot.
I'd seen men sit and gamble and make many
a shady deal.
I thought all were like this.
They'd gamble, swear, and steal.
One night during a census I
met a man and his wife.
They were different from any I'd met in my
whole life.
They were concerned about the
baby to come.

They said the boy to be born was God's
only begotten Son.
They said that He would make a way for
men to get to God.
It wouldn't be an easy route.
There'd be correction by the rod.
There'd be few who would follow.
Many wouldn't hear what He said.
They'd regret their callous attitude the
second they were dead.

The conversation was interrupted when the
baby's time arrived.
Though conditions were dirty the precious
child survived.
Wrapped in swaddling clothes and
placed upon the straw he did not cry at
all He came to fulfill the law.
The law of the prophets said a Messiah
would be born to remove
the sin of the world.
He'd be treated with much scorn. An
angel proclaimed His birth right up -
above my door.
It gave me a glorious feeling like I'd never
had before.
I had seen a side of man I
never knew existed.
The joys this night brought me could not
ever be listed.

Star of Bethlehem

I was the brightest star in Heaven;
placed in the sky at Jesus' birth.
When He was born I shed my light and
shined it down toward earth.
I guided the three wise men to the
place where Jesus was.

They brought rich gifts for Him but they
knew not His cause.
I was a bright Heavenly light. He
was the "Light of the World."
Since Satan likes only darkness his darts at
Jesus were hurled.
But I guided the wise men to
Jesus on that day.
Wise men still follow his light and never
from it stray.

A Candle

A candle's flickering light might
not seem like much to you but in the
absence of other light it would put some
things in view.
It could help you find your way and
show you where to go.
It would show barriers also;
pitfalls revealed by its glow. If
you were lost in darkness;
stranded on the sea of life a distant candle
could guide you slicing the darkness like a
knife.

It would show the way to others where
safety awaited you.
Jesus is like a candle which brings the
Christian path to view.
Born on Christmas morning He
shows the way to God.
He is the "Light of the World." If
we follow where He trod.
If we accept Him as our Savior He's the
light to show the way.
We'll never be out of step if
from him we do not stray.

Sheep

Some call us lowly and dirty; a
nuisance is what they say but they
shear us twice a year so in warm
clothes they can stay.
We're really not so bad though. We
just want the tender sprouts.
We don't always mind.
Our behavior causes doubts. One
day, I remember very well, we saw
an angel appear.
We sheep were good as gold all that day
due to fear.
As we listened to him talk he changed our
lives that day.
We heard about the Savior's birth and the
bed they made from hay.
We may look dirty and clumsy but we're
smarter than most men for we know Jesus
is God's Son and
He has always been.

Joseph and Mary

Joseph and Mary were engaged.
She was found with child.
Joseph was going to back out for he was
just and mild.
While contemplating these things an
angel of the Lord appeared saying,
Take Mary for your wife and do
not be affeared.
His Father is the Holy Spirit.
Mary shall bear God's Son.
He shall save His own from sin.
The victory will be won.
You shall name Him Jesus fulfilling

the prophecy of old; Behold!

A virgin shall bear a Son was
what the prophesy told.
They shall call Him Emmanuel;
itsmeaning is, "God with us."
Joseph obeyed the angel and
married without a fuss.
A Son was born as said. Jesus
was His name.

He proved He was God's Son but was
This, too, was prophesied.
crucified just the same.
It had to be carried out to make a way to
Heaven for all who do not doubt.

Shepherds

The shepherds were in the fields safely
guarding flocks of sheep.
An angel appeared to them and they, in
fear, fell asleep.
The angel said, "Don;t be afraid, I
bring great news of joy.
The Savior was born in Bethlehem.
He is a baby boy..
Wrapped in swaddling clothes.
In a manger he will lay."
Suddenly the angel was joined by an army
of angels that day.
The shepherds said to each other, to
They ran into the village and began
Bethlehem, "Let us go."
going to and fro. Lying in a manger as
said they found the precious child. They
told about the angels and the reason they
seemed wild.
All who heard were astonished.
Mary was proud in her heart.

Shepherds returned to the fields when it
was time to depart.
They praised God for the angels and for
being the ones they told.
They praised Him for sending Jesus and
keeping sheep in the fold.

Streets of Gold

When we shall walk the Streets of Gold
many truths will then unfold.
Christ, our Master and our Friend will be

Wherever we go He'll go along.
They'll be no end.
right with us.
His guiding power will keep us strong. In
shining light we'll see His face. We'll be
saved through His loving grace. On behalf
of his believers He'll intercede and for
them He will fill every need.

Prayer for Guidance

Lord. Have mercy on our souls. Set
our choice on proper goals. For our
sins accept confession. Guide us to
the right profession.
You know all our talents best and in
which field we'll be most blessed. We do
not wish, your will to shirk So, guide us
Lord, to proper work.

I Love to Tell Christ's Story

I love to tell Christ's story of
the Savior who died for me.
He could have stayed in glory but came
to set me free.
He came to save mankind from his

overwhelming sin;
to search and all the lost to find; giving
them the ultimate win.
He was rebuked throughout life and bore
much grief and pain
that we might have
His peace and might His kingdom gain.
The Lord is right beside me
throughout each passing day.
He helps me resist temptation and is with me
all the way.
Sometimes I do not follow the path
of the crucified.
He never never leaves me but stays right
by my side.
He stays beside me every day through all
my joy and sorrow and
I never have to worry.
He'll be right here tomorrow.
Some day when my work has reached its
very end I know
I'll be taken to Heaven to be with Christ,
my friend.

Take Us Home

When World War III at last breaks out let us
hear your returning shout.
Produce a long loud trumpet sound and
bring your angels all around. When our
work on earth is through take us Lord to
be with you. If our work down here is
done we wish to meet God's only Son.
We wish to gather to live above where
we shall live in perfect love. We'll have
blessings there in store and we shall live
forevermore.

Working For the Lord

Lord, we work not for praise.
We want your blessing all our days. We
hope to rise to Heaven above and to live
together in perfect love.
We will, by trusting, here below get to
Heaven where Christ we'll know.
Here on earth we will grow old but we'll
never age on the streets of gold.
We'll live forever with Christ, the
Son when finally
our battle has been won.

The Courage of Jesus

What courage and stamina;
He surely possessed to die on the cross that
we might be blessed.
Through hardships and sorrow He
showed the way to live with the
Father in that glorified day.
He showed the way and made it quite clear
that we might be saved and,
to Him, be near.
The pathway is narrow, straight
and quite long.
At the end we shall find that
sanctified throng.
This kind of sacrificial love has
never before been known but
Jesus suffered and died to
make us His very own.
In this fact alone
we should take much pride for
to save us from sin
our Savior bled and died.
It meant that much to Him, you see.
With a Savior so brave we
can't disagree.

A Wise Man

I was a member of the Magi. I
was said to be a wise man.
I'd been expecting the messiah as He
came to fulfill God's plan.
The prophecies said
He'd come from Bethlehem of Judea. His
coming had been expected; of the time we
had no idea.
When we saw a star in the sky that
was brighter than all the rest we left all
we had to follow it.
We knew we must pass the test. The
journey was expensive but we had
brought gifts to the king.
Gold, Myrrh and frankincense were the

presents we did bring.
We followed the star,
asking, where is the one
born king of Judea.
We hoped to find Him that way but Herod
had a different idea.
He asked us to report to him so he could
worship too but God revealed to us that this
wasn't what we should do.
When we found the child we gave
our gifts to Him.
We took a different route.
Herod's chance to find him was slim.
Later we heard that Joseph
had taken the child and fled. Herod had all
the children killed.
There was weeping for the dead.
As is true of Wise men everywhere we
believe in God's only Son.
We also know that the plan of God can't be
destroyed by what is done.

Why Me?

When tragedy strikes we
are tempted to ask,
Why did this
happen to me?
When it happens to the young we
ask, How could this be? One with
so much promise,
whose chances were outstanding.
We wonder why he'd die.
How could God be so demanding?
Though he was just loaned to us we feel
this isn't fair.
We read about Job in the Bible.
He got more than his share.
We don't know the reasons now.
We can rejoice that he knew the Lord.
We can go to the Bible for
comfort and get
strength from God's Holy Word.

While I Was Yet a Sinner

While I was yet a sinner my
Savior died for me.
He loved me more than words can tell to
hang upon that tree.
He took my sins upon himself taking the
punishment I deserved.
He straightened out my wayward path.
The way's no longer curved. My
feet are on the straight and
narrow. It is the only way.
If yours aren't there they should be. You'll
wish they'd been some day.

Rededication Prayer

Dear Lord, When I stray from you, please
help me to come back.
Please forgive me of my sins and give me
what I lack.
I pray, Lord, not for earthly things but
courage strength and power, For you to
shine your light toward me and be my
guiding tower.
Dear Lord, you know that I am blind to the
things that I should do. I do those things I
know I shouldn't and not enough for You.
Dear Lord, I'm asking you right now to help
me be prepared;
And to be uncomfortable all day long until
Your word I've shared.

Our Samaria

The Great Commission says to preach to
the world and begin at home though Hell's
darts at us are hurled.
If we can't witness at home our faith should
be stronger.
We must pray until we can then practices
little longer.
After we witness at home we must lose
all our pride and go to our Samaria
where our faith is tried. The Samaritans
are a people of a different race,
a person to whom talking would be
considered a disgrace. This is why Jesus
put them second on the list. Prejudice,
like a cancer, will grow just like a cyst.

If they overcame this God
could, their talents, use. They
could witness to people and they
would never lose.
They'd be rewarded for

giving up their pride.
This is the reason Christ
suffered here and died.
This message was for Jews and it
still holds today.
Our Samaria might be the ghetto which is
not far away.
Or it might be the rich we
have learned to hate.
It might be those at work who
always come in late.
It might be the poor,
separated by class
the jobless or the homeless who
we daily walk past.
Until we're ready to show
these people love We're not fit
to serve God who is waiting
above.
Let us show our neighbors the love Christ
showed to us.
Let us develop love for those with whom
we'd rather fuss.
Let us reach to our Samaria wherever
it might be
and to conquer our prejudice and
nevermore flee.
When we break down barriers
making us feel that way.
We'll broaden our horizons without
further delay.
We must reach out to the world with
the message quite clear and witness
for our Savior
who is very dear.

When You Feel
Discouraged

When you feel discouraged
and far from the Lord come
back to Him.
Get strength from His word.
Believe by His teachings and
be much in prayer.
Your discouragement will vanish into
thin air.

Family and Friends

Families are important for a place
where we belong.
They help us mature
and become both big and strong.
They provide a place of refuge
which we all need so badly.
If we don't have this kind of place we'd face
the world quite sadly.
With an understanding family we can learn
to face the world.
We gain comfort from this unit when
problems at us are hurled.
We can have our disagreements and
fuss with all our might but we know we
are still family and things will be
alright. Friends are important too. on
them we can rely.
We help them and they help us. At
least we should always try. Friends
are usually chosen for something
both enjoy.
It may be a certain sport, or
game or car or toy;
Something they have in common;
perhaps a common cause
brings them together and
causes them to pause.
Pause from their busy schedules. They

pause for a special reason; then they
become acquainted. working together
For a season, friendship begins to
grow. As they depend on one another.
Soon they treat their acquaintance like
a sister or a brother.
Each has made a friend; someone
with whom to share; to bear their
burdens and joys; someone they
know will care.
Friends and family help us get by
when things get rough.
They help us grow up stronger.
They help us to hang tough. We
all need friends in life at one
time or another.
If you want to have many why not
make him a brother?
If you're part of God's family you have
friends you've yet to meet in
every town and country and on
almost every street.

God's family is very large.
On common ground they stand.
They join together in prayer and
lend a helping hand.
If you make your friend a
brother or sister in the Lord
God's family will be larger and you'll
both grow in His Word.

Thy Boundless Love to Me (Paraphrased)

Jesus' love cannot be measured: Nor be
imagined nor detailed. Make my heart
to thee more treasured,

and Thee alone will there be hailed.
Now I am yours, yes only thine.
Be thou the source of strength
that's mine.

Empty my soul of everything: Fill
it with your abiding love.
May your great love in my heart ring. Help
me treasure things from above. Take all
my worldliness from me.
May all my words and acts please thee.

Your love is filled with compassion.
In your presence I have no fear.
Care and fear you make old fashioned
when your comforting grace is near. Jesus
help me to keep my sight and wants only
on what is right.

Starting a Bus Ministry

Christ told us to go and bring them in.
We thought,
"A bus ministry we'll begin.
Thoughts come quickly actions come slow
for the devil would rather we would not
go.
He'll block our pathway at every turn.
He doesn't want lost of the
Savior to learn.
He'll whisper, "Its way too much trouble."
When we get started his efforts will
double. He'll tell some to place obstacles
in our way so they'll vote to wait until
another day.
If he fails to swing the vote there He'll
make the task a hard one to bear.
The bus we can afford will be quite a
mess. It takes a lot of hard work we must

confess but with God's help we'll soon
overcome.
Our fingers and minds
might become numb. The
devil won't be finished with
us yet.
He'll cause objections, you can just bet.
Some may ask, Why
have another bus?"
There's plenty to carry all of us.

One will say, "I'll have none of it." and
he'll do his best to make us quit. God's
Word will keep us hanging in strong and
He'll fill our hearts with His dear song. His
work, regardless of how
hard and long. will continue for Christ
and is never wrong.

Unequally Yoked

Be ye not unequally yoked is
what Paul had said.
Don't yolk one who is alive with one who
is spiritually dead.
The truth of what Paul expounded is just as
true today
for one can't serve the Lord while being
pulled the other's way.
Be a separated people and a
good example set.
Don't sin against the Lord or you'll incur a
debt.
If you'll obey God's Word
He'll be your Father too.
You'll be His son or daughter and Heaven
will be in view.
Let us cleanse ourselves and live in
holiness and fear.

Let God's work be done and to Him
we'll grow dear.
We should never cheat or lie or sin when
out of view.
We don't come to condemn but to have
fellowship with you.
Some things we have to say might cause
a little grief but if they bring repentance
this will become relief.
We'll have no joy from sorrow but
want all to be saved.
Godly sorrow leads to repentance to
those who then behaved.
I didn't rob your happiness with motives
like a thief but that sorrow might cause
you to turn
scorn into belief.
Today as then sometimes we must make
one quite sad in order that in the end in
Christ he will be glad.

Sin in Our Lives

A man in a shack in the valley saw on the
mountain some gold.
It looked so pleasing to him.
It was a beautiful thing to behold.
After a lifetime of envy he desired, the
castle, to see.
He found but a shack glowing
with reflectivity. Sin is like
that in our lives. It has a
fascinating appeal.
It lures us in lust to its trap but its pleasures
are not real.
We find that our sin stained lives
deserve the death penalty but Jesus
went to the cross so
we might worthy be.

We must give account to God for the things
that we have done but we know if we trust
Jesus each of us
will become His son.
We cannot transfer our guilt or blame
others for our sin but if we confess them to
God
The victory we will win.

Sunday School

Some think when they miss church that
they are being "cool."
Some who attend miss blessings by
skipping Sunday School.
If you are serious at all about serving
Christ our Lord
You'll join in for Sunday School and study
from His Word.
Come, Hear about the Savior and the things
that He has taught.
The fellowship is outstanding
and you'll learn quite a lot.
If you fail to attend
you won't know what you'll miss so make
a habit of coming.
You'll be blessed. I'm
sure of this.

A Spot in the Cemetery

That spot in the cemetery where the dead
are in the ground
is a lonely place indeed with
scarcely a soul around.
There may be one here or there placing
flowers on a grave.
The souls of some residents are gone to
where people crave.

103

They're gone to be with the Lord for He
came to be their escort.
To take them to their mansions in
Heavens glorious port.

He shall wipe away all tears.
Every eye will remain dry.
There will be no tears in Heaven.
Christ is the reason why Those
who hadn't accepted the Lord
have an ordeal to go through.
Their future is outer darkness and with
scorching heat there too We know
there are more there
because they followed the wide way for it
leads to destruction where many will go to
stay.
The atheist will wake up there and
find out he was wrong.
He'll wish that things were different.
That's where his kind belong.
All liars will be there also for Jesus said
they would;
unless they repented as the
Bible says they should.

Atheism

The worst moment for an atheist
say some who are quite frank is when he is
quite grateful and
has no one to thank.
That might be a bit perplexing and it
really seems quite bad.
It is not really his worst moment
though it might make him sad. There
will be a worse time.
Everyone ought to know.
He'll be in a casket all dressed up

with no place to go.
This is what he thought through life and
many others as well
but he has a final destination in the
devil's Hell.
The only thing that matters when we
take that final breath is what
we did with Jesus here before we
entered the state of death.
He said, "I am the door, the
truth and the way.
He's the only way to Heaven so
repent without delay.

What Would Jesus Do?

When you make a decision
do you ask, "What Would Jesus Do?"
Do you try to please the Savior in all
that you say or do?
If you knew the answer you'd get
would it make a difference at all?
Would you change your mind or
doggedly make your call?
To know to do good and to not do it the
Bible says it is a sin.
We should want to please the Savior and
others attempt to win.
If others see us do our will and put what's
right aside will they
use us as an excuse not to make
Christ their guide?
Will we become a stumbling block to those
we are trying to win?
This action will be accounted to those who
accomplish it as a sin.

Treatment of Others

Treat others the way you'd be treated.

Don't be unfair and refuse to budge.
Remember God keeps the score and He'll
ultimately be the judge.
If you take advantage of others you
might seem to get by with it.
Remember, God knows your motives.
Your life will end in a bit
then you must answer this question; Did
you do right by your fellow man?
Did you do your Christian duty?
Can Christ say that you filled His plan?
Will He say to you, "Well Done!
Enter into a state of rest?
Will He say, "I never knew you. Depart
into Hell you big pest."

The Serpent

We were once beautiful creatures with two
legs on which to walk.
We were very cunning and we
could even talk.
One day the devil entered a
member of our kind
who approached the first woman.
She didn't seem to mind. He
made her question God;
wondering if He was good or if His orders
were meant to be as she understood.
She questioned if His command was to keep
them from fun.
The devil said they'd know
good from evil when done.
She decided he was right and
ate the forbidden fruit
then took some to Adam also and his mind
did pollute.
God cursed our kind for it taking away our
legs and feet.

He said we'd crawl in the dust and our heads
man would beat.
We've been like this ever since
because of one snake's deed. We
can't undo the curse he brought on
our breed.
If you doubt this story boas and
anacondas will stun.
They have a toenail on each side and hip
bones in their skeleton.
Why would these be there if
they had no legs or feet?
So the Bible is correct again in it there's
no deceit.

Nehemiah

I was the son of Hacaliah, exiled
in after Jerusalem's fall.
Babylon was captured by Persians and we
prospered, one and all.
As King Artaxerxes I's cup bearer, I
contacted the king each day.
My kinsman was Hanani from
Jerusalem.
I asked how the settlers fared.
He said the survivors of the exile great
trouble and shame shared.
Jerusalem's walls were broken. The
gates were destroyed by fire. I was
deeply disturbed by this,
knowing conditions were so dire. I fasted
and prayed and recalled
The promises to Moses God made to
redeem the Children of Israel.
My thoughts too deep to invade.
I decided to go there myself.
The king asked why I was down. I
said, Jerusalem lies in waste.

Could I go to the town.
The king wrote letters for me to governors
and the keeper of parks to provide me
with timber I needed.
With an escort I disembarked.
When we got to the city
we rested quietly for three days then at
night we made an inspection of the
damage the city displays.
I called Jewish leaders together saying
rebuilding should start.
we organized volunteers and assigned
groups to do each part.

They responded eagerly but some leaders
objected.
I said it wouldn't be done meagerly. The
walls were halfway erected. The builders
were discouraged.
Opposition threatened the work.
With security they were encouraged. Armed
guards around them did lurk. Guards were
present all the time.
Each worker was armed.
They were to assemble quickly so nobody
would be harmed.
With these measures the opposition
withdrew threats to intervene.
They invited me to meet with them. My
distrust could easily be seen.
Sanballat resorted to gossip. saying
against Persia we'd rebel. Then they
said I was in danger and should seek
sanctuary for a spell.
I said I would not run from them for they, no
doubt, were paid it to say.
We completed the walls and gates and had
dedication day.
We had the purification ceremonies

processions marched around the wall
headed by priests
with thanksgiving and feasts for all. I
appointed gatekeepers and guards.
Hanani was to keep the city secure,
to close the gates before sundown and
reopen in the morning for sure.
With the city safely behind walls I had a
census taken to compare with the number
who returned.
I invited leading Jews to come there.
It was to be the "Holy City." Ten
percent of Jews were to come.
After being there twelve years I
returned to Persia with some.
During my absence standards in
Jerusalem declined.
When I returned I carried out reforms
needed at this time.
They corresponded to the covenant signed
by leading men
under the supervision of Ezra the scribe
who was here then.
I was horrified to find
a room for keeping the sacrifice had been
placed at Eliashib's disposal
I had to look twice.
A wealthy Jewish landowner, his
furnishings were moved out. It was
restored to it former use. It didn't
matter that he had clout.
Most of the Levites had left due to a lack
of money there.
They were brought back and a tithe they
were told to bear.
Farmers brought goods on the Sabbath.
I put a stop to that, but when they said
fish were brought in I ordered the gates
to stay shut.

I denounced mixed marriages and
expelled Hehoida who married a
Samaritan daughter of Sanballat and
moved him when he tarried.
I desired to restore purity in
the religious arena there.
I wanted to be remembered by God for
always trying good news to bear.

Troubled Waters

When waters of life are smooth we feel
close to the Lord.
Its easy to trust Him then and to
believe His word.
When a ripple disturbs the water we take
the trial in stride.
We can lick our problems with
Jesus on our side.
When the tempest starts to howl and the
surface is really choppy
Our faith might start to waver,
church attendance might get sloppy. When
the water really gets rough and the winds
begin to howl
We feel like giving up on life, like
throwing in the towel. Jesus can
calm the storm.
He has the world in His palm. The
placid waters will return. Once
again they will be calm.
When we return to the Lord again we'll
know and feel His grace.
We'll feel better back with Him.
Everything will take its place.

The Difference Between a
Toad and a Frog

Nobody would mistake a cat for a dog but
many refer to the toad as a frog. There is
more difference between the two than
there probably
is between me and you.
For the frog is green, and wet and spry while
the toad is brown,
and rough and dry And the frog has skin
between his toes while the toad has warts
up to his nose.

The Brown Pelican

The brown pelican like his cousin the white
swims close to the shore and makes quite a
sight.
He doesn't net fish for his food, for
him, diving suites his mood.

A Snake

The snake, whether female or male has
only a head.
The rest is tail.

The Alligator

If you stay a little while
you might just see a toothy smile. Its
the alligator's smile, you see, for
crocodiles live in the sea.

The Turtle

An animal which you all know well
spends his life within a shell.
When the sun shines very bright he
climbs from the water in plain sight. If
you surprise him or get too near he will

simply disappear
For he will never really feel like being
served for your next meal.

The Gar

The oddest fish you'll see by far is the
slender, ugly gar.
Its ugly head is full of teeth which
ring its mouth much like a wreath.
No hook his jaw will penetrate and so he
only steals your bait.

The Snowy Egret

The egret which is known as snowy has
feathers which are very showy. Indeed,
for these, it has been shot till near
extinction this bird got.
Finally before it breathed its last for its
protection laws were passed.
Its numbers gradually increased and its
existence had not ceased.
Populations haven't grown enough to
overcome those times so tough.

The Snail

A curious creature is the snail. It
has no arms or legs, or tail;
But one large foot on which to crawl. A
shell on his back and that's about all.

The Sea Gull

"Sea Gull" refers to a group of birds.
There are many kinds.
Most people call them gulls and I
guess they don't mind.
Laughing gulls and herring gulls, even
terns, you see.
Most don't know the difference.
I guess that's true of me.
Many do not like them and
here's the reason why.
As food scarcens and flocks enlarge they
come down from the sky.
They often go to garbage dumps and
parking lots for food.
The thought of eating garbage makes many
people brood.
Adaptations like these will assure survival.
Because they weren't too proud they'll not
have any rival.
Though this nasty habit does not agree with
most.
These places have much food and make a
welcome host.
These habits don't take away from their
beauty and grace.
They are picturesque
and occupy nature's unique space.

The Greater Egret

The Greater Egret stands so still while
poised ready to make a kill.
He patiently waits as still as can be for a
small fish or two, or maybe three. He
suddenly jerks all in one motion so quickly
his prey never gets a notion That his life
will be over in a
second or two.
One gulp for the egret and then
he's through.

The Pied Billed Grebe

The pied billed grebe is a
duck-like creature.
The shape of his bill
is his number one feature.

The Spoonbill

The spoon bill is a lovely bird. His
voice is seldom ever heard.
While ecologists everywhere are
whining his population is declining.
He cannot catch enough to eat. For
this he might meet his defeat
For he's a very unusual bird and the way he
fishes is absurd.

The Kangaroo

The Kangaroo's endurance is a fact.
When people arrived he was in the act.
He is able to exist on grass which is dry.
He's nimble and quick and very spry. His
number have grown over time and he is as
silent as a mime.
His kind is diverse in all habitats.
Some are only the size of little rats.
Others weigh as much as a man.
They can store water like a camel can.
They are agile and quick as they hop.
If man tried to compete he'd
probably drop.
As mankind exploits their home in the sand
they've adapted and
covered the land.
One thing which to them isn't very good
is that man often
hunts them for his food. Due
to their endurance they still
survive.

We hope that they always will
stay alive.
We wish to salute today the kangaroo; with
agility, endurance,
and beauty too.

The Red Shouldered Hawk

If You look carefully you might see a
red shouldered hawk
in the top of a tree.
He sits way up there and looks around for
tiny creatures which abound.
He does not care for bread or cake but
sometimes feeds on the lowly snake. He'll
sit in the tree with a gallant air knowing
he'll spot a meal somewhere; He'll glide
right down with graceful ease and pick the
snake up,
if you please
Then he'll return to eat his meal which he
has earned for he doesn't steal.

The Gallinule

The gallinule is a beautiful bird which
might be seen or even heard.
He wades the edges in the weeds.
The food he finds there suits his needs.

The Black Skimmer

The Black Skimmer, quite a little
sneak. He captures tidbits in his beak.
He swiftly flies and drags his bill through
the water as he catches his fill

The Swallow-Tailed Kite

The Swallow-tailed Kite so
high in the air
looks completely at ease as he
glides way up there. He is
dressed completely in black
and white
and with his design he
makes quite a sight.
His tail is v-shaped and
really quite long.
He glides so high you
can't hear his song.

The Crow

A bird all black from head to toe is
one we refer to as the crow.

The Spider

The spider has eight legs, you know. He
makes a web with his big toe. When every
thread is in its place he sits and shows his
ugly face.
He waits for insects, large or small which
he will roll into a ball.
He'll save it for some future feast for he
might catch another beast.

An alligator

I saw an alligator's hide. He
opened his mouth very wide.

He looked up with a toothy grin and said,
"Feel free to drop right in.

The Anteater

I heard someone begin to shout, "An
animal with long claws and snout." His
favorite food consists of ants. I wouldn't
want his
lunch in my pants.

A Grizzly

Let me make this short and distinct. The
Grizzly is about to become extinct.
Indeed, unless his numbers soar. The
grizzly bear will cease to roar.

A Lion

I heard an angry lion roar.
Then I heard it more and more. The
frightening sound did scare me because I
don't know where
he might be.

Grizzly Bear

Once I was a grizzly bear
Ferocious and outspoken.
Now I am a koala.
My spirit has been broken.

A Guppy

Once I was a guppy. Peaceful
as can be.
Now I am a Tiger Shark

filled with ferocity.

Grizzly Looking for a Meal

In the deep forest Grizzlies
looking for a meal
As hunger dictates.

Ant

An ant is a hard worker.
Why can't man be the same?
Some want only a handout
without a bit of shame.

Mankind in the Web of Life

Mankind is only a thread in
the Web of Life.
As animals become extinct
the web fills with strife.
Each species is greatly needed to
keep the web in tact.
If too many threads are broken it
destruction would be a fact so it behooves
all of us to protect endangered ones.
Let's join hands to help them and let's stick
to our guns.
Some will always say. "The
cost is way too much."
Others, "I'll lose my livelihood if
we do such and such."
Some sit back and demand the feather,
horn, or hide.
It matters not to them If
extinction they decide.

Greed is always plentiful and always
close at hand.
but when they face extinction they
won't feel so grand.
If it hurts their feelings in spite of all
their wealth
We must set limits now to protect all
nature's health.
All animals are interdependent and
connected in some way.
By ensuring each species survival we'll live
another day.

Green Heron

The green heron moves as fast as a streak
and catches minnows in
his beak then he waits patiently for
more while perched right
on the sandy shore.
For many hours he might wait for
fish considered to be bait.
When, by chance, one swims his way it
seldom ever gets away.

Anhinga

The anhinga dives and spears his fish which
make for him a tasty dish.
His bill he uses for a spear whenever
fish get very near then he quickly brings it
up and has his dinner or his sup.
When he can't eat any more he
surfaces and wades ashore.
He spreads his wings so they will dry and
shows that he's not very shy.

Denning Bears

Its time for the bears to den; fat
from the summer feasts.
Some say they hibernate becoming
slothful beasts.
It's really not hibernation. If
you enter they will arise. They
might toss you out much to
your surprise.
Their cubs are born in there; while
they're denning up, you see.
They don't want to be bothered by the likes
of you and me.

Spawning Salmon

Salmon swimming upstream to spawn
climbing up ladders made for fish
The rivers should be clean free from debris,
we wish.
The adults seek the very stream where they
hatched years ago, swimming upstream to
lay eggs which we refer to as roe
The trip is so exhausting by the time the
process is through the adults lay down
and die and their life long quest is through
The eggs hatch when its time; the
hatchlings are called fry. Some
grow up to go to sea. Most will be
caught or die
Survivors, after several years return
where their eggs were lain.
Overfishing is a threat and polluted water too.
Eagles and bears will get their share.
We hope some will get through.

Red Wolves

Wolves were returned to Cades cove after

being wiped out long ago.
They were domestically raised but they
didn't fail to grow.
They reproduced and raised young but a
problem came into the plan.
These domestically raised wolves had lost
their fear of man.
They moved out of the boundaries and onto
private land.
Domesticated animals were
easily caught
and tasted mighty grand.
When the farmers came outside to
investigate the sound
the wolves did not run
but bravely stood their ground. They
had hunted wild animals; turkey,
rabbits and deer.
The survivors had to be recaptured because
of men, they'd lost their fear.

Monkey

I am a monkey with a tail. I am
as agile as can be. I want to
talk to you right now about a rumor
concerning me.
That rumor says that man evolved from a
monkey like me one day.
that's true why do we still have monkey
here with us to stay.
Evolution involves a mutant gene which,
the species, improves.
Because he's better adapted the change
rapidly moves throughout the race until
Soon all the animals there share that
advantageous trait.

To the facts you must heed.
They could never evolved from our
kind, you see
for evolution is within the species, New
species don't come to be

The Bald Eagle

The bald eagle, symbol of our land looks
very strong and very grand Yet many
young will never hatch. some will die
from every batch
For poisons have weakened the egg's thin
shell and we're supposed to
never tell
The power of this lethal stuff until we've
spread more than enough
To destroy this magnificent creature. Then
what kind of bird will this nation feature?

The Everglades; Piney Woods

Away out here in the wood things
seem to be the way they should.
This placid scene that God has made seems
too peaceful to invade.
Yet even here within the park thoughtless
man has left his mark. Wherever you go
you'll find his litter which makes
ecologists very bitter. Yet even through
this mess we make glides the smooth and
graceful snake.
An alligator in the slough
might sit right there and pose for you; And
the anhinga might just scoff with wings
extended to dry off.
A wood stork dressed in white and black
might fly away
and not come back

The beauty here is everywhere. How
long will it remain so fair?
For men with dozers, spades and picks can
turn the forest into sticks;
Fill the lake and fill the slough and hide
the beautiful from view.
All this to crowd more people in.
The very idea is a sin
For though to some we seem to gain to
others it will cause great pain;
To the animals its very clear.
You'll have to move,
You can't stay here, But Where? Oh
where? We hear them say.
There's no place left for us to stay.

The White Pelican

A white pelican fishes as
many men do.
He'll net his fish and
when he's through
He'll stop until he eats them all; the
very large and the very small.
He can hold in the pouch beneath his beak
enough food to last
at least a week.

When he wants to net some more he simply
cruises near the shore;
But with his fish comes DDT which was
not meant for him, you see.
It washed into our streams and lakes and
stayed in the bodies of fish and snakes, it
weakens the eggs
until they break,
The birds existence is at stake.

113

Christmas Tree

The Christmas Tree so pretty and bright
has always presented a beautiful sight.
How long will we continue to plunder our
natural resources with this big blunder?
Not only are we wasting a tree but the gas
used in transport is
important to me.
When Christmas season ends so fair we
burn them adding smoke to the air. This
waste is not necessary, you see.
It could be reduced with a make- believe
tree.

Everglades-Endangered Land

Along the trails of the Everglades, a touch
of nature still pervades.
All around are wild things with graceful
bodies and beautiful wings.
There are ugly creatures like the
possum and nature's beauty in every
blossom
Which from the land spring, untouched
by civilization which ruins so much.
At night you might see many coons and
during daytime ducks and loons. And
alligator or a crocodile might smile up at
you through a toothy smile.
If you gaze into the water you might just
glimpse the playful otter.
All is not safe in the Everglades for
civilization soon invades
This peaceful scene that God has made with
jetports where there once was shade.

Everglades Story

If through the Everglades you pass
you'll see an ocean of sawgrass.
When in a hammock you stand you'll
see trees, tall and grand.
You'll see the importance of elevation for
hammocks form another nation than the
sawgrass where water flows; where the tiny
creature often grows; But if birds and gators
are for you then you must visit the nearby
slough.
Here birds exist in untold number and
alligators around them slumber
While waiting for a fish or snake to swim
too close for then he'll wake And capture
him with one quick snap; then lie right
down and take a nap.
You'll see the anhinga who knows
no fear dive into the water his
beak for a spear.
He'll swim so close to a nearby fish
which he plans to stab for
his next dish.
He'll stab the fish right through the side
then surface to give him an airborne
ride
To the edge of the water or to a tree
where he'll swallow him for all to see.
If you tried you could not make
him fly.
His feathers are wet and need to dry. He
holds his wings out by his side until they
become completely dried.
Then he might leave and fly away or he
might decide he wants to stay.
Gaze as carefully as can be an American
Bittern you might just see. His colors
resemble the grass and weed. If you don't

know
you'll think he's a reed.
He'll stand so still the whole long day
when wind blows grass
he'll even sway.
Swimming or wading or eating grass a
gallinule you might just pass.
If he's all dressed in black and white a
Florida Gallinule is in your sight But if
the colors are purple and green a Purple
Gallinule is what you've seen.
With these birds searching for grassy loot
you might just spy
the American Coot.
Along with him you might just spy a
Pied-billed Grebe if he doesn't fly.
Butterflies can quite often be seen among
predators which
are often mean
if you glance into water clear bass, gar and
bream, swim very near.
All these things and others too compete
for dinner in the slough.
If you're lucky you might see a raccoon
climbing his favorite tree,
if you seek a possum or a raccoon you'll
go at night and not at noon. These
mammals are an unusual sight unless you
travel with a light.
If you can spend more than a day you'll
want to visit a pond or bay. You might
find the great Wood Stork silently doing
his only work.

Great Blue, Green-backed, or Little
Blue are herons which
might be there too.
Tricolored herons might also wade in sunny
waters or in the shade.

You might see pelicans, brown or white,
magnificent birds,
and a beautiful sight.
A cormorant might swim and dive for fish
it catches while alive.
Behind the pond, far from the rest
stands the huge Bald Eagle nest. Keep
your eyes peeled all around if you
travel further down.
On the edges you might see a hawk or
buzzard in a tree.
Drive back up through the
park at night;
deer and bobcat you might sight.
Owls are common in night-time flight.
Their eyes are adapted for low light. As
you drive through the northern gate you'll
want to return.
You just can't wait.

God's Handiwork

Every day I look and I'm proud to say I
have seen God's
handiwork on display.
Across great canyons, in
each formation,
I've seen much beauty in our
great nation.
The grand Canyon, giant of them all;
beautiful Bryce Canyon with its orange
wall; Zion Canyon; Olympic; and Cedar
Breaks; Lassen volcano with its
beautiful lakes; Sunset Crater, a
cinder cone;
and Dinosaur Monument with
all its bone;
Crater Lake, a crater within a crater, the
large one came first,

the small one later;
Death Valley, well known for its borax
mine and the twenty mule
teams in a line
With temperatures so hot that life is rare but
burros and snakes
can be seen there;
The Sequoia trees, largest in the world reach
toward the sky,
branches unfurled
With trunks so large that a single board
could make a driveway for my Ford;
Yosemite,
known for its waterfalls;
for the great Half Dome with its rocky
walls; Sentinel Dome with its twisted form;
black bears appearing when days are
warm.
Mount Ranier with it snow capped top
where glaciers form as its major crop
Yellowstone, home of the great bull moose
where the mighty elk wanders loose. Old
Faithful, a geyser, shoots to the sky which
puzzles some who wonder why;
Jackson Hole with its aerial tram; Flaming
Gorge with its mighty dam; Mount
Rushmore with its familiar form; Tioga
Pass seen during a storm; Denver Museum
with its many displays: the Denver Zoo
where the tiger stays; Wisconsin Dells
with its dangerous ledge;
Fort Bliss with an unusual hedge. The
Everglades with birds without number
walking close to where the gators slumber
Where the bald eagle builds itmighty nest;
Spoonbills fishing
where they think best.
God's handiwork is everywhere.
Its up to us to keep it there

and preserve this heritage which we know
for those who will be here when we go.

Step Poem

Male Bears
Under a tree
Growling. Slashing. Fighting Grizzlies

This Land Was Ruined by You and Me

As I was walking that ribbon of highway
I saw above me the smoggy skyway. I saw
below me the trash filled valley. This land
was ruined by you and me.

I've roamed and rambled and I've followed
my footsteps to the blackened sands of
her oil slicked waters
and all around me a voice was calling This
land was ruined by you and me.

As I was strolling the blackened
seashore with a gas mask on me I
wanted no more:
But all around me a voice was calling This
land was ruined by you and me.

Chorus
This land was your land This
land was my land From
littered roadways to the tin
can island;
From smothered cities to the oil
filled waters;
This land was ruined by you and me.

My Country is a Mess

My country is a mess cause people just don't
stress keeping it clean.
Land where we have no pride;
Where sloppiness abides; From
every mountainside
Let Cleanness ring.
If we don't clean this mess We'll
soon be in distress.
We'll suffer soon.
We can't afford delay. Its
not a game we play.
From every mountainside Let
Cleanness ring.

Our health is what's at stake.
We must clean up and make
her clean again.
We must start now to clean so beauty can
be seen.
From every mountainside Let
Cleanness ring.

Oh ugliness of Garbage Piles

Oh ugliness of Garbage Piles; of
litter covered ground;
of multicolored H2O Which
we see all around.
Oh painfulness of air we breathe; of
chemicals that kill;
of red tides in the mighty sea; of smoke the
air to fill
Oh horrors of the billboards high that hide
the fields of grain;
of smoke that billows overhead and fills

our lungs with pain

Chorus:
O citizens! O citizens! when will we all
awake?
and stop this mess and cleanness stress
before it is too late.

Everglades-Florida's Treasure

The Everglades, A Florida treasure Should
be protected by every measure. The resident
wildlife needs support.
Populations decline as jobs we court. The
Florida Cougar and the bear are almost
gone. Few are there.
Birds, once common, can't be found.
Deer no longer there abound.
Developments thrive on land well drained;
agricultural jobs with innocence feigned.
Pollution comes from cattle and sugar.
They are the Everglades' booger.
Cattails grow where nutrients abound filling
areas where birds
should be found.
Pollution abounds and laws
are ignored.
Poisons from fields in waters are poured.
These nutrients must be removed.
Danger to vegetation has been proved.
Once native plants are extinct They
can't be replaced for they are distinct.
If we let this boundless treasure be lost it
can't be replaced at any cost.
We'll find this will help determine
our fate.
It can't be renewed when it is too late. We

117

can't destroy an ecological link without
paying a price,
more than we think.
Animals continue to vanish, we know
because selfishness has
stolen the show.
Their people cry, "How can they
take the land for which we pay?"
The land, however, we recently
drained and due to this the
environment's strained.
The Kissimmee, a meandering River;
straightened for they'd money deliver.
They can buy those who lead and
ruin our treasure because of
greed.
They continue a daily routine to
pollute.
They buy more time not giving a hoot.
They don't seem to care about
what is said
Or that the Everglades is as good as dead.
Water quality declines and wildlife too but
they continue with what they do.
They wrote "The Everglades Forever" They
really mean "Everglades?
Never!" Sugar cane farmers don't
do enough.
To part with profit for them is tough.
Greed runs their effort.
It's clear to see. They don't look out
for you and me.
Their token efforts they say are great Are
really small; not what they state.

They'll ruin Florida and not
really care;
return home taking our money there. They
cause the animals to become extinct for the

almighty dollar but they don't think that we
are also in
the web of life.
The animals extinction will cause
us strife.
What does it profit them if they gain all
then lose their lives
for a price so small?
They will find out they cannot buy Their
way to the home
I have in the sky.
God commanded us to take care of His
creation everywhere.
Some will cry out; they'll even yell from
the abode they earn in Hell.

Threat to Tiger Creek

A sand mine in the area of Tiger Creek,
Would be foolish but many fail to speak.
When it comes to this people should holler.
Some would back it for their God, the
dollar, Once destroyed they'll say, "It's a
mistake." Can we restore wildlife or a
healthy lake.
Mines would destroy Lake Patrick and Lost.
Sacrificing these,
not counting the cost.
Some sacrifice animals for the dollar sign.
Man's place in the web is not very fine.
Some kill animals, watch their last breath.
That way seems right but it's end is death.
Get sensible. Say. "No" to mining sand.
Based far away they care little for the land.
Nature's beauty can be seen out there.
If we buckle under it won't remain fair.
Man will destroy for the money it'll bring.
They see profit but don't feel the sting Some

118

would enter Heaven with picks ruining it
and turning forests into sticks.
Dig land and trees and destroy the slough
ruin God's creation hiding beauty from
view.
They'd promise to reclaim and
beautify it near the road like the
phosphate pit.
Look at the land behind the hill. Find ruined
land just waiting for fill.
They'll remove sand and tree and stump.
Some might become a scenic
dump. To the animals this message is clear,
we're taking over.
You can't stay here. Where can we go?
We might hear them say.
Destroyed habitat leaves no
place to stay.

Wetland Heritage

Our wetlands are a heritage we can't afford
to lose.
Our quality of life will suffer if we continue
them to abuse.
They're valuable natural resources and
productive also for food;
for recreation, wildlife and water and
things that make life good.
Without them some would suffer.
Part of life would be gone.
Some people would ruin nature and think
that they had won.
Wetlands are more productive than our
richest farms
for food and furs and animals. Their
ruin should sound alarms.
Many people are complacent pretending
that all is fine while filling in our wetlands

and worshiping the dollar sign.
Fishing, hunting and recreation are things
that are at stake for once destroyed we
cannot construct a natural lake.
Oh, we can make a lake, a
marsh or a slough
but life there won't be the same In
spite of all we do do.
to us they may look alike but to the animals
its clear.
What takes nature eons can't be created in a
year.
Once the wildlife disappears it is
gone forever.
It will not reappear; not in
a lifetime! Never!
Past mistakes can be improved like
rerouting the Kissimmee, Prevention is
best, however,
and it will always be.
An ecological blunder can't be totally
erased. If animals are pushed to extinction
mankind's been disgraced for every link in
the web of life
is important as can be.
When one is gone all must change
including you and me.
Its time for us to face the facts that all living
things deserve a place
to live and breed.
This right we must preserve.

Crawfish

A crawfish depends on wetlands to allow a
quality of life.
Many depend on them to feed their children
and their wife.
In Louisiana crawfish bring in one

hundred million dollars a year. The
destruction of their wetlands would
end many a career.
The intrusion of salt water kills fresh water
life.
The protection of these wetlands is worthy
of some strife.
Flood control and industry is
important too, you see.
With planning they can co-exist.
This should fill us with glee its worth any
cost to preserve these
lands so fair.
To the animals its life or death. Lets
show them that we care.

Wetlands

We must encourage preservation of
wetlands everywhere for they should be
important and the object of our prayer.
We've witnessed their destruction by
the Army Corp of Engineers.
We cant let this continue and our eyes not
fill with tears.
These lands we are destroying can never be
restored.
To try is better than nothing but
preservation is the word.
One ounce of prevention, as the saying
goes, is worth a pound of cure and will
prevent woes.
If we cant coexist with nature, in spite of
what you think, we'll also be numbered
among the species to become extinct.

Pothole Power

Our potholes in the west are a value to us
all and when they are destroyed our fuss
should not be small for the greedy farmers
say they must cultivate this land for more
crops.
This attitude we should hate.

One half of our nations waterfowl Use
potholes in which to breed.
disappearance of potholes
puts water birds in need.
Once present in countless numbers
they can easily be counted now. We
must reverse this trend for our own
good somehow.
Hunting, fishing and trapping all rely on
the wetlands.
We must stop their destruction to meet
needs and demands.
For recreation they're indispensable if our
children will enjoy
the wildlife some now see.
Conservation we must employ.
We urge the U.S. government to buy
much Midwest land;
to dig new and larger potholes and protect
them from farmers' hands.

Kissimmee

A river in old age meanders
back and forth.
These meanders have a purpose.
They have a lot of worth. The
Army Corp of Engineers in
order to save land.
Straightened out the river to meet their
new demands.
This mistake proved costly known as the

C-38 blunder prove that meanders are
important while
man's efforts only plunder.
With the help of Marjorie Douglas
Governor Graham caused
The Army Corp's of engineer's proposal
to be paused.
By constructing dams called weirs he
caused water to flow
into dried up ox bows where it
should always go. Its trip
through the ox bows purifies
the water there.
When the river was straightened pollution
was too much to bear.
We learned that the river
affected all the glades
by straightening its channel we
did God's world invade.

Dangerous Wastes

We dump chemicals in the oceans.
We say that they do no harm.
If we realized the threat incurred it would
give call for alarm.
Radioactive chemicals in deep water. We
feel our troubles are washed away.
It might show up in fish and turtles that
swim in the gulf or bay.
These might come back to haunt us though
we don't know what else to do. We need to
dispose of them properly when their
usefulness is through.

A Tree

A tree's beautiful in many ways; a shelter
from the sun's rays;
a provider of fruit which taste good; for
paper; or building material, wood; a
beauty at Christmas, pretty and bright; a
rest for birds in their long flight. Roots
prevent erosion;
sap for turpentine.
Maple syrup from sap, tasting very fine;
leaves make mulch;
wood provides heat; natural rubber; nuts
and dates to eat.
Uses are too numerous to list, you see.
We encourage each to plant a tree.

Everglades: Worth Protecting

The Everglades is worthy.
It should be saved at any cost.
Many would disagree causing a
paradise to be lost.
These greedy ones are blinded to the beauty
of God's design for,
in their greed, all they see is a
great big dollar sign.
They've tried to develop the
land. They've drained it to
raise crops. They dug ditches
and built dikes watching the
water level drop.
They've tried to dry up the glades and
when ordered by the court to release an
amount of water their mission they'd not
abort.
They released the water all at once
drowning many birds and deer.
They tried to kill off the wildlife and
things ecologist hold dear.

Perhaps they could then step in and make
their monetary gain,
but to naturalists everywhere their
victory would bring pain. Because
their plot was foiled as the courts
took nature's side
they regrouped and attempted to destroy it
with pesticide.
It seems they'll never stop. and
leave it to the fish and otter
but what will it profit them to
develop without fresh water.
Before we let them succeed we
must stop to count the cost.
We'd all be losers in the end if
this paradise were lost.

You're a Grand Old Earth

You're a grand old earth but
you're polluted earth
and may citizens clean you
up now. For the health we
love is the reason of our
concern for your beauty and
care

Every nose breathes in the
pollution my friend.
And each one of us must pay.
For in careless deeds
we are sowing seeds which will send us all
to our graves.

Recycle

When you throw something away

think, Can I recycle or reuse it? Our
landfill sights are running out.
We can't afford to abuse it.
Landfill sights are expensive for they must
be lined and vented.
The garbage must be covered to assure it
is not scented.
In many places suitable land is non
existent or extremely rare.
To fill them up with recyclables would
really be quite unfair.
Recycling materials can help to
extend a landfill's life.
It can save natural resources and
end ecologist's strife.
Recycling a ton of newspaper saves forty
four trees from the ax.
It makes a lot of sense. We
can't afford to be lax.

Trees are a renewable resource but they take
time to grow.
Aluminum is non renewable yet we
throw cans to and fro.
Even if the ore was unlimited
Failure to recycle wouldn't be funny. The
electrolysis used to refine it cost many times
more money.
The ore is not unlimited though, when its
gone, you see.
Mining all the garbage dumps would be an
impossibility.
Some sites are being mined.
Thirty-year-old garbage to reuse. They
have run out of dump sites.
By recycling we can't lose,
If our current dump sites would last thirty
yers or more and we reduce trash by half
we'd have sixty years in store.

Section D Students

The students who enter my classroom.
   The ones who are in it right now Are
the ones who keep me going when
   they ask me Why?, What?, or How?
They keep me searching for answers to
   questions I never thought of;
Not merely because it's my duty; I
   do it because of my love.
A love for those who come searching, for
   those who want to know why;
A love which would not be in me if
   Jesus hadn't chosen to die;
But because of Him I owe it to those who
   come to my class
My best effort to answer each question out
   of debt to the past.
Each question they ask is a challenge for I
   must be cautious and sure
To answer it right and completely for this
   in itself is the cure,
The cure to ignorance and apathy the thing
   that will set them all free
For they'll eventually question
   existence which will lead them
   directly to thee.

Hospital Remembrance

Its no fun to be in the hospital, but when
you need to go take the Lord in with you.
   He'll comfort you, you know.
   He'll be right with you always so put
      your trust in him.
   He'll guide the surgeon's scalpel, You
   wont be on a limb in his hands you'll

rest. Safe and secure you'll be.
Cheer up and smile for soon you'll be
   out here with me.

Santa and His Gifts.

Christmas is the time when Santa will come
   with a bag full of toys,
   a doll or a drum.
He brings gifts for all girls and boys. Adults
   have parties,
   but he brings kids toys. When, at the
      parties,
   adults have their glee he comes and puts
      gifts in under the tree.

He only gives gifts to those who
   behave so the gifts for adults he
      gets to save,
   When people get older they
      cause shame.
   They say they never believed
      his name;
   He saves all his gifts for girls and boys.
   They get all his love and
      presents and toys.

Father's Day

A father's love is always there. It
   knows no bounds, you see.
   Even when you fail him his
      love will be with thee.
   He'll be saddened by it, but it
   won't affect his love for you.
   He'll be sorry about your failure, but
   he'll be there when you're through. It's

like the love of God the Father for each
of us down here For when we know
we've failed it's hard to draw quite near.
When we come to our senses like the
Prodigal Son that day
We'll come back the our father and say all
we have to say
We'll find he will forgive us. Hell
accept us back, you know Because
his love is like that and because he
loves us so.
Because of this we wish we could go
to him and say.
"We hope the Lord will bless you.
Have a happy Father's Day.

Thanksgiving

Thanksliving. means so much to me.
In the home of the brave
and of the Free.
A time when men will stop and
pray thanking
God for the blessings of the day Not
only for riches and earthly wealth but
freedoms enjoyed and good health,
For the freedom to worship as we choose, a
freedom we hope we'll never lose. We
sometimes take things for granted like the
harvest
after the seed is planted.
Each year we stop for one whole day to
give thanks and take time to pray.
For this special day we should thank God
in a land where
Satan receives applaud.
A land where some seek wealth and fame
and forbid the mention my Savior's name.
When Thanksgiving day rolls around

thank God for blessings that abound, For
the citrus trees with their golden crop. for
the phosphate pit with its endless drop,
For fuel for cars and heaters to burn, for
schools where children come to learn.
We have so much to be thankful for.
All these things and many more.

Each day, for us, should be Thanksgiving
as we practice the art of true
Thanksgiving.
We appreciate and look with pride on this
day which our nation
has set aside.

Mother's Day

Mother's Day is set aside for us to honor
mother.
It is her day. It's meant for her.
It's not for any other.
Honor her for she loves you and does a lot
for you.
Honor her by doing all the things she says
to do.
Mother's love is always here. It's
with us day and night.
There is no way to measure it.
Its end is out of sight.
Next to God's our mother's love is
strongest of them all.
She works for us and never tires. In our
eyes she's very tall.

Attitudes

We all have different attitudes and
sometimes they will change.

We all have different tolerances.
Each has a different range. Many
seem to always have an attitude of
prayer.
If others hear an unkind word we can watch
their tempers flare.
If you are one whose attitude goes from
one extreme to the other
You need to bow your head in prayer or
apologize to your brother.
As a Christian we ought to have a small
attitudinal range
Some fluctuations are necessary but
seldom extreme change.
Circumstances should not dictate the
attitude we show.
We should live above circumstance to
prove, the Lord, we know.
With Him as our Master we always know
who holds our hand.
If we let him control us he'll
make us feel just grand.
Who can be against us when
Christ is on our side?
We should not let petty matters
take us for a ride.
There's nothing man can do to affect his
destination. If we are right with God we're
above the situation.

Sorrow

Sorrow is never deeper than
when a loved one dies.
In these times, especially, the soul
for comfort cries.
It cries out long and loud. The
sorrow is very real, But only
God can comfort the sorrow

that we feel.
He said He'd never leave us. We
found he told the truth.
For us to not believe Him
would be a bit uncouth.

Evolution

Some say that early man
began as a tiny single cell.
He went to two then four and continued
thus to swell.
He kept this up repeatedly getting larger all
the time
Till he became a monkey and then began
to climb.
He lived up in the tops of trees climbing
without fail
Until he awoke one morning without his
lengthy tail.
He climbed down from the tree and he
walked upon the ground
Then he began to lose his hair and man
was to be found.
I believe it happened in
the Bible way.
For a monkey is a monkey and
that's the way he'll stay.

A Writer's Life

A writer's life is quite unique. If
you'd care to take a peek
You'll find the reason this is so by the
rejections he can show.
Rejected for this.
Rejected for that; too long, too
short, too thin, to fat. My

goodness, you say,
"This is good. It ought to be published if
anything should
But markets are limited and
hard to find.
This places the writer in quite a bind.

Requirements of a Writer

Writing: A pleasure. The pen: a tool.
Experience: A necessity.
An idea: A jewel.
They are important to a writer. With
less many failed who were brighter. It's
also important to have something to say
or an experience related in an unusual
way.
Grammar and spelling are
important as well.
Some have succeeded
who couldn't spell.

Rudolph

Rudolph grew both fast and strong but with
others he just didn't belong.
His nose glowed. He was a little bit shy
and the other reindeer said,
"Oh my!" They told him he was an awful
sight. Calling him Glownose they wanted
to fight.
He tried to hide that horrible glow or
cover in up so it wouldn't show But
everything that he tried to do
would rub off so the
light shined through.
He finally decided to run away.
With that red nose he couldn't stay.

He packed his belongings
deciding to go.
He'd wait till dark so
they wouldn't know.
When all was quiet he started away.
He didn't get far when he
heard one say.
"What's that red light way out there?" First
one then the others started to stare. When
they saw Rudolph with his staff, they all
stared.
They started to laugh.
They laughed and then they shouted while
Rudolph hung his head and pouted. When
others played ball taking their places
wishing to use him as one of the bases.
When they lined at Santa's sleigh they
pushed Rudolph out of the way: mocking,
teasing they treated him bad until this little
reindeer became very sad. Then it
happened on Christmas Eve night. Fog
settled in and extinguished their sight.
Santa was frantic. His sleigh could not run.
If he could not go kids wouldn't have fun.
His sleigh was packed. He frantically
waited til Rudolph's nose made other's
outdated. Santa noticed his glow showed
the way so he put Rudolph in front of the
sleigh. With Rudolph there they took each
gift.
When they returned the fog wouldn't lift.
Rudolph was a hero and they let him know
it wasn't bad to have a nose with a glow. In
Rudolph's eyes there now was a gleam The
others elected him head of the team.

Now, Isn't this just a little like us? With
those who are different we sometimes
will fuss.

Remember their difference might allow them to do something we might wish that we could do too.

Leaves

Dark golden leaves
Whisper along furrows.
Singing harvest time.
Fall drifting down Along
summer roadbeds.

The Storm

Wind howling through a broken pane.
Thunder vibrating through droplets of
rain. Doors banging again and again.
These are the things that
bring me pain.

Lightning striking at my feet.
Rain pounding on unharvested wheat.
Lakes forming in every street.
Flooded playgrounds spell defeat.

Water seeping beneath the door.
Weather reports in a continuous roar.
Forecasts predicting more downpour.
Sadness deepening more and more.

The Sun

The sun is a pretty sight but it is always
rather bright.
It hurts your eyes to take a look. It
gives us energy so we can cook. It
gives us day and it gives us night. It

makes things better for our sight. It is
necessary for plants to grow.
Without it we'd have no grass to mow.

A Reefer

He lit up a reefer. He
took a few puffs.
Along came a cop
and applied the handcuffs.

Summer and Winter

Oranges are like summer; tangy,
fresh, and sweet. Apples are like
winter,
a cold refreshing treat.

Santa

There once was a very fat man who had
a bold gift-giving plan.
He delivered a toy to
each girl and boy.
Saying, "I'll do it each year if I can."

Wrong Dive

Diving from the highest board Jere
arched high above the surface.
She flew gracefully And then She
seemed to hang in the air.
Coming down hard on her stomach She
doubled over in pain.
She straightened out, Gave a
few kicks
And rose to the surface.
Gasping loudly for air

She kicked a few more times, Reached for
the pool's edge,
Pulled herself from the
water And fainted.

Forest

In the deep forest; Grizzlies
looking for a meal;
As hunger dictates.

A Science Student

A science student once came. I
forgot but he had a name.
Simple minded at best he
failed every test.
His grade level remained the same.

Lab Student

A girl once came to the class. She
mixed up an obnoxious gas.
She started to shout As
the odor went out
For she knew that she wouldn't pass.

Handwriting

Handwriting Scribbly lines Characters
connected
Letters joined to compose words.
Handwriting.

Teenager

Once I was a teenager.
I thought drinking was cool..
Now, I'm in the cemetery. My
friends know I was a fool
Omit line.

Metamorphosis

Once I was a fawn dependent on my
mother. Now I am a great big buck
dependent on no other.

Fish

Beneath seas surface Fish
swim seaward seeking
sustenance
In summer shadows.

Ferocity

Once I was a guppy peaceful as can be.
Now I'm a tiger shark filled with ferocity.

Paperback

Once I was a paperback with romance,
crime, and strife.
Now I am the Good Book and contain the
Words of Life.

Embryo

Once I was an embryo
as my genes were being sorted.
Now I am a blob of waste
because
I was aborted.

I was a human being still
forming in the womb.
I'll never take a breath because I
am in a tomb.
I was God's marvelous creation all my
fingers and toes were there.
That was before my mother proved that
for me she didn't care.

Molecules

Molecules Tiny, microscopic
Moving, Flying, Energized
A free flying object, Molecules

Airplanes

Airplanes, flying, gliding, soaring Like
eagles slicing through the sky Free from
gravities pull.
An automobile, free to move
But only on the earth.

Teachers

Teachers; Caring,
Sharing,
Molding minds of children.
Improving lives. Helping
people.
Teachers.

Loneliness

I saw loneliness face to face.
He was frail and weak.
He turned and shuffled away.
I saw his greenish eyes and paled skin.

I heard him whisper hesitatingly And I
felt sorry for him.

Snowflakes

Snowflakes Soft, Cold Floating, Falling,
Piling up, Beautifully white,
Snowflakes.

Moon And Sun

The moon is like the winter; cool
yet often white.
The sun is like the summer; hot,
steamy, and bright.
The moon is like a sloth; slow
moving and serene.
The sun is like a lion; crouching, pouncing,
mean.

Mountains

Mountains, Beautiful,
Graceful,
Majestic. Inspiring. God's handiwork for all
to see.
Mountains.

Anger

I saw anger clearly.
He was enormous and frightening.
He turned and lunged rapidly. I
viewed his shocking red hair.
I heard him rant and rave and I felt terrified.

Ocean's Edge

At the ocean's edge Pounding, roaring,
sloshing in
As the tide changes.

Thunderstorm

In the darkened sky.
Pounding, Flashing, Striking, Blinding: As
rain falls from the sky.

Gossip

Some people will gossip all
day long.
They think they are smart but
they are wrong.
They talk and talk the
entire afternoon.
To want them to stop is to
wish for the moon;
They talk all the time but
have little to say.
We know when life's over they'll
get their just pay.

Retirement

We must begin to prepare For
retirement now.
But preparation is rare For we
really don't know how.
We feel there's no need For
retirement is far off   So
preparation is a deed
Which we quite often scoff.
There is plenty of time.

Right now we have to work.
Up the ladder we climb And
preparation we shirk.
Habits we now form Will
continue on with us. They will
be the norm.
With retirement we won't fuss.
We must begin now To
be ready, then, for it. We
need to take a vow
To start now and not to sit.
Learn to lead in life Not
by it to be led.
It will minimize strife
If you'll only use your head.

The Decision

Sitting quietly Contemplating
evil They wanted done. I
froze.
They wanted me To ruin a
person With false gossip.
I wouldn't
Standing straight I told them
I couldn't do Their evil
plan
They said It was for
The good of all
My God said,
"No."If he's that bad
He'll slip up on his own.
Without my help.

Why should I Frame a
person Due to gossip
That may be wrong?

If they want It done so badly
They can do it. I won't

A New Baby

Love is expressed in many ways By
creatures in the wild
But in man's life its best expressed By
the arrival of a child.
The happiness that a baby brings can't be
stated in a word.
Joy will grow through the years if he's
nurtured in the Lord.

Turkey Day

Some say Turkey Day when
Thanksgiving we celebrate.
Some think of pilgrims and of
their fate.
They thanked God then On Thanksgiving
Day.
They set it aside so they could pray.
Today some in their effort from
God to stray
Have renamed Thanksgiving As
"Turkey Day."
We all know how stupid domestic
turkeys are
but with the name changers they
are up to par.

Verse for a Wedding Card

May the sun never set on
your marriage
May its light be never failing: May
happiness follow you always and may
yours be a life of smooth sailing.

Juice Lab

Sample the pulp. Is it clean?
Are there impurities to be seen?
Is there dirt or seeds or bits of peel?
How does it look? How does it feel?
Has it separated? Does it gel? Read
the OHaus at the bell.
Is there too much water or
not enough?
What are the uses of this stuff? All
these questions come to mind. While
doing my job what will I find?

Gifts for a Promotion

In the tense moments
when you feel half dead
here's a bottle of aspirin to ease the pain
in your head.
When the orders are many and you push
for the prize

Visine is needed
for your blood-shot eyes. When
your voice is scratchy and
ready to stop
reach for the Halls, the
best cough drop.
When your stomach churns and the
goal almost fades reach for two
comforting wafers of tasty Rolaids.
After they do their job but you have no
time to eat get satisfaction on your way
with a snackers treat.
When your musical runs down at
your party's late hour
Here's spare batteries to supply
added power.
Remember this as you go with
the setting of sun that the jobs
never over till the paper work
is done.
(toilet Paper) Warm up with hot cider.
It gives energy too.
Give yourself a short break cause
there's more work to do

Thoughts About Getting Older

Its appointed a time to be born. We
get older though we don't try. Like the
flowers we soon age and begin to get
quite dry.

Some say life begins at forty.
To others that's "Over the Hill,"
These flowers have passed their prime but
they are with us still.

Many times we must face The
truth about our age
For history doesn't stand around but
turns another page.

There's a time to be happy and laugh;
A time to be sad and weep.
There are times when we wished our ages
we could secret keep.

The flowers may look aged and they are
past their prime.
There are also some among us Who
would like to stop at times.

We used to be so happy when another
birthday came;
Now we wish when they come they'd bear
another's name.

One little, two little, three little birthdays.
Stop me when I've said enough.
I thought I could count that high but the job
is rather past.

Birthdays come and go and no one
seems to care.
Tell us how many this will make.
That is, tell us if you dare.

Fellowship

After you're saved and baptized the next
thing you should do is to join with other
Christians and study
the Bible too.
Forsake not this practice.
That's what the Bible has to say.
This fellowship will help you grow and

help point out God's way.
By fellow shipping with others we'll
grow and they will too.
We'll find new ways of coping by
learning how others do.

Snow Outside My Window

The snow coming from the sky
Looks beautiful and white.
When I look from my window it presents
a pretty sight.
It covers all the grass and it covers all the
ground.
As it is covering all these things
It doesn't make a sound.
It looks so pretty as it falls. Its
beauty is untold but when you
go out in it
it makes you very cold.
You can pack it tight together and
form it in a ball.
You can make a snowman with it.
You can make him short or tall.
You can use a carrot for his nose and a
corncob for his pipe.
Use coal for eyes and buttons.
Don't worry! He won't gripe.
He'll stay right where you put him till
the sun starts shining bright.
Then he will start to shrink Till
he disappears from sight.

The Tree in my Yard

I have a little lemon tree. Its
fruit is sour indeed.

It will set your teeth on edge.
In its center is a seed.
You might ask these questions.
Why should I keep it around?
Why should I let it live?
Why shouldn't it be downed?
Well, if you squeeze its juice adding
water and some sweet.
You'll have drink that is delicious
though the fruit's not fit to eat.
Its blossoms are quite fragrant and
beautiful to the nose.
Its more fragrant than most its sweeter than
the rose.

Hungry Sparrow

A sparrow flew over the snow
searching for something to eat.
He flew through the woods then he went
down the street.
He searched high and low for an insect or
some bread.
He found nothing to eat though people were
well fed.
He was tired and hungry but
famine stalked the land. He
looked to people for help but no
one lent a hand.
He became exhausted and because he was
not fed he fell in the snow.
When found he was dead.

Book

I have pages and a cover.
I might be short or thick. You
might browse slowly or
maybe you'd go quick.

I might be fiction and funny.
I might be sad and true.
I might be old and ragged or maybe
bright and new.
You might find me difficult or so easy you
might laugh.
If I'm too hard for you, you might read
only half. If you accept my challenge
and do as you should do
you'll look words up and learn and finally
you'll get through.

A Falling Star

I saw a falling star shooting
through the sky.
I watched it till it disappeared.
Then I said, "Oh! My!"
I searched the sky for it.
I looked also on the ground.
I searched everywhere
but the star could not be found.

Wind Through The Trees

I sat quietly listening to the wind through
the trees.
I heard rustling of the leaves as they
twisted in the breeze.
The wind grew stronger still. I
heard a brand new sound.
I heard a large branch snap then tumble to
the ground.
Leaves flew through the air.
They left a naked tree.
The branch held them captive.
The wind had set them free. They

fluttered to the ground.
They flew rapidly down the street.
Then they ceased to move and they lay
beneath my feet.
Wind still sounded in the trees. No
rustling leaves were heard.
In the naked branches swayed the nest of a
lonely bird.

Time to Retire

Retirement is a special time; a
time that's worked hard for; a
time for an end of schedules; a
time to enjoy life more;
a time to relax and rest; a
time to be at ease;
a time to enjoy your family and to do just
what you please;
a time to smell the roses and for relaxing
by the pool;
a time to forget frustrations; a
time to keep your cool.

When You Look in the Mirror

When you look in the mirror do you like
the one you see?
Would you befriend that person or would
you choose to flee?
If you don't like that person there's
something you can do.
You can make that person better because
that person's you.

When you improve one thing It

will bring happiness
then improve other things.
You'll experience success.
Soon you'll like the person you see looking
back at you.
You'll be happy and more popular for
others will notice too.

As you like that person better your attitude
will change
The way you think of others and feelings
you'll rearrange.
When you like yourself better you'll be more
likable too.
Your successes will multiply and change
your point of view.

Its a Girl

Its a girl! Its a girl!
Is what someone said.
With a cute little curl on
top of her head. It's a girl!
It's a girl!
Born on this day Its a
girl! Its a girl!
we heard someone say. She
has many dimples all over
her face.
She's the cutest little girl you'll
ever embrace.
A bundle of joy.
Happiness without measure.
Its a girl! Its a girl!
She's really a treasure.

Nobody Special

I'm nobody special. I'm
just plain old me.
I just do my job And
let others be.
I'm nothing outstanding But
my job, I do.
I leave when I'm finished; When I
am through.
I'm nothing outstanding but I do as well
on my evaluations
as those who excel.

Inspector

As an inspector I strive to
do my best.
I titrate drop by drop to read accurately
each test.
Sometimes working long hours;
sometimes just a few I faithfully
perform with agency goals in view.
I do many extras to keep a neat lab.
I fill all the bottles when
they just need a dab.
When recognition time comes
I read page after page and find once again
that I'm just average.

Evaluation Day

My evaluation says average.
But I can plainly see
I work faster than some with
more ability.
I'm more dedicated and have
better style.
I work better and harder and
go the extra mile.

I fill all reagent bottles which
others don't do,
but I am just average when the evaluation is
through.
I work the computer and accuracy
stress.
when some leave the lab it is a mess.
On the evaluation equality is
a must.
We're all given average to my disgust.

Halloween Night

On Halloween night
when goblins are out
Some people scream
while others shout.
Some come yelling trick or treat,
They look for candy before they
retreat.

Tenth Anniversary

Our tenth anniversary!
Already! Oh my!
When you're having fun The
time sure does fly.
Though there's sometimes been sadness and
tears.
Our love has grown stronger With
the passing years.
Marriage to you is a fine thing.
I hope you will know the
love this card brings.

Disappearing Pencil
(Use with magic trick)

Our life is like a pencil; Our
talents like the lead.

Much good or bad can be done by what is
done or said.
Each has special talents.
For God they should be used.
We are told of a man whose talents were
abused.
This man hid his talents so others could not
find.
His talents were confiscated No
trace was left behind. Some don't
use their talents represented by the
lead.
They concentrate not on it but on the
eraser end instead.
They try so hard to erase
the good that others do that their talents are
replaced
by eraser number two.
We don't want this to happen.
We want ours to show. We
must always use them,
and cultivate to make them grow.

Rainbow Rope

(To be used with a magic Trick) There
was once a family closely knit by family
ties.
They went to church one day and heard the
pastor's cries.
They listened to his message. Their
attitudes were changed.
The even found their family ties had been
rearranged.
They found their ties were different.
Their family ties seemed longer.
Though arranged differently the ties had
become stronger.
They continued attending church Till one

day they were saved.
This again changed their ties and the way
that they behaved.
Again their ties were stronger.
In fact it now appeared Since
joining with God's family
the knots had disappeared.

Lightning

In the darkened sky.
Pounds, Flashes, Strikes, Blinds.
As rain falls from the sky.

Promises

A man is as good as his word
and never any better.
Any promise that he makes
Should be kept to the letter.
If he says one thing he'll do then he does
another thing.
He can't be worth a grain of salt, His
friends he'll only sting.

Rope

(To be used with a magic Trick)
There was once a family closely knit
by family ties.
They went to church one day and heard
the pastor's cries.
They listened to his message.
Their attitudes were changed.
The even found their family ties had
been rearranged.

They found their ties were different.
Their family ties seemed longer.
Though arranged differently the ties had
become stronger.
They continued attending church Till
one day they were saved.
This again changed their ties and the way
that they behaved.
Again their ties were stronger.
In fact it now appeared
Since joining with God's family the
knots had disappeared.

Dog

They say a dog is man's best friend and
this I can believe.
His tongue will never gossip. His
faith will never leave.

A Gossip

A gossip is the kind of person people
can do without.
For a simple act of kindness will be
spread all about;
not as an act of kindness but as a
scandal. Oh so big!
A reputation has been killed.
The grave is left to dig.

An Unkind Word

An unkind word can't be recalled
regardless of the desire.
It would be better left unsaid. Where
friction Is, there's fire.

Rumor

Some might listen all day long
to hear a juicy rumor;
but they'll separate the best of friends.
It'll grow much like a tumor.
If you hear an unkind word don't breathe
Its best that another forget it.
Do not slander your brother.

Its often said and it is true about the word
that's gone around;
and that is this,

"You can't sling mud without losing
precious ground.

Water

We take for granted running water but
when we must do without we realize our
lack of thanks for what comes from the
spout.

Retirement Activities

We can ruin our leisure and these
activities spoil if we work too hard at
them and turn fun into toil.
When sports become professions with
perfection as the goal pleasure disappears
when we swim,
or golf or bowl.
Leisure and work are needed each other to
compliment.
One gives meaning to the other this is the
way they're meant.
Leisure is not the reward for a
life of industry.
It won't be forthcoming if
work is all we see.
We must take time now for a
hobby and a game or
in retirement we'll find that we'll
work just the same. Retirement
is a time to broaden our outlook.
We can also learn new hobbies or maybe
how to cook.
Its not for resignation or to sit and vegetate
but to be filled with excitement so much
that we can't wait.

Life in the Lab

Life is hectic in the lab As
we know so well.
You weigh the sample carefully then you
hear the bell.
The oil is ready at the sound.
We don't want it to burn.
The acid is being figured but, before
we can turn the phone rings.
A blender wants to know if everything is
checked out.
If the acid is too low. The
C-3 is boiling away. It
must be ready to stop.
but before we take it off we

hear the flask go, "Pop."
The inspector gets a shower of hot juice
mixed with glass.
The blender calls again to
give some more sass.
You say, "Just hold your horses. I'll
call you when I'm through.
He says he wants the results now. As if
you've nothing else to do.

Victim

If you are on a date
and your heart is full of song.
Then your date gets ideas that you know
are wrong:
get up and leave right then or say,
"No!" and really mean it or say, "Take
me home right now." or, "Take your
act and clean it." Don't let things
happen because you'll be the loser.
If you're a victim of a crime report it. Be
the accuser. If you don't it could happen
again and again to you or to other people
who become victims too.

Daughter

A daughter's a wonderful thing; a joy
to behold.
They bring happiness with them as the years
unfold;
but trials come with them.
Such is life, you see.
Sometimes we're made to wonder what
they'll grow up to be.
Sometimes the things they do make us
swell with pride.

At other times we wonder what's going on
inside.
Sometimes they study hard and really make
the grade.
At times of failure they're
completely unafraid.
Sugar and spice and everything nice?
We could disagree;
But when we consider everything we're
happy as can be.
We see maturity coming on in the things
they do and say.
At times they act like children in a world of
play.
Sometimes the two are so entwined we're
astonished and confused.
The maturity we thought was
there is totally abused.
At other times we marvel at wisdom
beyond their years.
The pride springs up within us.
Our eyes fill up with tears.
When we're wondering how to
keep this gal-in-line.
We're thankful that she's our daughter;
our God-given Valentine.

Inner Motivation

Inner motivation affects our actions and
the types of jobs we take.
If our attitudes are not right a mess of the
job we'll make.
If we act according to God's
own Holy will.
we'll do the job He has for us and
His position fill.
We won't be slothful or lazy but diligent
and true.

We'll do our best in everything and be
faithful to God too.
A person with no hope is often in
despair but hope and joy are ours
when Christian love we share.
William Carey said expect and attempt great
things for God.
If we fulfill God's will
we won't look for man's applaud. In
troubled times which will come we must
look to God above.
With His help we will endure and increase
in brotherly love.
If our eyes are stayed on God we have a
hope that's sure.
This type of hope we have is
one that will endure.
Persistence in prayer provides power
which will lead to victory.
Our prayer may be all that's needed to win
one soul to Thee.
Romans 12:11 & 12
says we are all a part of
one body in Christ
and each can't be the heart. All
members of the body have
different jobs to do.
Each job is important. Each is
necessary too.
Each posses different gifts which should
not be abused.
Each person is very valuable and each gift
should be used.
Diligence can cause result's in
service for the Lord.
If we're diligent in service we'll study
God's Holy Word.
A person's diligence will cause him to

prosper in his work for one who is not
diligent will, his duty, shirk.

Friends And Family

Families are important
as a family to whom we belong.
They help us to mature
and become both big and strong.
They provide a place of refuge which we
all need so badly.
If we don't have a place like this we'd face
the world quit sadly.
With an understanding family we can learn
to face the world.
We gain comfort from this unit When
problems at us are hurled. We can have
our disagreements and fuss with all our
might;
but we know we're still a family and
things will be alright.
Friends are important too.
On them we can rely.
We help them and they help us. At
least we should always try.
Friends are usually chosen for
something both enjoy.
It may be a certain sport; or
interest, car or toy.
Its something they have in common.
Perhaps a common cause brings
them together for a time and
causes them to pause from their
busy schedules.
They pause for a special reason; then
they become acquainted working
together for a season.
Friendship begins to grow as they

depend on one another.
Soon they treat their acquaintance like a
sister or a brother.
Each has made a friend; someone
with whom to share: to bear their
burdens and joys; someone they
know will care.
Friends and family help us get by
when things get rough.
They help us grow up stronger.
They help us to hang tough.
We all need friends in life at
one time or another.
If you want to have many why not make
your friend a brother?
If you're part of God's family you have
friends you've yet to meet in every town
and country and on almost every str0eet.
God's family is very large.
On common ground they stand.
They join together in prayer and lend a
helping hand.

A Snowman

I started as a snowflake and I
covered all the ground.
More of me came falling down landing
without a sound.
I piled up on the ground till I was several
inches deep.
When people came I thought I'd be piled
up in a heap.
The kids surprised me then. They
rolled me into a ball.
They made two more snowballs. When
stacked up I was tall.
They used coal for buttons and a large
piece for each eye.

piece for each eye.
I enjoyed it when they did this.
With eyes I began to spy
They made a mouth for me and gave me a
corncob pipe.
I began to talk with them but I never
voiced a gripe.
A button became my nose.
It was flat and sort of thin but it gave me
personality and a
good feeling within.
With all the work they did on me I couldn't
let them down so
I began to walk
then to jump and dance around. I
danced with them all afternoon and
well into the night.
The next day I was left alone and the sun
became quite bright.
The water began to run off me.
My mind began to muddle.
I shrank and shrank and shrank till I
became a puddle.

The Wreath

The wreath, plain or decorated usually
comes in a circular form.
Its placement on a door gives a
feeling that is warm.
It says, "Welcome" to all who see
reminding them that Christmas is
near. It reminds us that Jesus was
born to remove all sin and fear.
He came to save from sin
Without Him, we'd go to Hell.
If we trust Him to Heaven we'll go.
We should, His message, tell.

141

Elves

At Christmas we think of elves; not as
mischievous as in lore but as helpers of
Santa Claus as his
gifts get more and more.
They help make all the presents which
Santa will bring.
They help him pack his sleigh.
They also help him sing.
We often picture them with beards;
Often long and white.
To picture them with Santa Claus is a very
happy sight.

Straw

I remember as some grass seed we
would joke with one another.
We bet on who'd sprout faster and
who'd outgrow his brother.
After we were growing men came and cut
us down.
They dried us and stacked us up then took
us into town.
When we saw the others with us placed in
a manger for cattle feed we bet on who'd
be eaten first for this pastime we had a
need.
We needed to do something to
pass the time for us.
If not, the waiting would kill all. The
anxiety would make us bust. We saw
some people come in.
The manger they did clean.
They weren't dirty like the others.
They didn't look real mean. They
picked us out of the hay. They
said that we were soft. They got

more to go with us
from out of another loft.
We wondered at their choosiness.
What animal were we to feed?
Soon a baby boy arrived and
then we learned of the need.
They had no bed for him.
The manger became His crib.
We were the mattress in it; the
swaddling clothes his bib.
We later learned the baby was God's own
precious Son.
His ministry on earth to men would soon
have just begun.
We knew we had a part in it. We
were proud as we could be.
Even if animals ate us now we had served
humanity.
After Joseph and Mary left and took the
child away we were thrown out of there
with other wasted hay.
We passed what we had done to the new
plants that grew.
They were envious of us but now our life
was through.
Many generations have passed since
that blessed day.
Our descendents still talk about us and the
roll that we did play.

Santa Claus

My name is Santa Claus. I
am slightly overweight.
On Christmas Eve I deliver presents
to every state.
With my sleigh packed with toys I
work the whole night through.
Nobody knows the work that's done or the
things I have to do.

Whenever I pose for pictures I
look quite big and fat.
If you saw me afterwards You'd
say where's Santa at?
I lose so much weight during
the Christmas Season
that you'd never see me afterwards and
now you know the reason.

Reindeer

We like to work for Santa Claus.
We get to rest most of the year but we were
jealous when others came They'd take our
job was our main fear.
Santa brought one named Rudolph.
His nose glowed a brilliant red.
We weren't threatened by him or by what he
did or said.
We thought we'd have a little fun so we
teased him about his nose.
We left the others alone a while, He
was the target that we chose.
We continued to mock and tease him.
Joking a lot with what we had to say but
he became so depressed he decided to run
away.
We saw him when he left.
We continued to laugh at him.
We said his chances of escape with that
red nose were slim.
Then on Christmas Eve one year the fog
had shut us down.
Santa's sleigh was packed but he viewed it
with a frown.
Then he saw that Rudolph's glow cut the fog
and showed the way.
Santa quickly hooked Rudolph up in front of
the team and sleigh.

After we delivered the gifts
Santa praised Rudolph a lot.
He said Rudolph's place in front was, for
him, a permanent spot.
Now we were very gloomy that we had
treated him so bad.
Now that he was in charge the
rest of us were sad. We knew
all our lives that wrong never
pays.
We'll regret teasing Rudolph for the rest of
our days.

Santa Filling the Stockings

After Santa tumbles down the
chimney with a boom; or, as
he does in Florida,
comes through the Florida room; he
goes to the mantle or wherever the socks
hang then he stuffs goodies in
them, enough for a whole gang.
He knows if you've been naughty and he
knows if you've been nice so he fills the
good child's stocking.
He doesn't care about the price. If,
however, you've been bad,
you might not find the toys for Santa
sees you all year long and gives
to good girls and boys.

Mistletoe

A piece of mistletoe might
look innocent as can be.
You might think nothing of it
while its hanging in a tree

When Christmas season rolls around you'd
not want a piece to miss for rumor has it
those beneath
must give each other a kiss.

Dorothy

There was a young lady from Oz. She'd
kill the witch for a cause.
She was taken from home by
an ugly old gnome.
She killed the witch without pause.

Three Bears

The three bears left their home.
They went out for a walk.
As they went through the woods they
carried on some idle talk.
Back at their home a girl named
Goldilocks soon came.
She was tired and hungry. The
house called her name.
She knocked but no one answered.
She entered and it felt good.
She found three bowls of porridge. She
saw them from where she stood.
She ate some from the big bowl but the
porridge was too hot.
She sampled from the small bowl. It was
too cold to hit the spot.
She took some from the other bowl.
It was good and tasty.
She was then so tired
to sleep she was quite hasty. She
tried Poppa Bear's bed but it was
hard and rough. She tried Mama
Bear's bed.

It wasn't hard enough.
At last she tried the baby's bed.
It felt just right
so she went right to sleep. From
sleep she couldn't fight.
The three bears returned home from their
little stroll.
They went to their porridge and looked
into every bowl.
Poppa Bear said,
"Someone's been eating Mine."
Baby Bear looked at his
and said, "Someone began to dine."
Mama Bear looked at hers and
said, "Someone ate it up.
The cereal is all gone
and the juice went from my cup. Poppa
went to his bed and said, "Someone has
slept here."
Mamma said," Someone's been in mine and
exited from the rear."
Baby Bear went to his bed.
Goldilocks was still there.
"Someone's still in my bed,
shouted Baby Bear."
They all gathered around her to view the
unusual sight.
She awoke and saw them and she was
filled with fright.
She saw them gather around and heard
what they had to say then she got out of
the bed and quickly ran away.

A Drug

I'm an illegal drug People say
you need me but
Far from them you should strut.
they just want your money.

144

I'm not good for you.
Their words are not true. I'll
make you an addict and ruin
your life too.
I'll make you act crazy and do things that
are wrong.
You'll get into trouble. I'll
take away your song.

A Christmas wish to the School

We want to wish you all the best and we
have a special reason.
Vacation time is almost here. It is
the Christmas Season.
A thanks to all the teachers for
being here to teach.
Thank you for every girl and boy who you
have helped to reach.
Thanks to the custodians for keeping our
rooms neat and to the lunchroom workers
for the good
things we had to eat.
Thanks to our migrant advocate and to the
library personnel and to our police on
campus we all wish you well.
To our secretaries and
student services
and our administrators too we say a special
Merry Christmas.
Thanks for all you do.
To this special little group whose
influence is all around
we want to say right now that
Santa's come to town.

Student Success

We have come to the completion of
another school year.
We've tried to get the students ready
for their career.
They will sooner than you think be
out on their own.
They'll ask themselves where their
school years have flown.
They'll face the cruel world whether
they're ready or not.
If they learned all their lessons what they'll
need they've got.
Although teachers try their best to teach
the students right
if a student doesn't learn
parents often want to fight.
It doesn't seem to matter to some if their
children are mean and rude. Some
parents, as a matter of fact, can be
rather crude.
Other parents do their best to teach their
child respect.
Their children are the ones who are most
often correct.
Their children are polite and obey most
every rule.
They'll be more ready for life than
those who think they're "Cool."
They will take advantage of the
knowledge they possess.
In the market for jobs they'll
achieve success.

Senior Citizens

As life expectancy increases senior
citizens increase too.
what to do.

With ever increasing numbers we wonder
How should we house these people?
We justifiably ask.
There are many possibilities to
this most difficult task.
Should we tolerate the slums
Letting houses deteriorate?
Should we give money for repairs before it
is too late?
Should we build houses for them and
make them all the same?
Should we let them struggle through and
say, "They are to blame?"
What service should we do to help these
people live?
What is the outer limit?
How much should we give? Are
nursing homes good?
Should we put the people there?
What are the solutions? How
well should they fare?
If they stay in their homes should we send a
daily meal?
Should we send doctors and nurses to check
on how they feel?
Should we pay their utilities to keep them
cold or hot?
Should we have restrictions on
what to pay or not.
Should we meet every need always coming
on the run to provide our elderly with their
place in the sun? Where do we draw the
limits between legitimate needs and do we
refuse requests when they come from greeds?
These questions are very real to us and to
them too.
We must search for answers so we'll know
what to do.

Land of Hershey

In the land known as Hershey once
upon a time
There was a little chocolate drop about the
size of a dime.
He was sad and lonely for this reason.
He did confess that he quite often melted
and became quite a mess.
He was sad until he married.
Then he was proud to tell that the wife of
his dreams was a rigid candy shell.

COMMUNICATION

Its important to properly communicate.
We must be plain and clear.
Its important to be understood If we're to
get ideas in gear.
Fax machines are available
To communicate with and teach.
We can communicate with work
Even when we're at the beach
The computer eases the process
With programs such as E-mail.
If the message is unclear Our ideas may
not prevail.
Time and energy can be saved By
proper communication. Define
new terms clearly
In every situation.

There are two important factors; These
are senders and receivers. Our
perceptions and filters interfere And may
make others unbelievers.
When politicians speak to us We
filter what they say.
Infomercails tell us many things But
their reasons get in the way.
We must think ahead about
Things we must communicate
Anticipate their reactions And
response to your debate.
Senders must plan their thoughts To be
clear and concise.
Be aware of your listeners.
Communication is a device. Ask
your listeners questions To check
their understanding.
Be clear and relevant.
Don't be overly demanding.
Keep in mind their terminology.
Don't use words they don't understand.
Repetition might be helpful To
help give them a hand.
Be an active listener.
Ask questions and paraphrase.
Don't sit there passively As if
you're in a daze.
Take responsibility to understand. Make
sure the message is clear.
Open communication is important In what
we say and hear.
Verbal, vocal, and visual are important to
the process.
All three must blend together And
be balanced for success. Body
language is important too And so is
tone of voice.
It can make the difference Between their
final choice.

A Notorious Liar

It has been said of one that he'd rather climb
a pole and tell a lie than to stand flat-footed
on the ground
and on the truth rely.
We don't understand this person but we've
all met them at work.
He says he's a team player, but his
duty he'll often shirk.
When asked where he'd been he said, in the
office I was.
If you say, "Your truck was gone.
He'll argue with you because he'll say,
"You just pick on me.
You're always keeping track.
You check your watch when I leave and
also when I come back.
I told you I had to go to the bathroom.
I also had to mail a letter.
You act like I'd do something wrong.
You should know me better.

Are you going to tell the boss?
What is wrong with you?
You're not a team player
Why do you care what I do?
It makes no difference to you
if I am seldom there.

I do my part of the work
so why should you give a care?

Work

When you work an eight hour shift do you
spend eight hours there or do you stay four
at the most and treat other workers unfair?
Do you expect them to cover and say that

147

your job you do?
Can you honestly claim your check
saying you should get more than you do?
If your fellow workers were like you
would anyone answer the phone or would
the lab be empty
with each following a will of his own?
When someone asks where you've been do
you jump to
conclusions and yell?
Do you challenge your fellow workers, get
mad and forbid them to tell?

Gossiping

I know an elderly widow who could be
really good but she's a constant gossip and
she pries more than she should.
She knows everybody's business and
she fills in the empty gaps
with imaginary juicy news then on the
neighbors door she raps.
She gossips about the mail
each of her neighbors receives.
She claims to be a Christian but is hurtful
and deceives
She's busy all the time usually on the gossip
line if you go and talk to her she says
everything is fine.
She pinches pennies so hard holding on to
every cent.
About this gossip problem she
really should repent.

Work Ethic

Where has the work ethic gone? Why

do people just want their pay? They
want to be gone all the time so they
won't be in work's way.
They want others to do the work and to
cover for them too.
They want to collect a pay check. when
the week is through.
They use any excuse to get out.
If you object You're not being fair.
If you don't cover for them
they say you're not a team player.
Where do they get this idea;
that they should be free to roam?
If that's all they want to do why don't they
just stay home?
Its that guy who is not a team player.
A team player shares the work.
He doesn't leave the work to others and
continuously his duty shirk.
He doesn't go out to eat saying
he had to mail a letter then
come back and eat your lunch. This
makes him to sin a debtor.

The Adventures of Gaw

There once was a boy named Gaw H
went out to smoke one day
He continued each day until his
addiction got in the way.
He was puffing upon one with friends when
the pastor walked
through the door.
His pastor told his parents
for he wanted him to do it no more.
The next Sunday when he
went to church
He preached on the danger of
smoke not naming

The next Sunday when he
went to church
He preached on the danger of
smoke not naming
Gaw but he spoke of the flaw and he said
the matter was no joke.
He got mad at the pastor for this He
said the Pastor had brew in his cup.
He said it was brew, not water and said that
the pastor covered it up.
The people never bothered to check to see if
the rumor was true.
They spread the word to the others to make
sure that everyone knew inner ear
problems bothered the pastor who
staggered somewhat
when he walked
People said he'd been drinking.
It overshadowed his spiritual walk.

They continually whispered to others and
some stayed, you see.
At each telling the story increased. This
added to the smoking boys glee. The rumor
ruined the man because so many whispered
the lie.

There was many a sad goodbye. The
The pastor finally resigned.
boy slipped deeper in sin. He was
seen by a leader of town.
He told the boys parents who sighed and
left wearing a terrible frown.
Gaw was punished real good.
The one who reported him he knew. He
started a rumor again, but was discovered
before he was through.
The town rejected this boy.

They'd never believe him again. They
tried to make amends to the pastor but
could never remove the stain. A
newcomer came into town. He heard
about Gaw and his lip.
He asked about Gaw's last name.
and discovered his last name was Sip.
Everybody in town knew the story. They
swore never to listen again.
They would check out every story
because they remembered the pain.
Everyone knew that lying was wrong.
Some thought of Gaw as a dip. They
made a joke of his name and
referred to this act as gossip
(GawSip.)

Once I Was a Child Once

I was a child crawling
on all fours.
Then I was a teen starting
boisterous roars. Next I
entered adulthood facing
foreign wars.
Now I'm in old age entering
uncertain doors.

Skunks

Mama skunk has twin sons. For
names she was in doubt.
She finally decided to call one "In," The
other she called, "Out."
In always stayed inside while Out

went outside to play.
In went out not to return on that
most memorable day. Mama
sent Out out to find In and
return.
Out came back with In. before
her back was turned.
Out found In so quickly Mama
asked, "Was he that distinct? How did
you know where to look?"
Out merely said, "Instinct."

Work Ethic (Ideal)

Everybody on the job should be
a team player, you know.
He should stay for the whole shift and
not run to and fro.
He should not take advantage;
leaving another to man the phone
while smoking or chatting with others while
one does the job alone.
He shouldn't go eat with a friend while
leaving another to do the work.
Helping attitudes should prevail. You
shouldn't, your duty, shirk.
This slogan says a mouthful
Its one we sometimes hear by some who
want to just sit
While the other must use high gear.
Some want the other to run.
while she be allowed to wait. Or
to analyze all the samples while
she sits and debates.
If everyone would pitch in the work
would get done well.
Then all could sit and talk while moral on
the job would swell.
When one goes off and stuffs his face then

comes back and begs from others. The one
who stays behind and works wonders why
he bothers.
Sloths make life miserable for all.
Nobody wants to work with Him. He
claims he's looking for work Chances
of finding a job are slim.

Fall Leaves

Leaves lose their green color
during the season called Fall.
Some retain the red.
Others lose them all.
Some are brilliant yellow;
Some a blend of the two.
Some are turning brown.
They'll fall in a day or two.
The trees are growing dormant due to the
shortening of the light.
Soon it will get colder and leaves
won't be in sight.

They'll have fallen to the ground The
trees will be quite bare.
Fall colors will have vanished;
some say into thin air.

One Day Too Long

Autumn colors slowly progress.
You wait for them to peak.
Tomorrow will be the day: is
what you hear and speak.
You decide to wait another day for the
colors are getting strong.
Suddenly it began to snow.
You'd waited a day too long.

When you went out in the morning with a
camera in your hand you expected
magnificent colors.
They really should be grand. You find the
leaves are falling and the colors fading
fast. You watched as the peak came. Now
it is in the past. You anticipated the day
for colors to come on strong but you
found on getting up that you had been all
wrong. This was very disappointing.
Consequences weren't great. Some put off
coming to Christ. Each day could seal
their fate.
Many feel that there's still time. They'll wait
another day. If the Lord returned tonight
They'd have eternity to pay. It would be
disastrous if they were a day too late. It
would mean eternity in Hell for they'd have
sealed their fate.

Friendship

Friends are wonderful people who
care about you;
They'll listen to problems
and share excitement too.
They understand how you feel and
empathize as well.
They cheer you up when sad
and share joy when swell. They
laugh with you at times but its
not to ridicule.
Their criticism's meant to help.
It is a learning tool.
They help you improve though it
might hurt like a rod;
but if it is done in love it
might lead you to God.
Jesus is our greatest friend.

He loves us more,
you see than anyone can imagine; He
died for you and me.
Our sins had separated us from Him
forevermore.
The wages of sin is death with punishment in
store.
He came as God and man to make, for
us, a way to enjoy
Heaven and forever with Him stay. He
was ridiculed by man who nailed Him to
a cross.
He suffered and died for us so we wouldn't
be forever lost.

A Friend

We can be ourselves with
one we call a friend.
A friend will share our feelings and still
care in the end.
With them we are free to laugh,pout, or
giggle. We know they won't leave if we
choose to wiggle.
We can act grown up or play the baby's
part. Even when we get upset they know
we have a heart.
We enjoy his company.
Sometimes angry we might get We
might even get mad
but we'll get over it. We
might get serious or act
giddy as can be. We share
our feelings and our
insecurity.
We toase each other often but we
do it just in fun.
We might offer helpful criticism so
improvement will be done.

We care about each other but we
don't shut others out.
We increase our circle of friends.
That's what life is all about. We
help each other study and develop
a healthy mind.
We mostly treat each other in a way
that's always kind.

Friend or Foe

Knock! Knock! Who's there?
Is it friend or foe?
Even those I've known for years.
How can I really know?
A friend can keep a secret and stand by
when things are bad.
She'll laugh when you are happy and
comfort when you're sad.
She'll sacrifice for you at times and not
always demand her way.
She wants you to be popular and a
friend of yours she'll stay.
She'll let you have other friends. She'll
give you space at times. She'll help
with school work; cheering when
grades climb.
A foe will demand you
have only one friend.
She'll selfishly want you to be her
friend to the end.
She might start a little gossip to see where
it might go.
She'll want you to join in and tell others
all you know.
If you put your trust in her and her
methods you defend
eventually she'll turn on you
separating friend from friend.

Then you'll be all alone for the ones so long
rejected won't want your friendship now
saying
you got what they expected.

Seasonal Changes

The change seems imperceptible.
Green color begins to fade.
Yellows, ambers and reds appear. In
between are every shade.
The bright colors show up one day in all
their splendor.
Each is a painting by God.
He's painter as well as sender.
Each person viewing the beauty sees a
painting that is unique.
None will see it the same no matter how
hard they seek.
A few leaves fall to the ground; others
their colors enhance.
The picture changes dramatically in
autumns wonderful dance.
The beauty is there a moment then the
leaves begin to fall.
Soon viewers of the trees find there are no
leaves at all.
Snow covers the ground.
Landscape's changes are great. The
splendid painting stresses the cold, the
white, sedate.
God's beauty is here also then the snows
begin to melt.
Warmer temperatures come.
The change is clearly felt.
Buds emerge green again.
Spring is on its way.
Flowers of summer will bloom. The
paintings changes each day.

God is the ultimate painter.
Artists try to capture His glory. Their
paintings are pretty good at
mimicking God's story.

Snow Showers

I'm a little snowflake;
Cold, soft, and fragile.
When I get caught in currents I can
be rather agile.
When I am uplifted water
condenses on me.
I become encased in ice but look
like snow, you see.
When I fall to the earth I hit
as hard as hail
but I still look like snow. My
whiteness does prevail.
I differ from snow, however, because I hit
with power.
I don't get people wet.
They call me a snow shower.

A Snowflake

I'm a little snowflake. I'm
icy, light, and airy.
I float softly to the earth.
I make some people merry. When
I hit the ground if it is too warm
I melt then evaporate to
join another storm.
After land has cooled I lay on the
ground other snowflakes land and near
me can be found.
Some land on top of me
and start to make a pile compacting and
assuring that I will last a while.

Section E

Love – I Corinthians 13

If I speak with the angel's tongues and I
do not have love
it does no good to make a sound.
This won't lift me above.
If I have prophetic powers and all
mysteries understand
And do not have abundant love I won't
hear the heavenly band.
If I have all faith on earth enough
to move a mountain
And do not have God's special love I need
the Heavenly fountain.
Love is not jealous or boastful but is
patient and is kind.
Its not arrogant, rude or stubborn or
resentful when in a bind.
It does not rejoice in wrong but only in
what's right
When someone goes astray in this there's
no delight.
Tongues, prophesies and knowledge all
will pass away
Love will endure forever.
It alone will stay.

Acts

Jesus began many good works which must
be carried on.
Apostles were given this task after

he was gone.
After his resurrection he
showed he was alive.
He told them what to do until the
Spirit did arrive.
He said, wait in Jerusalem until the
promise is fulfilled.
The Holy Ghost will come.
Your trembling will be stilled.
Empowered by his Spirit they'd
continue Jesus' work
His acts would be their acts.
From his task they could not shirk.
Asking, Will you the kingdom of
Israel now restore?"
He said, "Its not for you to know
what my father has in store.
You shall receive power when the
Holy Ghost gets here.
You'll witness in Jerusalem and regions far
and near."
When he said these things he was taken
from their sight
A cloud which took him up.
It was the fairest white.
While gazing toward Heaven two men in
white were seen,
"Be about your business. Don't
stand upon the scene.
His return will surely come but no man
knows the hour.
He'll want you to be working. He
will supply the power." They
returned to the city.
To the upper room they went.
Men and women joined in prayer for the
Spirit to be sent.
When Pentecost arrived they
were all in one accord.

Suddenly there was a noise. A
rushing wind was heard.
It filled the entire house Cloven
tongues came.
Sitting on the twelve
regardless of his name. They
were spirit filled. Each spoke
other tongues
The Spirit told them what to say and
filled with power their lungs.
Men of every nation, their
native language heard. Each
heard his own dialect,
understanding every word.
They marveled at this miracle, but some
were quick to say,
The men are not sober so
early in the day." Peter
preached saying.
"These men are not drunk. Their
fast is in progress.
They have consumed no junk. If
they are drunk as claimed. It is
not with food or drink, but its
with the Holy Spirit.
Each was made to think.
Peter showed Jesus, describing
miracles as a sign.
He said, "You murdered him, and
say these are drunk with wine.
God raised him from dead and loosed the
pains of death.
He showed Jesus was Messiah by giving
back his breath.
This same Jesus who you sent to die
upon the rugged cross stands waiting to
forgive you.
You tried to cause him loss."
When they heard Peter's message they cried,

"What shall we do?" He said, "Repent, be baptized,
every believer among you. Be baptized in Jesus' name. You shall his gift receive."
Three thousand souls came forward saying, "We believe."

Psalm 104

Bless the Lord. He's very great.
His majesty is first rate.
He clothed himself with bright light. He stretched the heavens out of sight.
In the waters he laid his heavenly beams. The clouds are chariots pulled by teams.
The wind is like his mighty wing.
The angels daily His praises sing.
Before our planet had its birth he laid foundations of the earth.
Waters flooded over all the land. He spoke and there appeared both rocks and sand.
He set the boundary for the sea.
so earth might nevermore flooded be. In the valleys He made cool springs for creatures with and without wings.
To prove his work was not in vain he watered the countryside with rain. To grow He caused herb and grass for man or animal who might pass.
For man he made both sap and wine and bread and oil to make him shine.
He planted trees, cedar and fir, for birds to nest in as they were;
Rocks and hills for badger and goat; the moon he caused through sky to float. He

set the sun in the sky to shine and caused the seasons to get into line.
He made the darkness of the night. For animals He enhanced their sight.
He allowed them to see well After dark when lions roar and coyotes bark.
When the sun shines they hide in dens then man labors until daylight ends.
Oh Lord, Thy works are never small; in wisdom thou has made them all. Thy riches fill the earth and sea where all living things were meant to be.
All things wait on Thee for food and what you give is always good.
Troubles come when you hide your face.
They die when you remove your grace.
Thy creative spirit you send forth.
You renew animals of worth.
The earth trembled when you spoke. At your touch hills began to smoke.
I will sing praises to the Lord as long as I can speak a word.
My thoughts of thee shall be sweet. I'll be glad when the Lord and I shall meet.
Sinners will be consumed and be no more.
Bless the Lord forevermore.

The Book Of Matthew
Chapter 1

As had already been predicted Christ descended from Abraham.
The descendants are all listed till the birth of the spotless lamb.
Mary and Joseph were to be wed but she was found with child.
Joseph sought a private divorce. for he

was always mild.
An angel came to Joseph and changed his
entire life saying, "Do not fear
to take Marry for your wife.
The Holy Spirit is the cause of the child she
has within.
Her son will be Jesus.
He'll save people from their sin.
All this brought to pass
what a prophet had depicted.
So Joseph took her as his wife as the
Angel had predicted.

Chapter 2

Jesus was born in Bethlehem when
Herod was the king.
Wise men saw a new star and
began to shout and sing.
Where is the baby who is to be.
the king of all the Jews?
We followed his star to this place.
We've come to pay our dues.
When Herod heard their question it upset
this wicked king indeed.
He demanded to know the birthplace for he
was filled with greed.
"In Bethlehem,' they answered. "That's
what the prophet wrote." Herod asked
when it appeared for this news he'd take
note.
He sent them to find the baby and then to let
him know
So he could pack his gifts and
off to worship go.
They left following the star which ahead
of them was sent.
It stopped where he child was.
To that place they all went.

They, filled with happiness,
worshiped the Christ child.
Bringing gold, frankincense and
Myrrh Joy made them go wild.
God warned them in a dream of King
Herod's wicked plan.
They went a different way so they'd miss
that evil man.
After they had departed Joseph had
another dream.
"Go to Egypt because things
aren't the way they seem,"
They left hurriedly, without delay.
Herod had all males killed,
who were two years old or less.
Jeremiah's prophecy was fulfilled.
Now, When Herod finally died Joseph was
told to pack.
Take the child and his mother. and
make the journey back.
He heard the new king's name and was
afraid to settle there.
He went to Nazareth, instead. He
did so with much care.
This fulfilled a prophesy which called him
a Nazarene.
Man could not foil God's plan which
man had never seen.

Chapter 3

John the Baptist said, "Turn from sin.
The heavenly kingdom is near."
He was prophesied by Isaiah in
an ancient year.
He ate locusts and wild honey and wore
clothes of camel hair.
People came from all around.
They came from everywhere.

Sadducees and Pharisees came
to be baptized.
"You came to escape God's wrath but you
can't be disguised.
You do things for show you've
turned away to sin.
Don't tell about your ancestors for they
can't get you in.
God can take these rocks and make people
from all.
If you continue in your sins then
you are sure to fall Every tree
that bears no fruit will be cut and
burned.
You'll be cut off if you don't do things you
should have learned.
I'll baptize you with water
whenever you repent.
One who baptizes with fire of the Holy
Spirit has been sent.
He's much greater than I. I'm
unworthy to lace his shoes.
Put your trust in him and
you can never lose.
Jesus went from Galilee out to the Jordan
River.
He came to be baptized John said,
"You're the giver.
I need you to baptize me and yet you come
to me."
Jesus said, "This is the way that it ought to
be."
John agreed to baptize.
As he raised the blessed one a
dove came from Heaven. God
said, "This is my Son."

Chapter 4

A spirit led Jesus to the desert to be
tempted by the devil.
He fasted forty days and nights.
Satan said, "If you're on the level If you
really are God's Son make
bread from every stone." Jesus
firmly answered him,
"Man can't live by bread alone," Satan sat
him in a high place saying, "Jump!
Angels will catch you,"
Jesus said, "Don't test the Lord or your
blessings will be few.
He took Jesus to a mountain saying. "All
kingdoms that you see
Will be yours if you do this thing. fall
down and worship me."
Jesus said, "Get behind me Satan. for
the scripture demands, "Worship the
Lord God only.
Follow God's commands.
The Devil left and went away. Jesus
didn't yield, you see.
He heard John was in prison so he went to
Galilee.
He didn't stop in Nazareth but went to
Naphtali and Zebulon.
To fulfill Isaiah's prophesy all
of this was done.
He walked Galilee's shores and met Peter
and Andrew,
Two fishermen netting fish but the fish were
very few He said, "Leave your nets. I'll make
you fishers of men."
Immediately they followed.
not casting their nets again.
He found two brothers,
James and John, sons of Zebedee
With their father in his boat. He

said, "Come. Follow me." They
left their boat and father.
They yielded to his call.
They knew that he was right and his work
was never small.
They went all over Galilee preaching the
Good News:
Healing people everywhere. Many could
not refuse.

Chapter 5

Jesus saw crowds on a hill.
His disciples gathered around. He
taught, "Blessed are the poor. In my
kingdom they'll abound. Blessed are
those who mourn.
God will comfort one and all.
Blessed are the meek.
Their reward will not be small.
Blessed are God's pleasers.
They'll be satisfied.
Blessed are the merciful.
God's mercy shall be applied.
Blessed are the pure in heart for
they'll see God in Heaven.
Blessed are the peacemakers. Their
peace shall be like leaven. Blessed are
doers of God's will and those
persecuted for it.
The Kingdom belongs to them. They'll
undoubtedly adore it.
Blessed are ye when men revile and
falsely gossip of you.
Your reward will be in Heaven for
everything you do.
Ye are the salt of the earth but if it loses its
savor
With what shall it be salted for it

has lost its flavor?
Its good for nothing but is trodden
under foot.
It shouldn't be kept for food. In the
garbage it should be put. Ye are the
light of the world. Don't let your
light burn dim.
Place it where all can see. Let it
shine and honor Him. Let your
light so shine that all might see
the good.
Let it glorify your Father the way you know
it should.
I have not come to destroy but to
fulfill the law.
I'll prove every jot and tittle.
You'll never find one flaw.
All who break commandments and teach
others to do so
Shall be the least in Heaven.
I want you all to know.
Whoever shall do and teach this
shall be very great.
You should do them right now.
You shouldn't ever wait.

Chapter 6

Don't do religious duties so
other folks can see.
If you do, that is all that
your reward will be.
When you give to the needy don't make a
show of it.
The hypocrites do this performing
like a skit.
Remember this, that their reward has been
paid in full.
Do your good deeds privately and you'll

receive a pull
From God who sees in private and knows
the heart's intent.
His blessings for his people will continue
being sent.
Don't be like hypocrites
standing publicly to pray.
For they receive their reward on that
very day.
Pray in your room.
Close the door behind. Pray to
God. He'll reward for he is
always kind.
Father in Heaven may I bring
honor to your name.
Your will be done on earth as in
Heaven just the same.
Give us our daily food and
forgive us for all wrong As
we forgive others.
Help us to get along.
Help us resist temptation.
Keep us from the evil one.
Help us forgive others for
wrongs they have done.
If we forgive others you
will forgive us too.
If we won't forgive we're
told what you will do.
You won't forgive us.
The guilt will stay with us. If
we refuse to forgive we have
no need to fuss.
When fasting don't look sad like
hypocrites all do.
They do it for attention until
they are through. They have
received all the reward they'll
get.

Don't announce you're fasting.
Don't worry, stew, or fret. Your
Heavenly father knows
everything you do.
What you do in private, will be
in Jesus' view.
Don't lay up your riches where
moths and rust destroy.
Store them up in Heaven and
you'll be filled with joy. Eyes
are like headlights.
We know if they're clear The
whole body's full of light.
If they are dark we fear.
If God's light is not within how dark
your life will be
To light your darkened body my
Savior is the key.
None can serve two masters.
He'll hate one and love the other.
He'll despise one of the two and
treat one like a brother.
You can't serve God and money.
You know this is true.
Don't worry about your food whether it is
meat or stew.
Don't worry about your clothes; whether
they're the latest style.
Life is more than these so get
up with a smile.
Take a lesson from the birds for they don't
sow or reap.
But God provides and they don't
have to make a peep. You are
worth much more. God will
provide. Don't worry.
Don't worry about clothing, and don't be in
a hurry.
Take a lesson from flowers.

They don't toil for clothes
Yet Solomon in all his glory can't compete
with a rose.
God will provide for you if you'll
just do his will.
Which doesn't include worry. At
times we should be still.

Chapter 7

Judge not lest ye be judged; for
if you judge others You'll be
judged the same.
You judge yourself not brothers. You
view the speck in one's eye when a log is
in your own.
Hypocrites, Solve your problems.
Don't cast, at others, stones.
When you conquer your problems you'll see
others' more clearly.
Their problems may seem smaller if you
love them more dearly.
Don't give that which is Holy to
the wandering dogs And never
cast your pearls into the pit with
hogs.
They'll trample them underfoot then they
will turn on you
Keep pearls for worthy ones.
Keep them looking new.
Ask and it shall be given.
Seek and you shall find.
Knock, it will be opened.
Keep asking. God doesn't mind.
If a son asks his father for a
single loaf of bread
Will he give him a stone?
Will he merely shake his head?
If the boy asks for a fish will

his father give a snake?
He'd probably give fish, hush
puppies and cake.
If ye then, being evil will give a good gift;
Your father does better.
He has no need for thrift. What
you would like for others to do
for you.
Do these things for them.
They'll treat you well too.
Destruction's road is wide.
It'll attract many to its fate.
Heaven's gate is narrow. The
road is very straight. Beware
of false prophets who come in
sheep's garb;
But inside they are wolves and you'll soon
feel the barb.
You'll know them by their fruits. Grapes
don't grow on thorns,
Neither do you find figs
on trees which have sharp horns.
A good tree bears good fruit. A
corrupt tree bears bad.
Chop down one with evil fruit though it
makes you sad.
Not all who call me Lord will get inside the
gate He that does my father's will will get in
without debate.
Many will say to me, "We
prophesied in thy name
And cast out many devils.
Many have done the same."
Then I will profess to them
"Your name I do not know.
Depart from me, sinners for
yours was just a show.
Whoever hears my sayings and does them
without fail

This person is a wise man. In
the end he will prevail. This
man can be likened to a
house upon a rock. When
floods descended it
withstood the shock.
Every hearer who does things that
are banned
Shall be like the foolish man who
built upon the sand.
The rains and floods descended and the
strong winds grew.
The house tumbled completely,
salvageable things were few. The
people hearing Jesus were
astonished by each saying.
His teachings had authority and
likewise did his praying.

Chapter 8

Descending from the mountain
multitudes were seen.
There came a leper saying, "Lord,
Please make me clean." Jesus,
stretched out his hand. "Be thou
clean." He said.
The leprosy disappeared like he raised the
dead. Jesus said to him,
"See thou tell no man Show thyself to the
priest and obey
Moses' command." Jesus
entered Capernaum." A
centurion came and said, "My
servant has the palsy.
Come or he;ll be dead,"
Jesus said, "I'll heal him."
"I'm unworthy." said the man. "Just
speak. He'll be healed. Many are at

my command." Jesus marveled at
this. He said,
"Your faith is great. I've not seen such
faith in Israel even to this very date.
I say that many shall come from the east
and the west and sit with Abraham and
Jacob.
In Heaven they'll find rest.
Other children shall be cast
into the blackest dark.
Weeping gnashing teeth shall make their
ugly mark."
Jesus spoke to the man, "You
can be on your way. Your
servant is healed. You have no
need to stay."
The centurion turned to leave; to
Jesus he had appealed.
The very hour that he asked his
servant had been healed.
Jesus came to Peter's house. His
mother-in-law had fever.
Jesus touched her hand.
Sickness began to leave her.
She rose and ministered to them then
evening came
They brought many with devils which he
cast out by name.
By this he fulfilled prophesy which Isaiah
had spoken
That he'd take our infirmities, their
spirits would be broken. Seeing the
multitudes about he'd go to the
other side.
A certain scribe came to him.
"I'll follow you." he cried.
"Foxes have holes, birds have nests," is
what Jesus said.
"The Son of Man has no place to

even lay his head." Another
disciple said,
"Let me bury my father first." "Let
the dead bury the dead.
Follow or be accursed." His
disciples followed him when
he got into a ship.
A storm tossed the boat. It
began to toss and tip.
Jesus was sleeping.
Disciples to him cried, Save
us before we perish.
We fear we've already died.
He said, "Oh ye of little faith, arose and
calmed the storm.
The men marveled saying. "Winds
shrink from his form."
They reached the country of
the Gergesenes.
Two from the graveyard came who
were very mean.
They said, "Don't torment us before it is
our time." Jesus looked
About and saw a herd of swine.
The devils begged him, "If
you must cast us out Let us
enter the swine.
We'll make them run about.
Jesus said, Go then.
Go to the swine. Feel free.
They possessed the swine
who ran into the sea.
They perished in the waters. Their
keepers quickly fled.
They went into the city saying all the hogs
were dead.
They told what had happened to the
man possessed.
Jesus, please leave our land. This is

what they pressed…

Chapter 9

Jesus entered a ship and
came to his own city. They
brought to him sick. Jesus
showed them pity. "Son, Be of
good cheer;
Thy sins are forgiven thee." Certain
scribes said,
"He commits blasphemy."
Jesus asked them,
"Why think you evil now?" Is it
easier to forgive or say, "Arise
and take a bow.
You know my power.
Don't be filled with shock. I'll
now say to this man,
Arise, take your bed, and walk." The
man arose and departed going to his
own house.
They suddenly became as
quiet as a mouse.
The crowds saw these things and marveled
glorifying God
He had given Jesus power. They
followed where he trod.
Jesus left and collecting taxes was Matthew
to be seen.
Jesus said, follow me.and
I will make you clean.
Matthew rose and followed.
Jesus ate at his home.
Publicans and sinners came
and they did not eat alone.

The Pharisees saw this and to the
disciples ran.
Why does he eat with he ones
who we ban.
Jesus said, "A doctor comes not to
the well,
But to those in need.
My word to those I'll tell.
I will eat with them when they invite me in.
You should do so too.
Their kind you should win.
John's disciples asked why
His followers didn't fast.
Jesus said, "The bridegroom's here.
This thing shall not last.
When the bridegroom is taken their
mourning time shall come.
They will fast day and night.
Their hearts will be numb.
Nobody uses a new cloth to mend a
damaged rag.
The new cloth would shrink and
cause the tear to sag.
You wouldn't put new wine into
bottles that were old They'd
break open
before the wine was sold."
While he was speaking a ruler came and
said, My daughter was sick.
Now she lays dead. Come, lay on hands.
If you'll do it she'll live.
He said, if you will do it a new life you will
give." Jesus rose following him.
His disciples followed too.
A woman diseased for years stuck to
him like glue. She said as she went, "If I
touch him I'll be whole."
She went straight to him like a mare would
to a foal

She touched his garment.
He said, My dear soul. Be
of good comfort now.
Faith has made thee whole."
The woman was made well
because her faith was great.
After twelve years she was healed.
Her effort was first rate.
They came to the ruler's house.
Funeral noise was heard. Jesus
said, "She's asleep." They
thought this was absurd.
When they heard what he said they laughed
and offered scorn.
They said, "She is dead and we have
come to mourn." Jesus took her by the
hand. She woke up and arose.
His fame quickly spread abroad by every
one of those.
He departed and two blind men followed
after him
Crying, "Son of David.
Don't leave us on a limb." He
asked, "Do you believe that
I can make you see?" They
said, We believe.
That's why we came to thee." He
touched them and they saw.
He said to tell no man,
But they spread the news about.
All around they ran.
A dumb man was brought. By a
devil he was possessed.
They asked Jesus to heal him for he should
be so blessed.
Jesus cast the devil out. The
devil's spirit he broke. As soon as
Jesus finished the man arose and
spoke. Multitudes marveled saying,

This we've never seen.
Pharisees said it's Satan's power.
This is what we mean.
"Jesus went to all the cities in the synagogues
to teach.
He healed sicknesses
wherever he did preach.
He saw the multitudes and said a
compassionate word.
They were as scattered sheep needing a
shepherd.
He said, "Harvest is plenteous, but
laborers are few.
Pray for the Lord of Harvest to send
laborers to you.

Chapter 10

Jesus called his disciples
giving power from above To
cast out demons and heal from
a heart of love.
James, Peter, Andrew, Philip. and
Bartholomew,
James and John,Zebedee's sons,
Thomas and Matthew, Lebbeus,
surnamed Thaddeus and Simon the
Canaanite.
And Judas Iscariot,
the betrayer on one dark night.
These twelve Jesus sent
commanding them not to go Into
the way of Gentiles.
Samaritans they'd not know.
Heal the sick, cleanse lepers.
Make the dead to live.
Cast out devils everywhere.
You've received. Now give.

Don't save for your trip.
These words I won't repeat.
Don't take extra clothes.
A workman deserves his meat.
Each city or town you enter inquire
who's worthy there.
Come and salute his house.
Enter with prayer. If
the house is worthy let
your peace abide but if
it is unworthy
don't let your peace inside.
Whoever receives you not, if your
words they don't repeat.
Depart from that house shake the dust off
your feet.
Verily, verily I say to you when its time
for judgment day
Gomorrah will have it better than where
you refuse to stay.
I send you forth as sheep with wolves
lingering about.
Be wise and harmless.
Beware of men who doubt.
They'll testify at council,
in synagogues they'll scourge you.
You'll stand before kings.
Your friends, indeed, are few.
When they deliver you don't worry about
what to say.
In the hour that you speak
you'll be shown the way. The
Spirit will take over.
It won't be you who speak.
It'll be brother against brother. The
child's life will the father seek.
Children shall rise against parents
causing them to be put to death.
You shall be hated by all men.

They'll curse you with each breath.
If you endure to the end your
salvation will be assured.
It will be worth the suffering that
you have endured.
If they persecute you in a city then
to another flee.
You shall not cover Israel before
you'll be with me.
Disciples exceed not the master nor is
servant above his lord.
A disciple should be like him and
obey his every word.
Don't worry when doing my will to the
exclusion of your own.
All covered will be revealed; all
hidden will be known.
All things told in darkness shall be
spoken in the light.
What is whispered in your ear
announced without fright.
Don't fear those who kill the
body but are unable to kill the soul.
Fear him who can destroy
both casting them into Sheol.
Two sparrows are very cheap.
My father cares for them all.
Each of your hairs is numbered.
Your value is not small.
Whoever confesses me I'll
also confess him.
If you deny you'll be denied.
Your future will be dim If
you say you love me, but are
not willing to tell You
deserve the penalty which is
to burn is Hell.
Think not that I bring peace.
I come to bring a sword.

Believers will be hated by those who
excuse my word.
Man will be against father and
daughter against mother.
In-laws against in-laws and sister
against a brother.
A man's foes shall come from his
household you see.
He who loves relatives more is
not worthy of me.
He who does not follow me and
daily take up his cross
Is unworthy to come to Heaven.
It will be his greatest loss.
He who finds his life on earth shall lose
his eternal life
While he who loses it for my sake shall be
free from eternal strife.
He who receives me receives God
who sent me,
He who receives a prophet shall
receive the same as he. Receivers
of a righteous man shall receive
his award.
If you give water in a my name you
won't lose your reward.

Chapter 11

Jesus finished with them
then left them to preach.
John heard of his works and
sent some to beseech,
"Is it you we've expecting or should we
look for another?
Should we keep on searching or proclaim
you to our brother?"
Jesus said, "Go show John the things you
hear and see.

Lame walk, lepers are cleansed, deaf hear,
and the blind see,
The dead are raised and walk, the
poor are preached to.
Blessed is he who receives me and does
the things I do."
As they left he preached to many
concerning John.
"Why did you go to the wilderness arriving
before dawn?
What were you there to see? A
man wearing soft clothes
belonging in king's houses and
to the likes of those.
Did you wish to see a prophet?
More than a prophet is he.
He is the one written about, I
send a messenger to thee.
The one who will prepare the way for the
one God sends to you.
John is this messenger.
He has told you what to do.
Not one born to woman is
greater than this man
For John the Baptist has fulfilled his
part in my father's plan.
Even so, The least in Heaven shall be
greater than this one.
From the day he preached
until this day is done
The kingdom suffered attacks. Men
tried to seize it by war.
All the prophets told what
the kingdom had in store.
If you believe John is
the Elijah who was predicted.
Believe his message
and you won't be afflicted.
This generation is compared to

children in the marketplace Saying,
"We piped. You didn't dance.
This is a disgrace.
You have not lamented
when we have mourned."
John came not eating or drinking and this
one was scorned.
You did this to him, but
when God's Son came
He came eating and drinking and you
ridiculed his name."
He upbraided their cities where
mighty works were done
Because they did not repent when
confronted with God's son.
Woe unto Chorizin and Bethsaida for if
the works you saw.
Were done in Tyre and Sidon they'd have
repented under the law.
Tyre and Sidon will be better off when
judgment day shall tell.
You, exalted Capernaum will be cast
straight into Hell.
If the works which you have seen in Sodom
had been revealed.
That city would remain today its
judgments would be repealed. On
judgment day that city will be better
off than you
You've neglected all the things I
meant for you to do.
At that time Jesus said,
"I thank my father, Lord of all.
He hid things from the wise revealing them
to babes so small.
We do not know what is good but
God is always right.
Let this be the way.
It seemed good in thy sight. The

166

father gives all things. None know
him but the son. The father knows
the son and believers in what's
been done.
Come unto me all thee who labor and
I'll give rest.
Take my yoke upon you and
learn to do your best.
I am meek and lowly of heart.
I'll give rest to your souls.
My yoke is easy, my burden light.
Take it and reach your goal.

Chapter 12

Jesus went out on the Sabbath and
walked through fields of corn.
His disciples were very hungry and ears
from stalks were torn.
The pharisees said,
"On the Sabbath that's unlawful."
Jesus said to them, Forbid
them not to pull. Didn't you
read when
David entered the House of God.
He ate show bread of priests and did not
receive the rod.
Perhaps you have not read the priests
profane the Sabbath
In the temple of the Lord yet they don't
see God's wrath.
One greater than the temple is
right here in this place.
If you knew the truth you would
seek his face.
If you knew mercy you wouldn't make
the guiltless pay.
The Son of Man is Lord
of all even of the Sabbath day.

When he departed into a
synagogue he did go.
One there had a withered hand. They
said, "We want to know Is it lawful to
heal on the Sabbath?" They wished to
accuse God's man.
He asked, "Is there one here who is so
completely in God's plan
That if his only sheep
fell into a pit on the Sabbath day He'd
leave it there until the next before, on it,
a hand he'd lay?
A man is much more precious than
any of your sheep
So I'll do well on the Sabbath,
what you sow you'll also reap.
Then he said to the man, "Stretch
forth thy withered hand."
He did and it was healed. He
went out feeling grand.
The pharisees assembled to plot to
destroy God's man,
But Jesus withdrew from them.
The multitudes, after him, ran.
He had compassion on them.
He healed them on his own.
He asked this favor that they should not
make him known.

These things fulfilled what Isaiah had
spoken of old.
There's a reason each of these prophecies
was told.
Behold, my chosen servant in whom I am
well pleased.
Shall show judgment on Gentiles. Their
mind shall not be teased.
No man shall hear him in the streets.
He shall not strive or cry. He

shall not break a reed.
The smoke from flax won't die.
He turns judgment into victory.
In his name shall Gentiles trust.
This prophesy has been fulfilled.
God's work is always just.
A man possessed by a devil who could not
speak or see
Was brought to Jesus and from affliction
was set free.
All were amazed saying, "Son
of David this must be." The
Pharisees said,
His power is from the devil, you see.
Jesus knew their thoughts. He
said to them these things.
"A kingdom divided against itself to itself
desolation brings.
A house divided against itself can not for
long withstand.
If Satan casts out Satan his fall will
be just grand.
If I use the devil's power to
cast the devils out
Whose power do your children use as
they wander about?
But if my power comes from
God's own mighty hand God's
Kingdom has come.
You ought to feel just grand.
How can you enter a house to
spoil goods, you see
Except you tie the owner up so he won't
bring harm to thee?
He that is not with me,
against me he will stand.
He that does not gather
will be scattered through the land. All
matter of sin shall be forgiven, but don't

you dare to boast.
One that won't be forgiven is
blasphemy against the Holy Ghost.

For things spoken against me forgiveness
will be received.
Don't speak against the Holy Spirit.
Don't ever be deceived.
This act will not be forgiven. Pay
attention to this text.
Forgiveness for this won't come in this
world or the next.
A good tree produces good fruit.
The fruit of a bad tree is bad.
A tree is known by it fruit,
and by the quality it had.
You generation of vipers.
How can you speak good?
Your heart is evil and you don't do
the things you should.
A good man with a good heart brings
forth good things.
A man with evil treasures only
evil brings.
I say every idle word
will be accounted for.
You'll be justified by good words and
condemned if they are poor."
Certain scribes and pharisees said, "We
want a sign of thee."
But Jesus said to them, "A
sign you shall not see.
An evil and adulterous generation seeks
after a sign.
No sign will be except Jonah for the whale
on him did dine,
He stayed in the belly for
three long days and nights.
God's Son shall be in the earth three days

then he'll be all right.
In judgment Ninevah will rise and shall
condemn this generation
For a greater one than Jonah's here and
you ignore the situation.
The Queen of the South shall also rise this
generation to condemn.
She listened to the wisdom of Solomon.
One here overshadows them. A man loses
his unclean spirit and he walks through dry
places.
He seeks rest, but fails then his
steps to home he traces.
It is empty, swept, and garnished.
seven wicked spirits he'll find. He's
worse off now than before. This
generation puts him in a bind.

As he talked to these people;
behold, his family came.
The people called him out.
They called to him by name.
He answered them,
"Who are my brothers or my mother? The
ones who do my Father's will are they, not
any other.

Chapter 13

Jesus went out of the house and sat down
on the shore.
Multitudes gathered around and kept
coming; more and more.
He boarded a ship and sat.
On the shore the multitudes stood. He
taught them in parables saying: A
sower sowed as he should.
Some seed fell by the wayside.
Birds came and ate them all.
Some fell in stony places, sprouted, but

didn't grow tall.
The earth was very shallow. Their
roots could not go deep.
The sun scorched them.
Moisture they could not keep.
Some fell among the thorns. The
thorns choked them out. Others fell
on good ground and they began to
sprout.
They brought forth fruit.
Some produced an hundredfold.
Whoever has ears hear
and take notice before he's old." The
disciples asked him later why, in
parables, he spoke.
He answered saying:
"To you the mysteries are no joke.
You know about heaven.
They wouldn't know what I say.
Whoever has little.
It will be taken all away.
Therefore I speak in parables so they will
understand.
Prophesy is fulfilled which was
written by Isaiah's hand.
By hearing ye shall hear but understand it
not.
Seeing ye shall see but won't
perceive a lot.
These people's hearts are gross.
Ears are dull of hearing.
Their eyes have been closed and have
stopped their peering.

Lest they should see with eyes and
hear with their ears;
And should understand,
be converted and shed tears."
Blessed are your eyes for

they've been given sight.
Blessed are your ears for
they hear what is right.
Verily, I say to you
many prophets and righteous men
Desired to see things you've seen but
have seen little of them.
They desire to hear things you heard but
their hearing has been lower.
Listen carefully because of this to the
parable of the sower.
When anyone hears the word and
understands it not
The wicked one will come
with a very wicked plot.
He'll take away
what was sown in his heart.
This was the seed by the wayside
which will soon depart.
The seed which fell on stone is he that
receives the word.
It takes root for a while, but
didn't make me Lord.
When troubled and trials arise he
quickly falls away.
The seed cast among the thorns is
he who accepts today.
Soon the cares of the world, the
deceitfulness of its wealth
Chokes out the word within killing his
spiritual health.
The seed on good ground is he who
understands all.
He takes root and brings forth fruit.
He obeyed God's call." This
parable he also said, "The
kingdom is like a man.
He sowed good seed but
his enemy had a plan.

He slipped into the field while
the farmer slept.
Sowing tares among the wheat then
from the field he crept.
The wheat grew up and bore fruit.
Tares grew in between.
Servants asked from where they came.
What's this that we've seen?"

He said, "An enemy did this.
"Should we pull the tares?"
'You'd also pull the wheat.
Roots tangle with theirs. Let
both grow up together. I'll say
then to the reapers. Gather first
all the tares don't cut any
keepers.
Gather them and bind them and
pile them up to burn. Then
gather up the wheat.
When its in the barn, adjourn."
Another parable He told likened
heaven to a mustard grain.
The seed is hardly visible,
but when watered by the rain
It becomes the greatest of herbs.
It grows into a tree.
Birds nest in its branches for
everyone to see.
A parable was told comparing the kingdom
of heaven
To what causes bread to rise.
He likened it to leaven. He
spoke all in parables.
Without them was little uttered.
This fulfilled the prophecy that God's
prophet had muttered.
"I will open my mouth. In
parables I will talk.

Uttering secrets unknown since
the formation of the rock."
Jesus sent them away.
He went in and stayed inside. Explain
the parable of the Tares, his disciples
quickly cried.
He answered them saying. "The
field is the world,
I sowed good seed before the
bad was hurled.
The devil sowed the tares,
children of the wicked one
The angels came to harvest
when the world was done.
Tares were thrown into the fire, so
shall the wicked be.
All offenders shall be thrown in.
Those who do iniquity.
They'll be cast into the furnace.
Wailing and gnashing teeth are near. The
righteous shall shine like the sun.
Let those who have ears hear.

Heaven is like a treasure hidden
by a man in a field. He sells all
to buy that plot so he could have
its yield.
Heaven is like a merchant seeking pearls
which are best.
He sold all to purchase that
which passed his test. Heaven
is like a net that was cast into
the sea.
They sorted the take keeping the best
for their fee.
The angels will sort the
wicked from the just.
The wicked will be judged for
punishment is a must.

Have you understood?
" They said, "We understand."
Behold every scribe instructed unto
the Heavenly land
Is like a householder
who sorts the new from the old.
When Jesus finished these parables he arose
and left the fold.
When he came to his country in the
synagogues he taught.
They were astonished because his
wisdom was a lot.
They asked, "Isn't this the carpenter's
son and the son of Mary? His brothers
and sisters are with us so why should we
tarry?"
Jesus said, "A prophet is not without
honor except near his home.
They didn't do many miracles there.
They left that town to roam.

Chapter 14

At that time King Herod heard
of my Savior's fame. He asked
if John the Baptist had come
back again.
Has he risen from the dead and
does a mighty work?
He had John the Baptist killed. He
felt like a jerk.
He had John put in prison for
Herodias' sake
John said it is unlawful his
brother's wife to take.
Herod would have killed him but he
feared the multitude.
They considered him a prophet and
considered Herod rude.

Herod's birthday came.
His daughter danced for him.
He promised anything she asked which
left him on a limb.
She said give to me John
the Baptist's head.
The king was bound by
what he already said.
He had John beheaded.
In prison he had it done.
His head was brought and
given to this one.
She took it to mother.
His body, disciples claimed.
They went straight to Jesus and told how
John was maimed.
When Jesus heard of this to a
desert place he departed.
When the people heard, after
him they started.
Jesus saw the people and he healed the sick.
At evening his disciples said,
"The multitudes with us stick." Jesus
said to them,
"Give them food to eat."
With five loaves and two fish.
Their needs we cannot meet.
" Jesus said, "Bring them to me."
He told them to sit down.
He took the two small fishes and five
loaves which were brown.
He looked up to Heaven; blessed the
food and broke it. He commanded
his disciples,
"Take food to them," he spoke it.
They all ate and were filled. They
collected what was left. They had
twelve baskets full, more than a man
could heft.

Those who ate their fill were
about five thousand men. Women
and children also ate.
All were filled and then Jesus
commanded his disciples
to get into a ship And go
to the other side. He'd also
make the trip.
He sent the multitudes home then
went out to pray.
He was alone at night.
Waves with the ship did play.

In the night's fourth watch Jesus
walked on the sea.
When the disciples saw him they asked,
"Who can it be?"
They thought it was a spirit and
they cried out in fear, But Jesus
spoke saying.
"Be ye of good cheer. It
is 1. Be not afraid." Peter
said, "My Lord,
I'll walk on the water when
you give the word." Jesus told
him to come.
He started on water walking.
He became afraid.
He began shaking and rocking.
He started to sink
and cried out, "Lord. Save me."
Jesus reached out and said, "Come, in
safety be."
He said, "Oh! Thou of little faith, why
did you doubt?"
When they made it back the
wind ceased to blow about. All who
were in the ship said,
You are God's Son.

On the land word spread of
what had been done.
The sick were brought to him.
They asked to touch his hem. All
who did were made whole.
Every one of them.

Chapter 15

Jesus came to the scribes and
pharisees who were saying "Why
don't your disciples wash?
From tradition are they straying?" Jesus
answered, "You transgress God's
commandment. Why?" Honor thy
father and mother.
Let the cursers die.
But ye say, Tell parents, "This is
for your good, you see."
Then honor them not and say this is
as it should be."
You've negated God's command and
done it by your law.
This can't be to your credit for it shows
a terrible flaw.
Ye hypocrites, Esaias
prophesied and rightly so.
They draw nigh with lip service but
their hearts go to and fro.
They teach commandments. In
vain they worship me.
He called the multitudes and said, "Hear,
understand, and see.
Its not what goes into the mouth that
defiles any man.
It's what comes from his mouth that defiles
him while it can."
His disciples said then, "You
offended the Pharisees."

Jesus said, "So be it for
I'm not here to please.
A plant not planted by my Father shall
be rooted out.
Blind lead blind into a ditch and
listen to them shout. Don't you yet
understand what the mouth takes
in
Goes into the belly only. Its
not considered sin.
Things coming from the mouth come also
from the heart.
It is they which defile a man.
I'll say to him, 'Depart!' Out of
the heart comes evil thoughts
and actions too.
These will defile a man if evil he does do.
It does not defile a man to eat with
unwashed hands."
Then Jesus left that place to
go to other lands.
He went to Tyre and Sidon. A
woman came from the coast.
"O Lord, Son of David, I
need your mercy most.
My daughter is possessed." Jesus
had nothing to say. Disciples came
and said,
"Lord, Send her away." He said, "I
am not sent except
to Israel's lost sheep.
She worshipped him and said, "My
trouble is very deep."
Jesus said, "It is not good to take the
children's bread
And cast it to the dogs." She said,
"The dogs need to be fed.
They eat crumbs from the table. A
crumb is all I ask." Jesus said, "Your

faith is great,
as you pursue your task.

Because your faith is great I
will do the thing you wish."
Her daughter was healed that hour and ate
a hearty dish.
Jesus left that place coming
to the Sea of Galilee.
He went up on a mountain and sat down,
alone to be.
Multitudes came to him, the
blind, maimed, and dumb.
Many other afflicted came.
He healed every one.
The crowd was amazed at miracles
he performed.
They glorified God and after Jesus
they all stormed.
Jesus said to his disciples, "They've
been here three days.
I won't send them out hungry or
they'll faint along their ways." His
disciples asked him,
"Where can we get bread?
The crowd is very great.
What shall they be fed?"
Jesus asked the men,
"How many loaves have ye?"
They said, "Seven
and a few little fishes,you see." He
told the entire group to be
seated on the ground.
He gave thanks for the food then he passed it
around.
They all ate their fill.
They ate all they could hold.
Four thousand men; women
and children untold. They

gathered the scraps. Seven
baskets held their fill.
He sent them all away then
he went down the hill.
He boarded a ship
and from that place they went
To the coast of Magdala where a little time
they spent.

Chapter 16

Pharisees and Sadducees
asked Jesus to show a sign.
But Jesus said to them,
"You predict the weather fine.
Red sky in the evening, you say.
The weather will be fair.
In the morning,
'It will be foul if red is found up
there.Oh, You hypocrites.
You can read the sky.
and signs of the times
Now I ask you why?
You adulterous generation.
You seek after a sign. You
have that of Jonah.
You won't get more of mine.
They went to the other side with no bread, If
you please.
Jesus said, "Beware the leaven of Pharisees
and Sadducees."
They figured it was because they
didn't have bread. Jesus said, "Oh ye
of little faith,
Ye shall all be fed.
Don't you remember
the five thousand and five loaves
And how much we had left though
we had no stoves?

Remember from seven loaves and four
thousand were fed?
The baskets you collected
when by Me you were led.
Why don't you understand, of bread I
don't now speak?
The Pharisees and Sadducees have a
doctrine which is bleak.
At Caesarea Philippi they followed God's
chosen lamb.
He asked of his disciples, "Who do
men say I am?" "Some say John
the Baptist, others say Elias.
Some say a prophet.
Others Jeremias" What do
you say "Who am I, say
ye?" Who do you believe
that I am? said he.
Simon Peter answered when he saw Jesus
nod. "Thou Art Christ" he said. "Son of
the Living God." Jesus said to him,
"Simon, blessed are you.
Flesh and blood did not
put this in your view. God made you,
Simon, leader of the flock.
You are now Peter.
One called "The Rock."

My Church will withstand even the
gates of Hell.
I give you Heaven's keys for I
know you very well.
What you bind on earth shall in Heaven
be bound.
The things you loose here shall loose, in
Heaven, be found.
That he was the Christ should be
whispered to none.
He showed his disciples what he'd suffer

as God's Son.
He showed he must suffer,
be killed and raised the third day.
Peter scolded him saying, "It
shall not be that way." "Get
behind me, Satan, You're an
offense unto me. You love not
things of God, but just what
pleases thee. If anyone will
follow me he must himself deny,
Take up his cross daily and
never ask me Why?
Who saves his own life it
shall be to his loss.
If he loses it for my sake he'll gain by the
cross. What profit does he have if
he gains the whole world if,
on judgment day to
Hell his soul is hurled? With
angels and glory the Son of
Man shall come.
He'll judge each by his works,
each person, not just some.
If the scales of justice warrant
you'll be cast into Hell.
The Son of man shall come before some
hear death's bell.

Chapter 17

Peter, James, John, and Jesus
went to a mountain alone. He
was transfigured there.
With brilliance his face shown. His
clothes were purest white.
Two appeared unto them.
Elias, Moses, and Jesus shined just like a
precious gem.
Peter asked Jesus,

"Is it good for us to be here?" We
will make, if you want, three
tabernacles near..

One for each of you.
A bright cloud appeared.
A voice came from it as to them it
neared, "This is my beloved
son in whom I'm well pleased."
When the disciples heard it
they fell on their knees.
Jesus came to them and touched every
one. Saying,
"Be not afraid for I'm God's only Son."
When they lifted their eyes
they saw he was alone.
He said, tell no-one until He'd
rolled away the stone."
They asked, Why do scribes say Elias
must come." Jesus said,
"It shall be done.
He'll restore all, not some." I
declare that he's come.
They knew him not, you see.
When the Son returns
likewise it will be." Then
they understood.
Of John the Baptist he'd spoken.
There was a man when they came who had
been broken.
He kneeled before Jesus saying. "Have
mercy on my son,
A lunatic who falls
into fire is what's done. He saw
your disciples. They couldn't
find a cure, But I have faith in
you
Of you I am quite sure."
Jesus said, How long shall I be with you?

Bring this man to me.
I'll show you what to do. Jesus
rebuked the devil who left
him that hour.
His disciples asked, "Why did
all our efforts sour?"
Jesus told them solemnly. "Its
your unbelief.
I say to you its enough to
cause me great grief. With faith
you could say to the mountain
there Move over and that place
would become quite bare.

Nothing would be impossible if true
faith you had.
Prayer and fasting would help. It
wouldn't be considered bad.
While they stayed in
Galilee Jesus said
They shall not rest until God's
servant is dead. There is a man
who, God's Son will betray.
God's Son will be crucified, and rise
on the third day. They came to
Capernaum they had this to say,
"We are collecting tax. Does
your master pay?" Peter said,
"Of course and he started in
But Jesus asked, "Who pays?
Does a citizen?"
Jesus asked, "If strangers pay are
citizens quite free?
Do not offend these men so go
down to the sea. Catch a fish.
In its mouth you'll locate a
coin
Give it to them for the tax then
come and with me join.

Matthew 18

The disciples had been discussing
their fate.
They said, "We'd like to know in
Heaven who'll be great?"
Jesus took a little child and
sat him in their midst.
Unless you become as a child
you'll not in Heaven exist."
Whoever shall humble himself
and become as a child.
Shall be considered great.
His riches will be piled.
Whoever receives a child
in my name receives me.
But if he offends a child an
offense to me he'll be.
It's better that a millstone were
hanged around his neck. And
be thrown into the ocean off a
large ship's deck.
Woe to the world;
for offenses must come,
But woe to the offender
for he is quite dumb.

If a hand or foot offend cut them off as
well. Its better to be maimed than, whole,
to enter hell. If your eye offends you put
out its desire. It's better to miss an eye
than to be cast into fire.
Don't despise these little
Ones 'for I say unto you
They'll see me in Heaven.
You should want to too.
I came to the world to
save what was lost.

A man would search for a sheep in
spite of time or cost.
He'll leave the others there
searching from desert to bay
He'll look all night if necessary for the one
who's gone astray.
He will rejoice when it is found, more
for that one sheep,
Than for the ninety and nine which in the
flock did keep.
Your father in Heaven also
wishes to lose not one.
He'll celebrate like the father of
the Prodigal Son.
If thy brother's against you
go tell to him his fault
You'll gain a brother
if these things he will halt.
If your brother doesn't listen go
with two or three.
If he still won't hear
get the church to go with thee.
If the church goes and
he continues in sin
Let him be as a heathen. Don't
visit him again. What you
bind on earth shall be in
Heaven bound. But whatever
you shall
loose shall loose, there, be found.
Again I say to you if
two of you agree As
touching anything
it shall be thus for thee.
Wherever two or three are
gathered in my name.
I am in the midst
of them just the same.

Peter asked if one should forgive
another seven times. Jesus said
seventy times seven forgive him for
his crimes.
The kingdom is like a king who had a
servant brought,
who owed ten thousand talents. To pay
his debt he could not.
The king said to sell him with his
family too.
The servant begged saying,
"Have patience. I'll pay you." The
king forgave his debt and set the
servant free.
The servant found a debtor and demanded
the proper fee.
He laid hands on him and
took him by the throat.
The other begged for patience saying
he'd pay the note.
He had the indebted servant
imprisoned behind the bar Until he
could pay the debt. His mercy did
not go far.
When his fellow servants saw what this
man had done
They went and told the lord. They
went to him on the run The king said,
"You wicked one.
You had pity from me.
You should have shown some pity by
forgiving this one's fee?"
It made the king so angry he had
him thrown in jail My Father will
do likewise if forgiveness doesn't
prevail.

Chapter 19

When Jesus had finished he
went to Galilee.
Multitudes followed and he said, "From
ailments be set free."
The pharisees came to him trying to
tempt him there Asking,
"Is divorce lawful for
any cause you bear?"
"Haven't you read?
They were made female and male?
Marriage makes the two one flesh and it
should never fail."
They asked why Moses allowed it with
only a written letter.
"Moses knew your wicked hearts and let
you break this fetter.

At first it was not allowed
now, I say to you;
Except for fornication divorce is taboo.
If you shall be divorced
and then marry again,
You commit adultery and
live day by day in sin.
Whoever marries one who has
been divorced
Also commits adultery for
it is not endorsed." The
disciples said,
its not good to marry,"
Jesus said, "There are some who
could not, this message, carry.
There are some eunuchs
which to this position yield.
Some were made eunuchs
by others its been revealed. Some made
themselves eunuchs for the Kingdom's
sake.
He who can accept it should

this pathway take."
People brought children to him to
lay hands on and pray.
His disciples rebuked them.
Jesus said, "Let them stay,
The Kingdom of Heaven is made up of
such." He laid hands on them
To them this meant much.
After he had done this
Jesus departed.
There came one to him just
after he'd started Saying,
"Good Master."
Jesus asked, "Why did you say good?
There is none good but God.
Keep commands as you should." He
asked to which Jesus referred.
He said, "You shall not steal, You
shall never tell a lie.
Tell only what is real.
You shall not murder or
commit adultery.
You shall honor your father and
your mother, you see. You shall
love your neighbor The same way
you love you.
Always treat him like a brother in all
that you do.

The man said, "I have done all this since my
youth." Jesus said,
"Give all to the poor.
He thought this uncouth.
When he heard this he
sorrowed for his
possessions were great.
Rich find it hard to
enter the gate.
It is easier for a camel to go

through a needle's eye.
His disciples asked, Who
can be saved and why?"
Jesus said to them "With
men it can't be.
With God all things are possible.
He'll set captives free." Peter
answered, saying, "We have
forsaken all.
What shall we receive for answering your
call?" Jesus said, "Verily,
I say, because you've followed me
When God sits on his throne there will
be thrones for thee.
You'll judge Israel's tribes. Those
who suffer for my sake Shall be
rewarded.
Life shall be their take.
They shall enter my kingdom, a land where
there's no thirst.
The first shall then be last and the last shall
then be first.

Chapter 20

The kingdom's like a householder seeking
laborers for a day.
He sent them to work saying a penny should
be their pay.
There were some standing idle in the market
at hour three.
He sent them to work
saying he'd pay a proper fee. At
the sixth hour and the ninth he
also did the same.
He asked at the eleventh hour,
"You're idle? Who's to blame?
They said, "Nobody hired us." He
told them to go.

179

I will pay what is right for
harvesting what I grow."
He said to his foreman when
working time was done,
"Call the workers together and
pay them, every one."

When the last hired came
they were paid a penny.
The first hired thought they
would get many. They too
got a penny. When this had
been done They complained
about when they'd begun.
They said some only
worked for an hour
But their pay was the same.
They were very sour.
They said ones who worked
during the heat of the day Did
the most work of all. They
should get more pay.
The householder said, "I
have done no wrong.
You agreed to work for a penny
and to work that long.
I'm in charge of my money.
Is it not my own?
I have not wronged you so
why do you groan?"
Jesus took the twelve apart and stayed.
Saying the Son of Man
shall soon be betrayed.
The chief priests and scribes shall
condemn God's Son.
They'll deliver him.
Scourge and crucify this one.
Do not be discouraged or
wear a sad disguise.

I'll be placed in a tomb.
on the third day I'll rise.
Zebedee's children's mother came
to Jesus on the run,
Asking if the best seat in Heaven could
be for each son.
Jesus answered saying.
"You know not for what you ask.
To drink the cup
I must drink
is an impossible task.
To be baptized with my baptism You are
unable, now."
They said, "We will follow. We
are sure we know how."
Jesus said, "You shall be baptized with
that which I am.
You shall drink of the cup of God's very
precious lamb.

To sit on my right hand or my
left on that day.
I can't give these things. It is
God's right to say.
Others were told of what had transpired
Indignation was ignited.
Against these it was fired.
Jesus said, "Gentile princes exercise
dominion over them.
The great exercise authority. It shall
not be with my men. Whoever is
great here will minister to the
others.
Whoever is chief shall be a
servant to his brothers. Even so
the Son came not to be
ministered to But to minister
to needy and give his life for
you."

As they departed
a crowd trailed behind.
Two men cried,"Have
mercy because we are blind.
" The multitudes said,
"They should hold their peace.
" They cried out louder.
Their shouts did increase.
Jesus called to them,
"What do you want me to do?"
They said, "We'd like to see so
we can follow you." Jesus had
compassion,
and their eyes he touched.
They received sight
thanking him much.

Chapter 21

From Bethphage to the Mount of
Olives they came.
He said to two disciples, "Go
in my father's name. When
you enter the city as the gates
you pass
You will find a colt tied up with an ass.
Untie them and to me
bring them if you please. If
anyone asks why, say, The
master needs these."
He will send them with you.
All of this will be done
That prophesy is fulfilled
for, it, I won't be
shunned.

On an ass with her foal my
king comes to the meek
They listened and did just
as he did speak.

Bringing them they placed on
them their clothes.
They put Jesus on them.
Great multitudes arose.
Throwing clothes and branches on
which they would walk.
They cried, "Hasannah."
People started to talk.
They said, "Who is he?
Why is he coming here?"
They said, "He is Jesus.
Do not have one fear."
In the temple Jesus saw where
money changers were. He cast
out buyers and sellers as they
started to stir.
He overturned their tables
and the dove sellers' seats.
Saying, "My house is for prayer.
Its now filled with deceit."
The blind and the lame were
then quickly healed.
Priests and scribes saw their
motives were revealed. They
saw things and listened. In the
temple were sayings.
The priests knew that these
people were not playing. They
came to Jesus asking.
"Do you see their ways?" Jesus said,
From the mouths of babes
shall come praise.
He left for Bethany where
he lodged for the night.
In the morning he was hungry and
we looked for a bite.
He saw a fig tree on the way. There
was no fruit thereon.
It had plenty of leaves

but of fruit it had none.
He said, You won't bear.
Its leaves shriveled and dried.
Its branches drooped. It
wasn't long till it died. The
disciples marveled speaking
of its demise.
Jesus said, "If you have faith this
would be no surprise."

If you do not doubt
you'll do more than you've seen.
Tell a mountain to move.
The earth shall be swept clean.
All you'll ask believing you
shall soon receive. Remember
when praying you must also believe.
When he taught in the temple the priests,
to test him, came Saying,
"These miracles
You do them in whose name?
Jesus answered and said, I ask
you only one thing. Answer
my question then an answer
I'll bring.
The baptism of John; from
whom did it come?
From Heaven or from men?" They
were all quite dumb.
If we say Heaven he'll ask why we didn't go
near But if we say,
"From men," his own people we fear.
They answered saying,
"We can not tell you." Jesus said,
"Neither, then, will I answer your's too. A
man said to one son, 'Please work in
my yard. He said he would not then

worked really hard. He said to the
second son in my
yard you should work.
He said, "I will go," but his
duty did shirk. Which one
did the will of his dear dad?
Which one made his father feel
really quite bad?
They said the first did well.
Jesus said it too,
Harlots will enter Heaven
before the likes of you.
John came to you and you
believed not.
Among those who believed one
was a harlot.
A man planted a vineyard and
hedged about.
His wine press and a tower.
He had rented out.
He sent servants there to
ask for his pay.
They beat and killed him Where
they met him that day.
He sent other servants,
more than he first did. They
treated likewise. Their
bodies they hid. He said
they will honor for me, my
only son." They said, 'He is
heir. Let's kill him for fun.
Out of the vineyard they hid
him from view. When the
owner came
what will he do?"
They said, "Destroy them and
rent it to another, One who
would never cheat on his
brother."

182

Jesus said, "The stone that had been rejected
Became head of the corner in what God erected?
The kingdom shall be taken from you.
It shall be given to those who know what to do. People who won't kill the Master's dear Son.
Who'll pay their fair share for the services done.
Stumblers on the corner may shout a bit louder
But he on whom it shall fall will be ground into powder."
Chief Priests and Pharisees heard what he had said They would not rest at all until Jesus was dead.
Whatever they schemed the multitudes they feared.
They knew him as a prophet. He was, to them, endeared.

Chapter 22

In parables. Jesus said, "I tell you this thing.
The Kingdom's like a wedding for the son of a king.
Servants went to the guests.
They refused to come.
They said, The food is there.
Come, now, and eat some.
The guests ridiculed them and went their own way. Others took the servants and slew them that day. The king heard of this and sent out armed men.
Burning the cities where they had been.
He said to his servants,
The wedding is prepared. Guests are not coming.' At the banquet he stared. 'Go into the highways.
Invite all you find,
So they invited all there.
At the feast they all dined.
The king saw one present without wedding clothes.
He said, 'Why did you come?'
He quickly arose.
The king commanded,
Tie him tightly with lashings.
Cast him into darkness where teeth are gnashing.
Many will be called,' he said and arose.
But few will be chosen from the likes of those.
The pharisees took counsel and tried to trick him.
The chances they'd admit they were wrong was slim They sent disciples saying.
"Master, this we know.
You teach God's ways and care nothing for show.
Do you think it is lawful to pay Caesar tax?"
Jesus said, Why do you tempt me with these acts?
Show me your money. Whose image is there?" They said it is Caesar's. He said, Then it is his fare. You benefit from services.
He collects tax from you.

183

Belonging to groups means these
things you must do,"
They marveled at his answer then they
went their own way.
Sadducees came to him and had
this to say.

Moses said marry
a deceased brother's wife. Raise your
brother's seed
for the rest of your life.
There were seven brothers.
The first took a wife.
He was still childless
when he lost his life.
The second married her. He
died childless too.
The other five did likewise.
Now we ask of you.
After the last brother
was taken in death
The woman was deserted by
her own living breath. She had
seven husbands as, by Moses'
law, it should be; In the
resurrection,
who will be with she?"
Jesus said, "You err
in not knowing the word.
In that life people are as
angels of the Lord.
About what you've asked, Have
you read what God said?
I am God of the living and
not of the dead."
They were filled with awe
and with astonishment. The
pharisees gathered after they
had been sent.

A lawyer wishing an argument, put
him to the test.
Which commandment is greatest?
Which one is the best? Jesus
said, "Love the Lord with all
of your heart.
This commandment covers all
not just a part.
Not only with your heart but
with your soul and mind.
All others are found
in this commandment combined.
The second is like it;
love your neighbor as yourself.
On these two hang the law and
all those on the shelf." Jesus
said to them,
"I have a question of thee.
"What about Christ? I ask,
whose son is he?"

They said, David's. He said, "
Why does he call him Lord? He
made this statement.
It's from his own word. "The
Lord said to my Lord" is what
he did say.
David called him Lord.
Its still true today.
No man answered him.
Their tongues he ensnared.
They asked no more for not
one of them dared.

Chapter 23

Jesus spoke to the multitude and to
disciples too.. "Pharisees fill Moses
seat.

What they bid you do. Don't
follow for they don't do what
they say. They make strict
rules. Common people pay.
Making laws for men not
wanting to linger. As for
observing them,
they do not raise a finger. All
works that they do are so men
will know.
Their phylacteries and hems are enlarged,
just for show.
They seek for themselves the best
room and seat.
The names of Rabbi
and teacher each of them repeats.
Why call them Rabbi when
Christ alone is head. Call no man on
earth, father.
This is what I've said.
Call no one father because
he's up above. Don't be called
master for the master is love.
Whoever is great in my kingdom shall be
a servant to all.
Whoever exalteth himself shall be
humbled by fall.
Woe unto Pharisees. Hypocrites you
are.
You cause men to stumble those
who would go far. Your
damnation is great for you make
long prayer Devouring widow's
houses and hindering her there.

Woe to you Scribes.
Hypocrites you are. To win
one convert you'd travel
quite far. Then that convert

by what you tell.
You make more deserving than
you to enter Hell.
Woe to you all,
'It means nothing to swear'
when in reality you're bound
by the words you bear.
You are blind fools
and all should behold
The god of the temple
which sanctifieth the gold?
When you swear by the altar.
You're bound by nothing at all
By the gift and you're bound
though the binding be small.
You are blind fools
for is the gift greater
Or is it the altar to which you all cater?
Swear by the altar
and by what's on it you swear.
Swear by the temple
and by the dweller who's there.
Swear by Heaven
and you swear by God's throne and
not only the throne
but by he who sits thereon.
Woe unto you who tithe of mint,
cumin, and Anise
Of these small things indeed
you faithfully pay tithes.
Of judgment, mercy,
and faith which are under the law
you have overlooked.
It is a grievous flaw.
Of these weightier matters
had you not been blind.
You swallow a camel yet
you don't seem to mind.
Woe to you for you

stress cleanliness
But you don't seem to mind
the dirt and excess.
Clean within then
clean the outside also.
You do things backwards.
This adds to your woe.

Woe unto you whitewashed statues
of stone.
The outside looks clean but
you're full of dead bones.
Outwardly you look righteous,
but its truly a pity.
You are full of hypocrisy
and of iniquity.
Woe unto you for tombs
to prophets you build.
You decorate these as if you are
sorrow filled.
You say if we'd lived
then they wouldn't have been slain.
You admit you're their children which,
should cause pain.
Go finish what you started.
You will do quite well. You
serpents and vipers. How can
you escape Hell? I will send my
prophets.
You'll nail some to the cross.
You'll whip others in synagogues but it'll
be your loss.
The punishment for murders will fall
grievously on you.
From the murder of Abel to
Zacharias whom you slew.
The punishment will fall on the
people of this day For
unfaithfulness and sin though

you knew the way.
Oh Jerusalem, You kill and
stone those sent to you.
How often would I gather you as to
biddies the hens do.
Your house is desolate. You
will never see me
Until you say, "In God's name, Blessed
now is he,"

Chapter 24

He left the temple.
His disciples came to him.
They showed Jesus the temple then
he turned to them,
"Can't you see these things?" He said
with a frown.
I say, every stone will, one day,
be cast down." On the Mount of
Olives. His disciples came
saying,
"Tell us when these buildings will
start decaying?

Tell us signs of your coming. when
the world shall end." Jesus said,
"Don't be deceived or let your
minds bend.
Many shall come in my name claiming to
be me.
They shall deceive many. Don't
let this thing be. You'll hear
about wars and rumors of a war.
Don't be troubled then. The
end's not yet in store.
Nation will be against nation,
and kingdoms shall fall.
There'll be famines, pestilence,

and earthquakes great and small.
All these are the beginnings of
sorrows to come.
You'll be hated by nations.
They'll kill you just for fun.
Many shall be offended
and hate one another. False
prophets will arise and
deceive their brother.
Iniquity shall abound and
love shall grow cold He
who endures shall be
welcomed into God's fold.
In this world the gospel will
to all beings be preached
As a witness to nations
before the end is reached.
When you see the abomination
spoken of by Dan
Stand in the Holy place.
You will see his plan.
Let those in Judea flee to
the mountain top.
Those on the housetop should go
quickly and not stop.
He shouldn't take a thing
nor should he in the field
Return to his house.
He's forbidden to yield.
Woe to those with child and
for those nursing pray.
Pray that your flight's not
in winter nor on the Sabbath day There
shall be great tribulation such as never
was known.
Except the days be shortened no
flesh would stay on bone.

Don't believe one who says,

Behold, the Christ is here."
False prophets and Christs
shall make it their career.
They'll show signs and wonders.
The best they can select
If it were possible they'd deceive God's
very elect.
Behold I've said if they say,
'Come, you'll find him."
If they say, 'He is in chambers." Do
not yield to this whim.
As lightning flashes
so shall his coming be. Where
the carcass, is the eagles you'll
see. After the tribulation the
sun shall be dark.
The moon shall not give light.
Stars shall disembark.
Heaven shall be shaken.
Signs of God's Son shall appear.
All tribes shall mourn and God's
Son they shall hear.
They'll see him in clouds with
power and glory He'll send his
angels.
Trumpets shall tell the story. From all
of Heaven his elect will gather with
him.
Learn from the fig tree when it
has a tender limb.
When leaves appear summer is
at hand. When this occurs know
summer's in the land.
These will occur before this
generation passes away. Heaven
and earth shall pass but my word
will stay.
The day and hour when I'll return no man
shall beforehand know. My father alone

knows the time.
None else above or below. As the
days of Noah were so shall the
days be.
As were times before the flood this
also you'll see.
Eating, drinking and marriage, will be
in the end.
To escape, you know the way.

The flood came suddenly destroying one
and all.
So shall Jesus's coming be for
the great and small. Two will be
in the field. One left, the other
taken. Two will be grinding,
one saved, one forsaken.
Be ready for you don't know when he
shall appear.
If the thief's plan was known He'd not
have a career.
He will come unannounced when
defenses are down.
The faithful and wise from
Him get a crown. He'll
become the ruler
and he'll be given meat.
Blessed is he who is ready
for the Lord to greet.
The Lord shall make him ruler in
that great day.
The evil servant says,
his coming is in delay.
He'll smite other servants, eat
and drink in excess.
The Lord shall surprise him
and put him in distress.
Then shall he be judged.
His place is beneath, with

hypocrites, with weeping
and gnashing of teeth.

Chapter 25

Heaven is like ten virgins going
with a light.
To meet the bridegroom.
Wanting things to be right.
Five were wise, but the
other five were not.
The foolish took no extra oil. The
wise took a whole pot.
They slept for the bridegroom was
very much delayed.
At midnight his cry was
to be made.
They said, Go meet him and
everyone arose.
Finding their foolishness to
others really shows.
They demanded from the wise.
'Give us some of your oil.
You see our lamps are out. Soon
tempers would boil.

The wise to them said,
"We might all run out. So
they reluctantly retraced
their route.
The bridegroom came
while they were away.
They thought they'd get oil and
find things were OK. The wise
went with him,
those who did all things right.

The foolish returned but the door was
locked up tight.
They cried, 'Open up the door for
oil we've now got.'
He said, 'Depart, for I
know you not.'
Watch for you don't know
the day or the hour When the
Son of Man shall come in his
power.
The kingdom's like one when
a trip he'd take.
He called servants saying, 'Investors
I will make.'
He gave five talents, then two, to a
third he gave one.
When each received talents the
journey was begun.
He who received five
invested what he had. He
now had ten talents and he
was quite glad.
The one with two doubled his, making
four. The third dug a hole content with
no more.
When their lord returned before
him they appeared. 'I doubled
your money. for your wrath I
feared.'
The master said, 'Well done. You
have done quite good.
I'll make you a ruler for you did just like
you should.'
The man given two said,
'Master, I now have four.
I knew you'd be back so I
made two more.'
"Well done. You've been faithful with
these little things.

I'll make you a ruler.
Your joy will have wings."

The man with one said, "You are
a hard man.
Collecting money from each
operation you ran.
I hid it in the earth because your
kind I knew.
I give the same money you
gave me back to you." "You
wicked servant.
You knew I'd be grieved.
If you loaned it out interest
you'd have received.
To the ones who have it
shall be given.
He who did little from me
shall be driven."
When the Son of Man
comes in his glory He'll sit
on his throne.
We're told in God's story.
Nations shall be separated
by God's only Son.
He'll separate each;
judging them one by one.
Saying to those on his right, 'Ye
blessed, come in.
To the kingdom made since this
world did begin.
I was hungry and thirsty. You
gave drink and meat; I was
naked and you dressed me
real neat.
I was sick and you came and
comforted me;
In prison and you stayed until
I was set free.'

They'll ask, 'When and where did
we do this thing?"
'When you cared for a brother you
cared for your king.'
He shall say to the others.
"Depart into the fire.
The place of the devil. You
lived for desire.
I was hungry and thirsty and I
was denied:
A stranger and naked and you
refused a hide: Sick, in prison,
and lonely.
You failed to give time. They'll
answer saying. "When did we
this crime?"

He'll answer them, I
say now to thee
If you refused it to your brothers you
refused it to me.'
These shall go away into
everlasting fire.
The righteous shall have all
that they desire.

Chapter 26

When Jesus finished his
disciples met his gaze.
He said, "Passover is coming in
two more days...
The Son of Man will be
crucified on a cross." Chief
Priests assembled at the home
of their boss.
They discussed Jesus.
They wished this man to slay. But
they feared the people for it was a

feast day.
When Jesus was in Bethany
he stayed at Simon's house,
A woman with ointment his
head started to douse.
When the disciples saw this they were
indignantly and said, "What a waste."
With its price many could be fed."
Jesus heard this and said,
"Why bring this woman grief?
She has done good unto me.
Where is your belief?
The poor will be with you, but not
the Son of Man.
This ointment is for my burial.
Believe me if you can.
As a memorial to her my
people will teach.
They'll tell of her act wherever the
gospel they preach."
Judas Iscariot, one of the twelve, went to
the Chief Priests
To betray Jesus to them when
they'd finished the feast."
They bargained for silver. They
would give thirty. Judas then
sought a way to do his work so
dirty. The first day of the feast of
unleavened bread,
Disciples asked. "Where will the
Passover be fed'?"

Jesus said, "Go to the city. There
you'll meet a man.
Say, "At thy house we'll serve for his
time is at hand."
They prepared Passover in the
little town.
Then, with the twelve Jesus

sat down. He said,
"One here will the Son of man betray.
" Lord, Is it I? Is it. I?
They started to say?"
"The one who dippeth with me.
It is one and the same.
Woe unto theone who is
therefore to blame."
It would be better for him had he not
been born.
Jesus said this to them from whom he
would be torn.
Judas said to Jesus, "Master,
Is it I?" "Thou hast said."
Jesus answered with a sigh.
He blessed the bread
and passed it about, Eat,
this is my body. he said
with a shout. Then he
took the cup and held it
in the air.
He held it up and went
to his father in prayer.
He gave it to them and said,
Take all of it in.
This is blood that was shed for
remission of sin.
I shall not drink again of
the fruit of the vine
Until in my father's kingdom
When I'll drink the new wine."
They sang a hymn and to the
Mount they went. Jesus said,
"This night from me you'll be sent.
You'll be separated
and you'll run from my sight. It
is written, you will find the
shepherd I will smite.

After this the sheep
all scattered they will be."
I'll be raised and go before
you to Galilee.
Peter answered, "Jesus
I'll never be offended of thee."

He said,
"Before the cock crows three times
me you'll deny." Peter said,
"I'll not even if I shall die."
"They all said the same.
At least they would try. At
Gethsemane Jesus said, "Sit
here while I pray." His
mood was sorrowful and
had turned to gray.
He said, "My soul is sorrowful
unto death, you see.
Stay right here awhile. Pray
and watch with me." He
prayed, if possible
et this cup pass from me today.
Nevertheless, not my will, but
for your will, I pray."
He found his disciples
all were sound asleep.
He said to Peter,
Your watch you should keep.
Couldn't you watch and pray for
even one hour?
The spirit is willing but the
flesh has no power.
He went a second time to the
garden to pray.
"If this cup may not pass from me I'll do
as you say,
Thy will be done for it
must be that way. Their eyes

were heavy. He found them
asleep.
He left them and prayed for their
sleep was deep "Sleep now and
rest,
is all that He said The hour
is at hand
when I'll be with the dead. I'll be
betrayed this night; turned over to
sinners hands.
We must go for he's yielding now to
their demands.
While Jesus was saying this Judas, with
troops, came out
A multitude with swords and
clubs hereabout.
As previously arranged the sign of
betrayal was this
They'd grab the man Judas betrayed with
a kiss.

He greeted Jesus warmly and
then he kissed him.
He asked, "Why? Their mood had
turned a bit grim.
One drew his sword and, to
him came very near.
He used his sword to cut off one of the
priest's servants ears.
Jesus said, as a rebuke; "Put your
sword in its place All who live by
the sword shall die by it in
disgrace. Twelve legions of
angels could be sent to me
It wouldn't profit God, though and
it's not how it must be.
Jesus said, "Why do you treat
me like a thief?
I taught daily with you and you

never caused grief,
These things were done,
however, to fulfill prophecy.
The scripture said all
of his disciples would flee.
The multitude went to Caiaphas, their
High Priest.
Elders assembled but Peter's
anxiety increased. He followed
from a distance
to where the soldiers met.
He sat with the guards to see what
punishment Jesus would get.
They sought false witnesses to
make sure Jesus would die.
False witnesses came forward when the
priests gave sigh.
"He said the temple he could restore in
three days."
What is your answer about the accusation
that he says"
The High Priest said, "Are
You the son of God?" Jesus
said, "Thou has said,"
then gave a nod.
"After this you'll see
me on the right hand of power
And coming in clouds
which above you shall tower.
The High Priest said,
"A blasphemer is he
No more witnesses
are needed to blasphemy.

They said, "He's guilty. He
should surely die.
They palmed and buffeted him and
spit in his eye...
They said, "If you're Christ,

tell us who hit thee."
A maid told Peter,
"You were with Him in Galilee." Peter
denied it saying.
"I know not what you say."
Another said "I saw you with
this man one day." Peter
denied this."
Of him I've not had a peek." One
said, "You must be his. Listen to
how you speak," Peter cursed
saying.
"That man I do not know."
When he said it he heard the
rooster begin to crow.
Jesus had said, Before the
cock crows quite free. Three
times you'll me deny. Simon
Peter wept bitterly.

Chapter 27

When morning arrived Priests
and elders conspired.
They wouldn't rest until the
Christ had expired. They led
him away and to
Pilate they went.
If he'd demand death their time
was well spent. Condemnation was
shouted. when this, Judas had seen
he returned the silver to those
who were mean.
He said, I've sinned.
Innocent blood I betrayed." They said,
"Do you think we care?
Our hand won't be stayed." Judas threw
down the silver and hanged himself out
there.

They collected the silver showing
their lack of care. They said that
they couldn't put it in the treasury.
Because it was blood money coming
with misery.
They bought Potter's Field to bury
strangers in.
It was called "Field of blood." because
of their awful sin.

This fulfilled prophecy spoken by
Jeremiah one day, "They took the
same price that they had to pay.
For the price of one of value. They
took this price, you see. They
purchased potter's field said the
prophet Jeremy.
Pilate, asked, "Art thou the
King of the Jews?" Jesus said,
"Thou sayest." To Pilate this
was news.
To the Chief Priests and elders he had
nothing to say.
Pilate said, "Did you hear the
charges made this day?" Jesus
didn't answer him.
He didn't say a word. The
governor marveled,
for this seemed absurd.
Now, at the feast the people chose one
prisoner to release.
According to their custom which they
wished not to cease.
They had Barabbas locked up
in their jail. Pilate asked, "will
you waive Barabbas' bail?
Jesus had been brought due to
envy of theirs. Your wife has a
message which she now bears.

"Don't listen to evil accusations or
to wicked dares.
Have nothing to do with Jesus.
He is a just man today." They
said, release Barabbas and not
Jesus, we say. "Which one
shall I then release unto you?"
"Give us Barabbas." They said.
That's what you should do?"
They declared of this Jesus…
"Let him be crucified." Pilate
asked, "Why?"
"Crucify Him!" they cried.
Pilate saw he couldn't win against
the angry mob.
He washed his hands and said.
"You do the job."
They said, His blood is on
our family's head."
Pilate released Barabbas.
Crucify him then, he said.

The soldiers took Jesus to
the common hall.
A group gathered around, the
large and small.
They stripped him and placed on
him a robe of red.
They placed a crown of thorns upon
his precious head.
Bowing they placed in
his right hand a reed.
They said "Hail, King of the Jews; King
of the Jews, indeed."
Mocking and ridiculing they
spit in his face.
They stripped him adding
humiliation to disgrace.
Striking and scourging him their insults

they loudly cried.
They clothed him once again and
took him to be crucified.
They forced a Cyrenian,
His heavy cross to carry to
Golgotha where they
continued making merry.
They gave him vinegar to drink and
mixed it with gall.
He would not drink though the
amount was very small.
They crucified him
and his clothes they divided.
Throwing dice was the way who
got what was decided.
They sat down after hanging
a sign above his head.
"This is Jesus, King of the Jews"
is all that the sign said.
Two thieves were crucified, One at
each hand.
The people shook their heads.
All acted very grand.
"Thou can destroy the
temple and build it again.
Save yourself from the cross, the
cross with all its pain. The priests
and the scribes and elders mocked
him too. Saying, "he can't save
himself or that's what he would do.
If he'd come down off the cross we
would then believe.
He trusted God and now,
who does he believe?

The thief with him there
rebuked him, no less. The
land for three hours was in
much darkness.

194

Then Jesus cried out in a
voice that was loud.
"Why forsaketh thou me?
His head was bowed.
Some who heard him said,
"Now, To Elias he calls."
One offered him a sponge with
vinegar mixed with gall.
They said, "See if Elias
comes as his host."
Jesus cried out and then he
gave up the ghost.
The temple's veil, from top to bottom,
that very hour was ripped.
Partying stopped, the earth quaked and
many rocks were flipped.
Many graves were opened
and out came many saints.
They appeared to many and they
made no complaints.
When the people there
considered what they saw, each
one was shocked
and nearly dropped his jaw.
They fearfully said,
"Truly this was God's Son."
Many looked again to see
what had been done.
They followed Jesus when
they left Galilee.
Two women both named Mary and
others too, you see...
A rich man came at evening.
Joseph was his name
. He was a disciple.
From Arimathea he came.
He begged from Pilate to bury
Jesus dead body. He wrapped
it in linen for he was not

shoddy.
He laid it in his tomb hewn from
the rock.
A great stone was in front This
served as a lock.
The two Marys sat against
the sepulcher.
Priests and Pharisees with
Pilate did concur.

They said after three days
he said he'd arise.
Place guards so they don't come
steal away the prize. They might
come at night and take him away
Then claim that he has risen as he
said, on the third day.
Pilate said you can make it as
safe as it can be.
They sealed it and placed guards
there for all to see.

Chapter 28

At Sabbath's end,
at the approach of day.
The Mary's came
to the sepulcher to pray.
The earth quaked as an angel of God
came down.
He sat on the stone after
he rolled it around.
His countenance like lightning,
his clothing as the snow.
The guards shook with fear like
mortals would, you know.
The angel said he knew
what they had come there for.
You look for Jesus, he said but

he is here no more. Come, look
inside then go to his disciples
and say
he has risen from the dead and goes
to Galilee today.
They'll know him now as their
resurrected Lord.
They went with great joy at the
Heavenly angels word.
Jesus met them on their way and
he simply said, "Hail."
They hailed and worshiped
Jesus without fail.
Jesus said for them
tell the disciples, "Go to Galilee."
When they arrive there
they shall then see me.
On their way the guards came in
with the story.
Elders assembled and they said no
one should worry.
The soldiers were to say some men
came at night Stealing him while
they slept and took him from their
sight.

They said that protection,
their troops would provide.
They took the money,
went to the people and lied.
The disciples went as they
were commanded to do.
They worshiped Jesus,
but to some their doubts grew.
Jesus spoke saying,
"All power is given to me.
Go,teach all these things which you
now hear and see.
Teach them to all nations.

In God's name baptize.
Don't believe any of the soldier's lies.
Do as I taught you though
satan's darts are hurled.
For I will be with you even
Unto the end of the world.

<u>Matthew 26:1-51</u>
(Alternate reading)

Jesus said to his disciples. "It
will be as prophesied.
Two days from now at Passover
I shall be crucified."
The Chief Priests, Scribes, and elders
assembled in the palace.
They conspired to kill Jesus in the
home of Caiaphas.
They wanted secretly to take Him before He
could do more.
They said, "Not on the feast day.
There would be an uproar.
When Jesus was in Bethany at Simon,
the leper's house,
A woman with precious ointment,
God's Son, began to douse.
It was kept in an alabaster box. She
did it while he sat to eat.
The disciples asked, "Why waste it?
This question they did repeat.
They said, "You poured it on his head
and some went on the floor.
You could have sold it
and given the money to the poor.
When Jesus heard it he asked why
they couldn't see.
"Why do you trouble her?
She's done a good work to me.
The poor you'll always have.

196

I won't be here that long.
She's anointed me for burial.
She has done no wrong.

Wherever the Gospel is preached
they'll tell what she has done.
Do this in remembrance of her and
the victory she's won.
Judas Iscariot, One of the twelve
went to the Chief Priests
asking, "What shall I get to deliver him
after the Passover feast?"
They agreed to give this man, of silver,
the pieces were thirty.
He sought then a way
to accomplish his work, so dirty..
The disciples came asking where
to prepare the Passover meal.
He said, "Go and find the man.
Don't try to make a deal.
Say, "The Master wishes to prepare the
Passover in your upper room.
He says the time is close at hand
when he shall reach his tomb. They
did as Jesus commanded and the
Passover table was set. When
evening came he and the disciples
gathered there and met.
As they ate he said to them,
"Verily, I say unto you,
One of you shall betray me.
This one is in full view.
They were greatly sorrowful and
asked him, "Is it I?" Would
anyone really
do that and, if so, tell us why.
He answered them and said,
"He that dippeth his hand with me
Will be the betrayer of God's Son.

This is how it will be.
Woe to this one.
It'd be better if he'd was unborn." Judas
said, "Master, Is it I?
Am I to be that thorn?" Jesus
answered him, saying,
"It was you who thus has said."
Later, while, they were eating
Jesus took a piece of bread.
He blessed it and He broke it and
to the disciples he gave. "Eat,
This is my body
which is sacrificed for you to save.
He gave thanks for the cup.
This is my blood of the New Testament
saying, "Drink ye all that is within, Shed for
remission of sin.

I'll not drink of fruit of the vine.
I'll not again have some
Until I drink it new with you in my father's
great kingdom."
They went to the Mount of Olives after they
had sung a hymn.
"Because of me, this night You
will be on a limb." "The
shepherd will I smite.
The sheep are scattered abroad.
I'll rise and go into Galilee.
You'll know then that I am God." Peter
said, "Though all are offended I'll not be
ashamed of Thee."
Jesus said, "Before the cock crows
thrice you'll deny knowing me." Peter
said and the others did too."
We will never, thee, deny
We'll not be ashamed of you even
if it means we'll die. They went to
Gethsemane where Jesus told

them to stay.
He said, "Sit here and wait
while I go yonder and pray."
He took with him
Peter and the two Sons of Zebedee.
His heart was sorrowful. It
was clear for all to see.
He said, "My soul is sorrowful
even to the death today
Stay here and watch with me.
Tarry you here and pray.
Then he went further to pray he
fell and prayed on his face
If possible let this cup pass
but have your way in any case."
When he saw his disciples
he found them all asleep.
Can't you watch an hour?
I thought this watch you'd keep.
Watch and pray ye here that temptation
will not speak.
The spirit indeed is willing but the flesh
is awfully weak.
He went and prayed a second time
saying, "Father this is no fun.
But if this cup can't pass from me thy
Holy will be done."
He returned. They were asleep due to
heaviness of their eyes He left them
and prayed again repeating his
previous cries.

He said to his disciples,
"Asleep I'll let you stay.
The hour is now at hand when
one cometh to betray. He'll
deliver me to sinners.
Arise, let us be going.
He's waiting to betray me to

stop my life from glowing
While he was still speaking
Judas on the scene appeared.
An armed multitude was
with him for escape they really feared.
The one who betrayed him said,
"Whomsoever I shall kiss.
He's the one you want.
Capture him. Don't miss."
He came saying, Hail, Master and
kissed Jesus on the cheek.
Jesus asked, "Why do you come?
Your future will be bleak."
They came and captured him.
They began to take him away.
One who was with Jesus drew his sword
saying, "Let him stay."

Genesis 1-15
Chapter 1

In the beginning God made light and saw
that it was good.
He separated it from darkness
because he knew he should.
He called the darkness night and
he called the light day.
The earth was bathed in light
all day and all night in darkness lay.
After making the first day
he made the land and sky.
He had waters to congregate
so other places were dry.
He called the waters seas and the
land he just called earth.
He was pleased with all he'd done and
our planet had its birth.
He caused plants to grow

and made the tiny seed.
Which made plants like their parents which
later would be feed.
He placed two lights in the sky and
called them sun and moon. He made
the stars in the heavens, The fourth
day ended soon.

On the fifth day God made animals in the
sea and in the air.
He commanded them to multiply and
be found most everywhere. On the
sixth day God made man to rule over
all the earth
But man needed a companion so He
gave woman birth.
God made mankind the ruler over
animals, birds, and fish.
He gave him all these from
which to prepare a dish.

Chapter 2

The seventh day work was done so he
rested on that day
And sanctified it and said
it was to continue in this way. The
plants grew and bore fruit though
no rain ever fell.
No man tilled the earth,
you see, yet plants grew very well.
A mist came up from the earth and
watered all around.
It came from beneath, you see, and
covered all the ground. God made
man from the dust. From it He
made a living soul.
He planted a garden for him and gave him
full control.

God planted trees to bear fruit.
He planted the tree of life
And the tree of good and evil which
could fill mankind with strife.
A river watered the garden. God put
man there to till.
He said to leave one tree alone but from the
others to eat his fill.
If of the tree of good and evil mankind
should eat he'd die.
This was God's promise to man and
God can never lie.
God made animals and beasts.
To Adam they all came.
He had quite a job, you see. for to
each he gave a name.
When Adam had named every one the Lord
caused him to sleep.
From Adam's rib God made a mate
which he gave the man to keep. Adam
called her woman because she'd been
made from man.
The first marriage took place that day
because it was God's plan.

They both were naked as can be, but
they were not ashamed.
They had no evil thoughts, you see, so
neither can be blamed.

Chapter 3

The craftiest creature God made
was the lowly minded snake.
The serpent came to Eve and asked,
"Which fruit are you not to take?"
We can freely eat each fruit
except from one certain tree. If I
eat of it my God has said that

death will come, you see.
"It is not true." the serpent cried.
If you do what you should You'll
eat its fruit and be like God and
know evil from the good."
She believed the serpent,
ate and took some to her man.
They saw that they were naked so to
different trees they ran.
They sewed fig leaves together to cover
up their hips.
That night when God came walking these
words were on his lips.
"Why are you hiding? Don't you know, I've
come to talk to you?"
"Because we are naked, Adam said, we
hid ourselves from view." "Have you
eaten the fruit
from the tree I warned about?" "Yes,
cried Adam. Its all her fault," She did!
He began to shout.
God said to her, "How could you do a
wicked thing like this?"
She said, "The serpent lied to me.
Of this I do confess."
God cursed the serpent so that he
must crawl forever in the dust. And
from that day, to mankind, he'd be
forever cussed.
God told Eve when she had kids she'd
also have much pain
But she would love her husband so
she'd do it all again.
Because Adam listened to his wife he
must his lifetime toil.
He must pull thorns and thistles too if he'd
harvest from the soil.
"You'll struggle all your lifetime: even
to your dying day.

I made you from earth and
you'll return to clay.
He named his wife life-giving one
because she, his children bore. God
clothed them in animal skins which
they from that time wore. From the
garden God removed the first man and
his wife;
and sent an angel to keep guard and to
protect the tree of life.

Chapter 4

Adam knew her and she gave him a
little baby son.
His name was Cain. She had Abel.
A family had begun.
Cain cheated God though his farms cut
across the land,
While Abel became a shepherd and obeyed
the Lord's command.
The Lord accepted Abel's gift, but
Cain's gift he refused.
This made Cain so angry that
his brother he abused.
He killed him in the field one day and
placed him in a hole.
When asked he told the Lord he
hadn't hurt a soul.
God said your brother's blood calls to me
from the ground.
Because of this God said his land would
never more abound.
Cain told him, "Lord, my punishment is
more that I can bear.
I've lost my farm and people will try to
kill me everywhere."
God told Cain, "They won't kill you; in

200

daylight or in the dark
For I will place a sign on you, a
very special mark.
If anyone shall kill you then I
will make him grieve
For seven times your punishment is
what he will receive."
He left the Lord and went to Nod and
there he did remain.
His wife conceived and bore a son and
Enoch was his name.
Cain founded a city which he named Enoch
after his dear son.
After that Eve bore a son. She
said she'd finally won.

She said that Seth was God's gift
for the son which Cain had slain.
They were called. "The Lord's people"
during Seth's son's reign.

Chapter 5

Nine generations passed from the
time of Adam to that of Noah.
When God revealed that he had in mind a
special chore.
Now Noah's name meant relief for
he would be the first
To relieve all men from farming in
the land that God had cursed.
Shem, Ham, and Japheth were the sons of
Noah and his wife.
Noah was five hundred when
God chose to bless his life.

Chapter 6

Men increased in number

faster than had ever been.
Beings of the spirit world desired daughters
born of men.
Jehovah said that every man
must mend his awful ways
Or, in one hundred twenty years
God would end his days.
The offspring of these spirit beings and
their earthly wives
Were giants and you've heard some
stories of their lives.
When God saw man's wickedness he
wished he'd had no part
In their creation for, you see, they
had broken his dear heart. God
said that he must destroy all that
he had begun
For they cared not for Him but
lived only to have fun.
Noah's family pleased God with
everything they'd do
But men and women everywhere were
evil through and through,
As God looked over all mankind he
whispered down to Noah,
"I have chosen just for you a
very special chore.
I am going to destroy the earth
and all the people there,
But if you'll do the things I say
I will, your family, spare.

Make a boat of resinous wood and
seal it up with tar.
Make this ship a sturdy one for
it must travel far.
Make stalls on every deck of which there
shall be three
Make it exactly as long and high and

wide as I tell thee.
Construct a skylight near the top but not
too far below.
I'm going to send a flood and
just a few may go.
With your family bring on a pair of
each animal and reptile
And bring on food all will need and
you will ride in style.

Chapter 7

God said, "You know what I requested and
you've done very good.
Load up a pair of every animal, the
bad as well as good.
But of the ones which I have sent for
sacrifice or meat
Of them and birds take seven pairs for you
will have to eat.
This is so that after the flood you
will be sure to find Each and
every animal replenishing its kind.
In one week I'll make rain come
falling from the sky.
All animals, birds, and people that aren't
with you will die.
Noah finished everything the
Lord told him to do.
He was over 600,
but he was not yet through.
The subterranean water flowed and
rain fell from the sky
But God closed the ark tight so they
could all stay dry for forty days and
nights the rain kept falling down.
The ark was lifted by the flood and
drifted all around.

Twenty two feet of water was
above the highest peak. For one
hundred fifty days there was not
a leak.

Chapter 8

God did not forget the ones he
said that he would save.
They were tossed one hundred
fifty days
o'er many a fearsome wave. By
then the water went down until
they came to rest
Upon Mount Ararat's peak.
They ended their long quest.
Eight months later they went out and
the earth was dry.
God said to release the animals to
run, or crawl, or fly.
Noah and his wife and sons
and their wives left the ark.
The animals all left it too,but
each one had left his mark.
Then Noah built an altar and
sacrificed to the Lord. God accepted
his sacrifice and gave them his word,
"I won't again flood the earth wiping out
all things Even if they sin so much and do
many evil things.

Chapter 9

God blessed Noah and his sons and
told them to replenish the earth.
He told them to have children and value
each person's worth.

He said, "Animals, birds,
and fish will be now afraid of you.
Drain the blood before you eat for
this is right to do.
Murder is forbidden.
Guilty must be put away.
If animals or beasts kill you
must them surely slay. God told
Noah and his sons,
"I solemnly promise you
I won't send a universal flood
because of the sins men do.
I placed a rainbow in the sky for
all of you to see.
You'll remember the promise
which I have made to thee."
Shem, Ham, and Japheth.
Were sons to whom they give birth.
From these three sons of Noah came
all nations of the earth.
Noah planted vineyards,
growing fruit of the vine. One
day he lay there naked
when he'd consumed much wine. Ham
saw him and ran and told.
He thought the very worse.
When Noah heard about it upon Ham
he placed a curse.
He cursed the Canaanites swearing
they'd be enslaved.
He blessed his other sons cursing Ham
for the way behaved.

Chapter 10

Noah and his descendants spread
throughout the land. Lead
throughout the earth by God's
own mighty hand.

Chapter 11

The people spread out.
The language was common to all. As
they spread out they planned a city that
couldn't fall.
They talked about a tower to be
built right up to the sky.
To weld that city together so that
they would never die.
When God came to visit them.
Viewing what they had done He said,
"If they're successful they'll
politically act as one.
Let us confuse their languages so
they can't communicate.
They'll neglect this temple.
Its end will be this date.
They started speaking tongues and were
scattered around.
As their descendants filled the earth some
farmed and tilled the ground.

Chapter 12

God chose his servant, Abram, to
journey to a distant land. He'd
become a mighty nation and be
protected by God's hand Abram
departed immediately as the Lord
said to do.
He took Sarai, his possessions,
and nephew, Lot, too.
He went through Canaan's land.
He built an altar for his Lord.
In famine he went to
Egypt and made Sarai give her word
that she'd claim to be his sister and tell
nobody she was his wife

For she was so very beautiful that
he feared for his life.
He feared that they would kill him to
have her for their own.
If they thought he was her brother then
they'd leave him alone.
When they entered town, the
people saw her and stared.
Pharaoh took her for his own and
with Abram much he shared. God
sent a plague on Pharaoh and he
called Abram in.
He said, "Why did you lie to me
and cause me to do this sin? Take
her and get out of here," is what
the Pharaoh said.
"Take her and your possessions and
from our land be led."

Chapter 13

They left Egypt together.
They headed to the North.
Lot and Abram felt good for
they were men of worth.
They traveled North past Bethel to
where they'd camped before.
Abram found the temple
and worshipped there once more.
Lot's men fought with
Abram's over where they should graze.
Abram said, "Choose either land as
far as you can gaze."
Lot chose Sodom's valley. so
rich, and green, and nice.
Abram stayed in Canaan's land and
there he did suffice.
Lot left then God told Abram,
"Look as far as you can see. I'm

going to give you this land.
This is my gift to thee.
Hike around in all directions.
View what I'll give you."
Abram built an altar
and worshipped in full view.

Chapter 14

All cities of Sodom and Gomorrah
mobilized for war;
But, against a stronger enemy they
couldn't get through the door.
Abram learned they captured Lot and
put him with the rest
He took his men and chased them and
put their armies to the test.
He returned with everything. their
women and their loot. They gave
him bread and wine and threw in a
blessing in to boot.
Abram returned all
that he had regained that day.
Only what his soldiers ate would
he accept as pay.

Chapter 15

Abram was unhappy for he had no
son to be his heir,
But the Lord God said to him,
"Don't worry for I am fair."
He told Abram to count the stars that
were in the sky.
"I'll will give you a descendant for
every one you spy."
Abram asked. "How can I know that
these things are true?"
God told him to obey and

he'd know what to do.
God revealed through a dream
He sent to Abram's ears saying
Abram's descendants
would be slaves 400 years.

Matthew:3

People heard a wilderness voice
saying,"The kingdom is at
hand.Repent of sins and be baptized.
The Savior will enter the land.
This fulfilled Isaiah's prophecy of the
pleading wilderness voice. saying,
Prepare for the Lord.
If you do you will rejoice.
This was of John the Baptist
dressed in camel's hair.
His food was locusts and honey but
he really didn't care.
His concern was not with looks or
what he ate, you see.
His message was of the Savior
who was sent for you and me.
Preaching in Jerusalem and in regions round
about he baptized in the Jordan; His
message made them shout.
Then pharisees and Sadducees came the
baptism to receive
but Jesus knew immediately that
they did not believe.
He said, if you are true you'll bear some
worthy fruit but trees which do
not bear will have the ax laid to the root.
They'll be hewn and cast
into the midst of the fire.
I baptize you now with water.
There comes one who is higher.

One greater than I comes.
I'm not worthy to lace his shoes.
He'll baptize with the Holy Ghost.
With Him you'll never lose. Then
Jesus came from Galilee to be
baptized by John He said,
"You should baptize me for I am but
a pawn.
Jesus said to John
I need you to baptize me.
When John baptized Jesus
He said, "God set you free."
God's spirit came like a dove.
John's mind was now eased God said,
"This is my beloved son
In whom I am well pleased."

Philippians 4:4-9

Rejoice in the Lord all your life.
Fill your mouth with praise.
Let your moderation be known.
Soon will come the end of days.
Be anxious for nothing. Be
very much in prayer.
Make your requests known to God
Then leave your burdens there.
God's peace will come to you.
The world won't understand. The
comfort and joy you posses has been
given by God's hand. Things that are
honest and pure are of good report
and true
are things you should think on and
things that you should do.
Things received of God will be, for
us, release.
If you dwell on things of God then
God will give you peace.

Philippians 4:8
(Two versions)

Philippians 4:8 says our
thinking really should
be positive, true and honest;
on whatever things are good;
consider the pure and lovely:
dwell on them all your days.
Think things of good report of
virtuosity and praise.

We are told in Philippians 4:8 to
dwell on the positive side;
To set our minds on good for
trouble's way is wide.
If we set our minds on problems or the
way things can go wrong it will take
away our joy
and from our hearts the song.
We'll be wise to follow the
advice given there.
Think on the pure and lovely.
Burdens will be easier to bear.

Philippians 4:9

Rejoice in the Lord.
Fill your mouth with praise. Let
moderation be known.
It'll be the end of days.
Be anxious now for nothing but be very
much in prayer.
Make requests of God.
Leave your burdens there. Peace will
come to you.
The world won't understand the

comfort you posses that's given
from God's hand.
Things that are honest and pure are of
good report and true
are things you should think on and
things you should do.
Ones received from God will
be, for us, release. If we dwell on
things of God
He will give us peace.

John 1:1-2:25

1 In the beginning was the Word.
The Word and God are the same.
So God and the Word are one;
the same with a different name.
2 The same was with God.
In the beginning it was.
3 He made everything:
every object, law and cause.
4 In Him was found life;
the life was the light of man.
5 The light shines in darkness.
Darkness cannot comprehend.
There was a man from God;
John was his name.

7 He came to be a witness of
light from God which came.
He witnessed of this light
that all men might believe.
8 He was not that light but
the light he did receive.
He bore witness of that light
9 of God's light to all mankind.
It was sent for every man.
For everyone it shined.
10 He was in the world.

The world was made by Him
but the world knew Him not;
to them His light was dim.
11 He came to His own.
His own received Him not.
As many as received Him
each one He did adopt.
To them He gave His power.
His sons they became;
To all who believed Him;
All believing on His name.
13 They were not born of blood
Nor of the flesh, you see Nor
of the will of man
but by God with whom they'll be.
14 For the Word was made flesh
and dwelt among our race.
Glory of the only begotten;
full of truth and grace.
15 John bore witness of Him he
cried to mankind, saying This is
He of whom I spoke, for whom
we've been praying.
He that cometh after me is before me, you
see for He created the world.
He was and is before me. 16
We received His fullness;
His grace from God's face
17 for the law was given by Moses.
Jesus brought truth and grace.
18 No man has seen God;
This never has been done
but God has been declared
by His only begotten Son.
19 This is the record of John.
The Jews sent some men to
ask who he was.
They came from Jerusalem.
20 He confessed and didn't deny

That the Christ he was not.
21 They asked him who he was
for this is what they sought. They
asked if he was Elijah.
He said, Not so. Not so.
Art thou a prophet then?
To this he answered, "No." 22
Then said they unto him, Tell us,
Who art thou?
We must answer our senders
What sayest thou now?
23 He said, "I am the voice of one
crying in the wilderness;
Make straight the way of the Lord of whom
Isaiah did profess.
24/25 The pharisees asked,
Why do you baptize?
If you're not Christ or Elijah why do
you think you're wise?
26 John answered them saying,
With water I baptize thee but there stands
one among you.
You know not whom ye see.
27 Although He came after me.
Before me He's preferred.
I'm unworthy to loosen His shoes.
To Him you are referred.
28 In Bethlehem this happened. John
baptized those who came.
28 Next day he saw Jesus saying.
"Behold. God's lamb by name.
He is the lamb of God
who unto the world was hurled.
He takes away the sin of man.
Indeed, of all the world.
30 This is he of whom I said,
w after me there cometh one
who is preferred before me coming before
me as God's Son.

31 I didn't know this man
but to Israel He must be known.
I come baptizing with water those
who their God will own.
32 John bore this record, saying.
I saw God's Spirit descend From
Heaven like a dove
on Jesus whom God did send.
33 I knew Him not, You see.
He in whose name I did baptize said, If the
Spirit descends and stays He's my
chosen, You'll realize.
You baptize with water,
but He with the Holy Ghost.
34 This is the Son of God;
in Him I must then boast.
35 The next day he stood with two
Disciples whom he knew.
36 He looked at Jesus and said,
"Behold God's lamb. Its true."
37 The two disciples then
followed Jesus when He went.
38 He turned and looked at them and
asked from whom they're sent.
They said, Rabbi or Master
Where do you stay?
39 He said to them, "Come.
Come see. This very day.
They went where he lived and
stayed about a day
At 10 A.M. they left that place
after their brief stay.
40 One of them who heard John
was his brother, Andrew He had
followed Jesus
41 and showed his heart was true.
He found his brother, Simon and
told him, We have found The
Messiah which is the Christ.

Come and gather around.
42 He brought him to Jesus.
Jesus looked at him alone.
"You shall be Cephas
by interpretation a "stone."
43 The next day Jesus traveled
to the town of Galilee,
He located Philip there and said,
"Come, follow me."
44 Bethsaida was Philip's home;
Andrew's, and Peter's as well.
45 Philip said to Nathaniel,
"We found he who Moses did tell."
The prophets did also write
of the Messiah too which is Jesus of
Nazareth. Joseph's Son, That's who."
46 Nathaniel said to him, "From
Nazareth comes good?"
"Come and see.' said Philip.
He acts just like He should.
47 Jesus to Nathaniel said, an
Israelite with no guile.
48 Nathaniel asked how He knew.
Jesus answered with a smile.
"Before Philip went out.
Before he called on thee;
I saw you sitting there
under the fig tree."
49 Nathaniel said, "You're God's Son.
You are also Israel's king."
50 Jesus said, "Because I saw. You
believest now this thing?
Greater things you'll see.
51 You'll see Heaven open wide;
angels coming and going
from Heaven to my side.

John 2

1 The third day at a marriage in
Cana of Galilee.
Jesus' mother was there.
2 The disciples too, you see.
3 His mother said, of wine they
are completely out. Jesus said unto
her, What is this about?
My hour has not come.
5 His mother to servants said, "Do
what he says to do
for He is Spirit led."
6 There were six water pots to
cleanse and make Jews pure
of two or three firkins each, thirty
gallons, to be sure.
7 Jesus said, "Fill them with water."
They filled them to the brim.
8 Serve it to the governor so
they took some to him.
9 The ruler of the feast tasted the
water turned to wine.
He knew from where it came,
10 "Men serve their good wine early then
afterwards the worst
You kept the best till now and
served the poorest first. 11 This
was Jesus first miracle
in Cana of Galilee.
It manifested His glory for
everyone to see.
12 He went to Capernaum; His
mother and brothers too. Some
disciples went along and stayed
for days, a few.
13 It was the Jewish Passover.
To Jerusalem Jesus came:
14 animal sellers and money changers the
temple did profane.

15 He made a scourge of cords To
the sellers He went.
He drove them out with it.
They were to the streets sent
He poured the changers' money out and
drove them all out too.
They left in haste before Him.
Their tables He overthrew.
16 To the sellers of the doves
He said; Take my advice.
take these from the temple.
It can't be a place of merchandise.
17 The disciples remembered
that it had been written,
zeal of thine house hath eaten me.
His actions were befitting.
18 Jews answered and asked,
Do you have for us a sign since
you have done these things
which are so very fine?
19 Jesus answered them,
Destroy this temple here in
three days I'll raise it up.
Of this I have no fear.
20 Then the Jews said,
It took forty six years to build
and you say in just three days
you can build it if you willed.
21 Jesus spoke of His body,
not the one of stone
22 when he had risen from the dead the
meaning was made known.
They believed the scripture which
Jesus had proclaimed.
23 When He went to Jerusalem many
with him were named.
He came for the Passover.
Many saw the miracles He did.
Many believed on His name and in

His mercy hid.

Zaccheus - Luke 19:2-18

There was a rich tax collector who
went to see my Lord.
He was short and couldn't see, but he
had heard Jesus' Word.
He wanted to see Jesus.
He climbed up in a tree.
Jesus looked up and said, "Zaccheus. I
see thee." He said, Come quickly down.
To your house I will go.
Zaccheus was a tax collector.
Some thought he should say,
"No. "Zaccheus was filled with joy.
He came hurrying to the ground.
They said Jesus ate with sinners and this
word spread around.
Zaccheus, however, told Jesus
"Half my goods I'll give to the poor."
If I have falsely accused a man
I will, fourfold to him, restore
Jesus said to Zaccheus,
"Salvation has come to you for,
like other sinners
You've accepted the Savior, too.

Romans 1: 1-13

1 Paul, a servant of Christ; an
apostle who heard the call.
I was separated for service by
God who is over all.
2 Which He had promised by
prophets in His Word. 3 It
was written earlier
concerning Christ the Lord;

made of the seed of David.
In the flesh He came.
4 He was the Son of God.
5 All power was in His name.
6 To the Spirit of Holiness by
resurrection of the dead.
7 Apostleship was given to us because He
said. For obedience to the faith among
nations for His name.
8 You have been called also by
Jesus Christ, the same.
9 7 All He loved in Rome;
called by the Holy One.
Grace and peace be yours from
the Father and the Son.
8 First I thank my God through
Jesus for each of you. That
throughout the world they speak
of your faith too.
9 God is my witness.
My spirit serves Him now.
In Christ I pray for you.
Without ceasing somehow.
10 I ask Him for grace so
I can come to you.
11 I long to bring spiritual gifts so you will
serve Him too:
12 so you'll be comforted by a faith that
you will share.
Its common to both of you and is
the faith I bear.
13 I would not have you ignorant that I
wished to come to you
but I was prevented from it by the
work there was to do.

Romans 1: 10-2: 13

10 I requested to be allowed to

journey to where you are.
11 I long to see and talk with you but,
the distance is too far.
I wish to establish you by
giving a spiritual gift,
12 that we might find comfort
and your faith give me a lift.
13 I would not have you ignorant, my
brothers. I wished to come that my
faith might bear fruit and of
Gentiles I'd win some.
14 I'm in debt to barbarians and
also to the Greeks to wise and
unwise alike,
to all who've heard me speak.
15 I'm ready to preach the Gospel to
those who in Rome stay.
I need to preach Jesus and to
tell about God's way.
16 I'm not ashamed of the Gospel of
Jesus Christ, my Lord.
Its the power of salvation to all
who believe His Word; to the
Jew and to the Greek for that is
only right.
17 God's righteousness is revealed
from faith to faith in His sight.
The just shall live by faith as
it is written and it's true
18 God's wrath is revealed against
ungodliness and unrighteousness too.
19 That which may be known of
God is manifest to all
for God has showed it to them, to
each one, large or small.
20 The invisible things of Him from the
creation of this sphere are clearly seen
and understood;
by these its all made clear.

His eternal power and Godhead are also
made known to all
so they are without excuse who
don't follow Jesus call.
21 Because when they knew God
they glorified Him not
their imaginations were vain; on
their hearts was a spot.
22 They declared that they were wise but
became fools nonetheless.
23 They changed the Glory of God, an
incorruptible being, we stress

into the image of man,
to a corruptible creeping thing.
Whenever man does this a
punishment he'll bring
24 God gave them to uncleanness
through lusts of their hearts to dishonor
their own bodies between them and all
their parts.
25 They changed the truth of God into a
wicked perverted lie.
They worshipped the creature more than
God who's on high.
26 Because of their perversions God
gave them to affections vile. Even
their women change nature acting
against it all the while;
27 and likewise did the men
leave natural use of the woman.
They did what was forbidden and
performed with another man.
They'll have to pay the penalty for
the error of their way.
28 They didn't want to know God or hear
what He had to say.
God gave them a reprobate mind to
continue with their sin.
29 They were unrighteous.

Wickedness was within
Covetous and malicious; full of
envy and murder too.
They practiced deceit and gossip.
30 They hated what God would do:
were backbiters, despiteful and proud;
inventors of evil things:
31 disobedient, without
understanding: covenant breakers
with all it brings.
They were without natural affection;
implacable and unmerciful as well.
32 They know about God's judgments.
They're guilty and worthy of Hell.
Even knowing all these things they
continued to do evil.
They took pleasure in their deeds and with
those who did them still.

Chapter 2

1 Thou are inexcusable,
whoever does these things.
You've judged yourself and others with
the condemnation such brings.
2 We're sure God's judgment; is
according to truth for all;
His judgments are against them who
commit evils they think small.

3 Do you think you can escape
if you judge others for what you do?
God will judge you also.
His judgments are final when through.
4 If you despise riches of His
longsuffering and forbearance; and do
not know His goodness that leads to
repentance;

5 If your hardened impenitent heart
incurs judgment and God's wrath;
6 6 who rewards all people perfectly
each according to deeds he hath.;
10   to those who continue
patiently In the seeking of God's glory;
He'll give eternal life in Heaven
according to His age old story unto
those who are contentious;
who the truth do not obey; ones
who obey unrighteousness
His indignation and wrath will stay.
9 Tribulation and anguish shall
come to each evil doing soul to
the Jew and to the Gentile His
wrath will take its toll.
10 Glory and honor and peace
will come to those doing good;
to the Jew and to the Gentile
11 for God does what He should.
There's no respect of persons
12 for sinners without the law.
They'll perish without it too and
all shall see their flaw.
Those who sinned in the law shall be
judged by the same.
13 Doers of the law are justified,
Not just hearers about His name.

I Timothy

1 Paul, an apostle of Jesus Christ by God,
our Savior's command
and by the Lord, Jesus Christ, Our
hope is in His hand.
2 Grace, mercy and faith to Timothy, my
son, in faith, through the Word from God,
our Heavenly Father
and Jesus Christ, our Lord.

3 I begged you to stay at Ephesus as to
Macedonia I went,
that they teach no other doctrine than the
one which we were sent.
4. That they not give heed to fables and
genealogies which confuse,
but to Godly edifying which is
in the faith we use.
5 The end of the commandment is
charity from a pure heart
and out of a good conscience unfeigned
from the start.
6 From this they have swerved and
have turned aside.
They're filled with vain janglings and
have, the faith, denied.
7. They desire to teach law,
but don't understand what they say or the
things that they affirm thus from the way
they stray.
11 We know the law is good
if it is used properly;
if it is used the way it
was designed to be.
9-10 We know the law wasn't made for the
righteous man
but for the unrighteous ones,
They're why we need the plan. 11
According to God's gospel
committed to my trust.
12 Jesus counted me as faithful.
Faithfulness is a must.
13 I was earlier a persecutor trying
to cause the Gospel grief But, from
Jesus, I got mercy because I'd
acted in unbelief.
14 Exceedingly abundant with faith was
our dear Lord's grace
and the love which is in Jesus is

waiting for our embrace.
15 This is a faithful saying,
worthy of all acceptation that Jesus
came to save sinners.
I'm the chief among all nations. 16
For this cause I obtained mercy
that Christ's patience might be shown. to
them who believe on Him
that His pattern might be known.
17 Now unto the eternal invisible king.
God who is always wise; be
honor and glory forever and
also in men's eyes.
18 I commit this to you, Timothy
according to prophesies
that you might wage a good war
against the likes of these.
19 Hold fast to faith and
good conscience
which some have put away. They've
made a wreck of faith from which
they shouldn't stray.

20 One of these is Hymenaeus.
Alexander's on the same team.
I've delivered them to Satan so they'll learn
not to blaspheme.

Chapter 2

1 I exhort you brethren with all
supplication, prayer and intercession; to
give thanks for all men everywhere.
Listen closely to the lesson. 2
For kings and all in authority
also you should give thanks that
they'll lead a peaceable life with
godliness in their ranks.
3 For this is good and acceptable; its
the proper thing

to do in the sight of God, our Savior.
All things are in His view.
4 He wants all to be saved and the
truth to come to know.
5 for their is one god and mediator,
Jesus Christ will help us grow.
6 He gave Himself as a ransom for
all who have believed.
In due time He'll testify of
all who Him received.
7 By Him, I'm ordained to preach;
an apostle of Christ, the truth, to
take
His Word to the Gentiles.
To disobey would be uncouth.
8 I want men to pray everywhere; to
lift their hands in prayer. without
wrath, doubting, or worry but with
faith that He'll be there.
9 Let women be modest in dress, Not
striving to be a "10."
They shouldn't wear excess jewelry in
order to attract the men.
10 They should do works of Godliness.
11 and silence with all subjection
12 not usurping authority over men.
This should meet their rejection. 13
for Adam was made before Eve and
he was not deceived.
The woman was, however,
Satan's lies she had believed.
15 but through it all take comfort that the
way for all's been paved.
If you continue in faith and love in the end
you will be saved.

Chapter 3

This saying is correct, I say.
If a man has a desire to be a bishop, it is
good. It'll keep him from the mire.
2 A bishop must be blameless, the
husband of one wife; vigilant,
sober, apt to teach and behaving in
daily life;
given to hospitality and not
3 a striker, given to wine; not
greedy of filthy lucre,
covetous or brawling, but fine.
He should be a man of patience,
4 of his house he, the ruler,
should be having his children under
subjection with utmost gravity
5 for if a man knoweth not how to
rule a house of his own. How can he
care for God's house? These things he
must be shown.
6 He should not be a novice lest he be
lifted up with pride and fall into
condemnation and be on Satan's side.
7. He must be of good report of
them which are without
so he won't be caught in a snare
which the devil has set about.
8 The deacons must be grave.
Their tongues must not be double. Not
given to wine or filthy lucre for these
things will bring trouble;
12 holding to the mystery of the
faith and of a pure conscience be
13 and let them first be proved.
No blame must in them be.
11 Their wives must be grave;
sober and faithful in all things.
They must not be slanderers for reproach is
what that brings.
12 Let the deacons be the
husband of one wife.
Let them rule their household well so they

won't be filled with strife;
13 For they that use the office of a deacon
will purchase for themselves great boldness,
of Jesus faith they'll tell 14 These things I
hereby write
hoping to come real soon 15 but
if I should be delayed Just sing
out the Jesus tune.
You'll know how to behave in the church,
the house of God.
the pillar and grounding of truth so
you'll receive His nod.

16 Great is the mystery of godliness; of
this there's no controversy.
God was manifest in the flesh. The
angels in Heaven did see. He was
justified in the spirit; in the flesh
was manifest.
His word was preached to Gentiles.
In glory they became guests.

Chapter 4

Later some will leave the faith.
The Spirit does express.
They'll give heed to seducing spirits. Satan's
doctrines they will press.
2 Their consciences will be seared.
They'll speak hypocrisies and lies. 3
They won't permit marriage,
Abstinence from meats will arise.
God created these for us.
To abstain would be uncouth.
They're to be received with thanks by those
who know the truth.
4 for every creature of God is good and
nothing should be refused.
It's to be received with thanksgiving: if
refused His law's abused.

5 It is sanctified by God's Word and
also by much prayer.
6 If you remind one of this you'll
be a good minister there.
You'll be nourished in the words of faith of
the good doctrine
you've attained.
7 Exercise yourself in Godliness.
Old wives tales should be
disdained. 8 Bodily exercise
profiteth little but Godliness profits
much.
You'll have the promise of life now.
Eternally You'll have His touch.
9 This is a worthy saying and
should be accepted by all 10 for
because we trust in God our
reproach will not be small; But
He's the Savior of all men effective
to those who believe. 11 Command
and teach these things for Satan
will deceive.
12 Let no man despise your youth, be an
example in all you do;
in word, conversation and charity, spirit,
faith and purity too.
13 Till I come attend to reading; and
exhortation and doctrine of Me. 14 Don't
neglect the gift you have which was by
prophecy given thee.
With the laying on of hands 15
all these things recall. Give
yourselves to them.
Let your profiting appear to all.
16 Take heed unto thyself and the
doctrine you should do for in doing
this thou shalt save thyself and those
hearing you.

Chapter 5

215

1 Do not rebuke an elder as to
a father you should act. Treat
yourself with respect. To
yourself make this pact.
2 Treat older women as mothers.
Make this a surety.
Treat younger women as sisters and
with all purity.
3 Honor those who are indeed widows
4 But if they have relatives God
said to care to their jobs. It should
be them who give.
5 The desolate widows indeed who
trust God for their way. who
continue in supplications
and in prayer both night and day. 6 But
she who lives in pleasure, though she
lives she is dead
7 Charge them with these things to
be blameless as is said.
8 If any doesn't provide for his own and
those of his house as well;
He has denied the faith and is
worse than an infidel.
9 Do not take a widow in,
listen all who hears;
who wasn't the wife of one man and
reached the age of sixty years. 10 She
should be known for good works and
have raised
her children right.
She should have been kind to
strangers washing
saints feet without a fight.
She should have aided the sick and
have followed what is good. All these
things and more should have been
done if she could.
14 Refuse the younger widows:

don't allow them to tarry
for they'll grow cold to Christ then
they'll go out and marry.
12 They'll have damnation
because their first love they'll cast off
13 then they'll become idle and,
at God's Word, they'll scoff.
They'll wander from house to house.
They'll cease to be only idle but tattlers
and busy bodies.
Their tongues they will not bridle.
14 Therefore let them marry, guide the
house and children bear; give none of
them occasion to speak
reproachfully anywhere.
15 Some have turned already.
They've already turned aside to
chase after Satan
and God's commands defied.
16 If a believer has a widow let
him care for her need;
so the church can take care of them that
are widows indeed.
17 Let the elders who rule
well double honor receive
especially those who labor
and to Word and doctrine cleave.
18 "Thou shalt not muzzle the ox."
It says so in God's Word
for it says, "The laborer is worthy of
his reward."
19 Do not receive accusation
against an elder unless two or
three are present
to also bear witness.
20 Rebuke those who sin before all
that others may also fear.
21 I charge thee before God and Christ and
against angels who are near; that thou

don't show partiality
in doing all I've said.
22 Don't be too hasty with men or
partake in the sins I dread.
Keep yourself pure. 23
Drink a little wine.
For your stomach's sake a
little bit is fine.
24 Some men's sins are known
before the judgment day.
Some men keep theirs hidden.
Eventually they'll pay.
25 In the same way too some good
deeds are known but
eventually all good deeds and
the doers will be shown.

Chapter 6

Let all who are servants not
their masters blame
so doctrine won't be blasphemed nor that
of His dear name.
2 And those whose masters believe let
them despise them not
but do them faithful service
because they're a loving lot. These
things, I say, exhort and teach
them to each other. Spread
brotherly love around. Treat each
man like a brother.
3 If any man teaches otherwise and
consents not to right doctrine and
defies the Word of Christ
for this, to him's, a sin.
4 He is proud and knoweth nothing and
dotes about questions and strife
producing envy, strife and railings. Evil
surmisings come from his life.
5 Perverse disputations of evil minds

which are destitute of the truth.
They withdraw from Godliness which
proves that they're uncouth;
6 but godliness with contentment
brings great gain about;
7 for we brought nothing to this world and
can carry nothing out.
8 If we have food and clothing let
us therewith be content.
9 Those who desire great riches to
temptations snares are sent; drawn by
foolish hurtful lusts.
They are proud as well. They
drown in destruction and they'll
be cast into Hell;
10 for love of money is the root of
evil and of sorrow.
They coveted and erred from the faith and
will pay in Hell tomorrow.
11 Men of God shall flee these things and
follow after Godliness,
faith, love and patience;
meekness and righteousness. 12
Lay hold on eternal life.
Fight a faithful fight.
Thou profess a good profession and are
called to what is right.
13 I charge thee now before God who
gives life to all things: before Jesus
who before Pilate to a good
profession clings,
14 that thou keep my commandments
without spot or flaw
15 until Jesus Christ, the Lord, appears as
predicted in God's law.

16 He is an immortal being and
dwells in the light.
His honor is everlasting.

He's not been in man's sight.

17 The ones who are rich now
high minded they shouldn't be.
They should not trust in riches but
in the God they cannot see.

18 that they should be good and in
good works abide
being ready to distribute and
communicate without pride

19 that they should lay up a
foundation for time to come;
that they might gain eternal life and of
its joys they might have some.

20 Keep that committed to thy trust.
Don't use profanity or babbling's vain or
so-called contradictions of science.

21 Some erred with nothing to gain.

II Timothy 1-4

Paul, an apostle of Jesus Christ by
God's precious will
according to the promise of Christ which is
with us still.
to Timothy, my beloved son:
mercy peace and grace,
from God, the Father and Jesus, our
Lord whom you did face.
I thank God whom I have served with a
conscience pure and right. Without
ceasing I have remembered you in
prayer both day and night. greatly
desiring to see you,
being mindful of your tears that I
might be filled with joy after
these many years.
When I remember your true faith my
grandmother Lois did show then in my
mother Eunice and,

I believe in you also.
I remind you of your gift and
of the laying on of hands.
God didn't give us the spirit of fear
which abounds within our bands; but
His gift was of power and love and of a
sound mind, too.
Don't fear the Lord's testimony or of
me, a prisoner true.
Partake of the afflictions
which, due to the gospel, will come.
Depend on the powers of God. To do
otherwise would be dumb.

God hath saved & called us and with
His calling He did embrace. According
to His own purpose and according to
His grace.
These were given to us by Christ
before the world began.
They've been manifested by the
appearing of Christ, the man.
He abolished death and brought life and
immortality to the light through the
Gospel whereby
I was sent to set gentiles right. He
appointed me as an apostle, a preacher,
and teacher too
for which I suffer now,
but I'm not ashamed of what I do, for I
know whom I have believed and am
persuaded, I say:
He can keep what I've committed unto
Him against that day.
Hold on to my words which is
in Christ Jesus. Keep what was
committed by the Spirit which is
in us.
Phygellus and Hermogenes and all in

Asia have turned away.
Onesiphorus often refreshed me. May the
Lord's mercy with him stay. He was not
ashamed of my chains but looked me up
in Rome.
He ministered to me in Ephesus. May
God's mercy rest on his home.

Chapter 2

You, my son, be strong in Christ and
commit yourself to each
thing you've heard from witnesses and to
the ones who teach.
As a good soldier of Jesus you
must, hardships, endure.
One doesn't enter warfare then worry
about affairs of life
in order to please his enlister; to do
so would cause strife. If one
competes in athletics he will not
win the crown unless he obeys the
rules.
If not he will go down.
The hardworking, diligent farmer will
work until he drops.
He should eat them first and
enjoy the best of the crops.

Consider the things I say.
Lend an ear and hear me well. May
the Lord add understanding. May
He, to you, His message tell.
Remember that Christ Jesus is
from David's seed.
The Gospel says that He was raised
from death after He did bleed.
For this cause I suffer
a suffering that is sustained. I

am labeled an evil doer and
even have been chained.
Because of this I do all things for
the elect of God' sake
that they may receive salvation
and Christ's disciples make.
Remind them of these things.
Charge them before the Lord not
to ruin the hearers
by striving over profitless words.
Be diligent unto God.
Present thyselves approved unashamed
workers
who the Spirit himself has moved.
Rightly dividing the Word of truth
and shunning the profane.
Stay away from idle babbling
which increases without gain.
Their message will spread like cancer and
increase ungodliness.
Hymenaus and Phitelus do this.
Their message, God won't bless.
They strayed from the truth saying the
resurrection is already past.
They overthrow the faith of some upon
whom doubts are cast.
Nevertheless, God's foundation stands,
having received God's seal.
The Lord knows who are His. He
knows whose deeds are real.
Let everyone who names the name of
Christ, remain forever true.
Let them depart from iniquity in
everything they do.
20 A house has vessels of gold
and silver
and also of wood and clay.
Some for honor; some for dishonor; to
be used in a different way.

Cleanse yourself and be a vessel to
be used for honor and then Be
sanctified and useful for the
Master's work, we pray again.
Prepare yourself for Godly works.
Flee from youthful lusts.
Pursue righteousness, faith, love and
peace. These things are a must.
With those who call on the Lord, those
with a pure heart;
Avoid foolish and ignorant disputes
which cause some to depart.
God's servants must not quarrel but
be gentle to one and all, able to
teach and patient
in humility to great and small.
God will perhaps cause repentance so the
truth they can know
so they can escape the devil's snare and
his snares overthrow.
Be assured that in the last days perilous
times will come.
Men will love themselves and money
will make them dumb.
They will be boasters and
they also will be proud.
They'll be disobedient to parents and
they'll run with the crowd.
They'll be blasphemers and
unthankful, unloving, unholy
unforgiving and slanderers, without
self control and lowly;
despisers of truth and brutal, traitors,
headstrong and haughty;
Lovers of pleasure not God, foolish
ones and naughty: having a form of
godliness
but denying the power, you see.
From such turn away. From

such you must flee.
They creep into homes
and lead gullible women captive;
those loaded down with sin, who
with various lusts do live; always
learning but never coming to the
truth.
As Jannes and Jambres resisted Moses these
are quite uncouth.
They resist the truth and have corrupted
minds of the disapproved in matters
concerning the faith.
Their progress can't be moved. They
will progress no further than they have
already progressed.
Their folly will be known to all.
It will, to all, be manifest.
You've followed my doctrine
and my manner of life.
You have followed my purpose,
my faith, persecution and strife; My
longsuffering and my love;
11 my persecutions and afflictions too.
what happened at Antioch
and the thing they tried to do and
what happened at Iconium and at
Lystra what I endured and how the
Lord delivered me and how my
stripes were cured.
12 Those who live godly in Christ will
suffer persecution.
13 Evil men will grow worse with
no fear of retribution.
They'll deceive and be deceived
14 but you must never fail;
continue in things you've learned
and be assured I will prevail.
15 From a child you learned the
scriptures, You memorized
every word.

God's Word that make you wise to
salvation from the Lord.
16 All scripture was God breathed and is
profitable for doctrine to bless, for
reproof and correction
and instruction in righteousness; 17
that Godly man may be perfect and
his will never shirk;
but that he might be ready to perform every
good work.

Chapter 4

I charge thee before God and
Jesus Christ who'll judge
those who will be saved and
those who won't be budged. 2 Be
ready to preach the word
at all times with sincerity.
Rebuke, reprove, and exhort with
longsuffering and clarity.
3 The time will come when people will not
endure sound doctrine.
They'll seek those who affirm their
lusts and their sin.
4 They'll turn from the truth and those who
preach the Word.
They'll turn to fables accepting cults
with one accord.
5 Watch out for these people.
Endure afflictions for Christ, you see.
Do the work of an evangelist. Be
faithful to the ministry.

6 I'm ready to leave the earth.
My departure is at hand. 7 I
have fought a good fight
and finished the course so grand.
I have kept the faith.

I know the Lord will bless.
8 In Heaven I'll be rewarded with a
crown of righteousness.
The Lord, the righteous judge will
give it to me that day.
Not only to me, but to all that
love Him and know the way.
9 Live so you'll see me soon
10 don't forsake me like Demas did.
He loved the present world and
in Thessalonica he hid. Cresens
went from me also.
He went to Galatia.
Titus left as well going to Dalmatia.
11 Only Luke is with me still.
Bring Mark and come to me. He
is profitable to me now to
continue my ministry.
12 Tychicus I sent to Ephesus.
13 With Carpus I left my coat in view.
Bring it to me when you come and the
books and parchments too.
14 Alexander the coppersmith did
evil to me there.
May the Lord reward him as to evildoers
everywhere.
15 Be aware of him also.
He greatly withstood the Word.
All men forsook me there
because of what they heard.
I pray that God will not blame them
for the evils of this man.
17 The Lord stood with me anyway and
strengthened me by His hand.
He made my preaching known that the
gentiles there might hear. I was
delivered from the evil one from
whom I had much to fear.
18 From every evil work out there the

Lord will deliver me.
He'll preserve me for His kingdom.
I'll give Him the glory, you see. 19
Salute Priscilla and Aquilla and
Onesiphorus' household too.
20 Erasmus lives in Corinth.
I left Trophimus whose sickness grew.

21 Try to come before winter.
Eubulus will greet thee. Pudens,
Linus and Claudia are Christians
too, you see. 22 The Lord Jesus
Christ keep you till we meet
again. His grace be with you
also.
In Jesus name. Amen.

Miracles (John 2:1-18)

Jesus used His miracles to
show He was divine.
He healed the sick, raised the dead, and
turned water into wine.
At the wedding feast in Cana the
people's faith was tested For the
outcome of a miracle quite often
on faith rested.
He walked upon the water and the
raging storm He stilled.
He caused the lame to walk and the
hungry to be filled.
After multiplying loaves and fishes for the
people's nourishment
He said, "I am the Bread of Life who was
from Heaven sent.
So, you see, Christ's miracles were
powerful teaching tools
To point to His divinity for he
suspended natures rules.

Luke 1:1-55

1 For many have written down those
things we do believe.
2 Many eyewitnesses delivered the
things they did perceive.
3 My dear Theophilis, I
felt that I should write.
I understand these things
which came into my sight. 4 I
write now unto you
so that you all will know the
certainty of the things of
which, to you, I'll show. 5
Zacharias was a priest who
lived in Herod's day. With
Elizabeth, his wife he often
knelt to pray.
6 They were righteous people;
walking in God's command.
The Lord saw them as blameless as
they walked hand in hand.

7 They didn't have a child and
were getting very old Elizabeth
was barren
or so she had been told.
8 While executing priestly duties
according to God's Word
9 burning incense as was custom in the
temple of the Lord.
10 When he burned the incense and
the people prayed without 11 he saw
an angel of the Lord of this there was
no doubt.
This angel stood by the altar. He
stood there to its right.
12 Zacharias was very troubled and

was filled with fright.
13 The angel said, "Fear not."
Elizabeth shall bear a son.
I know it sounds absurd, but you
shall name him John.
14 He'll bring you both happiness.
There will be much joy.
Many will rejoice at the birth. of this
precious baby boy.
15 He'll be great in the Lord's sight.
Of him you'll want to boast.
He'll drink no wine or strong drink. He'll
be filled with the Holy Ghost.
16 Many children of Israel
to the Lord their God shall turn. 17
He'll go in spirit and power. The
spirit of Elias shall burn.
To turn the hearts of the fathers to their
children indeed.
Disobedient will turn to the just. Of
their wisdom there's a need. He'll
cause people to get ready and prepare
to meet the Lord 18 Zacharias said to
the angel, "How shall I prove your
word?
I am an old man now. My
wife is also old."
19 The angel said, "I'm Gabriel. I
have spoken what God told.
I stand in the presence of God.
He told me what to say.
I was sent to bring glad tidings and to
explain God's way.
20 Until these things take place You
shall not speak a word because you
didn't believe things given to me by the
Lord.
21 People waited for Zacharias
and wondered at his delay.

They marveled that he remained in
the temple where he did stay. 22
When he finally did come out and
they saw he could not talk they
figured he had seen a vision. for he
motioned as he did walk. 23 When
he finished in the temple and
returned to his house.
24 Elizabeth conceived while he
remained as quiet as a mouse. She
hid for five long months
25 Saying, "The Lord has dealt with me
to take away my reproach
and set my heart at liberty.
26 In the sixth month of her pregnancy
the angel, Gabriel, was sent.
God sent him to Galilee.
To Nazareth he went.
27 He appeared to a virgin.
To the virgin Mary he came.
She was engaged to Joseph.
The line of David was his claim.
28 The angel said, "Hail."
This message he gave her.
"You are blessed among women.
With the Lord you've found favor.
29 She was troubled by this saying
wondering about her lot.
30 He said to her, "Do not fear.
With God you've a special spot."
31 You shall have a baby.
It will be a son.
You shall name Him Jesus.
32 He shall be the greatest one.
He'll be called the Son of God.
He'll be greatest among men.
The throne of his father David will return
to his family again.
33 Over all the house of Jacob He

will rule forever.
His kingdom will continue
its ending will be never. 34
Mary said to the angel,
"How can this come to be?
For I'm not even married.
No man has been with, me?"
35 He said, "The Holy Ghost shall come
and overshadow thee.
Your boy will be the Son of God.
He will a blessing be.
36 You're cousin Elizabeth will
have a son also.
Many said that she could not. This
will God's power show.
37 Nothing is impossible
for God who made us all.
38. Mary said, "I'll serve the Lord;
Though I am very small.
Let it be done unto me
according to thy word. The
angel went away. That is
what Mary heard.
39 Mary soon got up
and proceeded to make haste.
She went to the city of Judah for
time she wished not to waste. 40 She
entered Zacharia's house.
To Elizabeth she called out. At
her voice the baby leaped. Of this
there was no doubt.
Elizabeth filled with the Holy Ghost.
42 To Mary she did say, Blessed's
the fruit of thy womb
You're blessed among women today. 43
Why does the mother of my Lord honor me
with a visit today.
44 As soon as I heard your voice My
baby leaped, I say."

45 Blessed is she that believed.
Her belief will come true.
46 Mary said, My soul magnifies God.
My spirit rejoices too.
48 For God regarded His handmaid.
All people shall call me blessed.
49 God has done great things.
His Holy name be blessed.
50 His mercy is on each generation and
all who his name fear.
51 He has showed strength this day and
scattered the proud from here.
52 He has put down the mighty and
lifted up the low.
53 He has filled the hungry. to the
rich He has said, "Go.
54 He helped His servant Israel.
His mercy will be recalled.
55 He promised Abraham's ancestors.
His promise has not been stalled."

Matthew 16-25

Pharisees and Sadducees came
desiring Jesus to show a sign. He
answered them all saying. "You
predict the weather fine.
In the evening when the sky is red you
say the weather will be fair.
In the morning you say it will be foul if
red is found up there.
Oh! Ye hypocrites! Ye hypocrites!
You can discern the sky.
Why not the signs of the times?
I ask you why? Oh why?
Wicked, adulterous generation
seeketh after a sign
You've the sign of Jonas.
You won't see another of mine.

They went to the other side.
They took no bread if you please.
Jesus said, "Beware of the leaven of the
Pharisees and Sadducees."
They reasoned to themselves saying, "Its
because we have no bread."
Jesus perceived this and said to them, "Ye
of little faith. Ye shall all be fed. Don't
you understand or remember the five
thousand and five loaves?
How many baskets did we take up
even though we had no stoves?
"Don't you remember the seven loaves and
the four thousand which were fed?
Remember the baskets of leftovers when,
by the Master,
you were led Now, Why do you not
understand of bread I don't now speak.
Beware Pharisees and Sadducees for
their doctrine is bleak.
When He came to Caesarea Philippi they
followed God's chosen lamb.
He asked the disciples saying. "Who
do men say that I am?" "Some John
the Baptist, some Elias,
other Jeremias or one of the prophets." He
said, "But who saith thee I am?
Just where are your thoughts set?
Simon Peter answered and said,
"Thou art Christ, Son of the Living
God." He said, "Blessed is Simon
Barjona. You've received my
Father's nod. Flesh and blood
did not show this.
God made you leader of the flock.
I say that you are Peter and
shall be called "The Rock."
Upon this rock I'll build my church. It
will withstand the gates of Hell.

I give you the keys to Heaven for I know
you have done well.
Whatever you bind on earth
shall in Heaven also be bound
Whatever things you loose,
loose they will be found.
He said the fact that He was the Christ
should be whispered to no one.
From that time on he showed them what
He must suffer as God's Son; how He
must suffer and be killed and raised on
the third day.
Peter took Him and rebuked Him,
saying things shall not be that way.
Jesus said, "Get behind Me. Satan!"
Thou art an offense to Me.
Thou savorest not the things of God but
only what pleases thee.
If any man will come after Me he
must, himself, deny.
He must take his cross and follow Me.
Never asking Why?
Whosoever shall save his life.
It shall be his loss.
Whoever loses his life for my sake shall
gain by the way of the cross.
What is a man profited if he
shall gain the world if on
judgment day
his soul into Hell is hurled? With
angels and God's glory the Son of
Man shall come. He'll judge each
by his works. Every person not
just some.
If the scales of justice warrant You'll
be cast into Hell.
The Son of Man shall come before some
shall hear death's bell.

Chapter XVII

After six days Peter James, John, and
Jesus went to a high mountain alone. He
was transfigured before them, His face
bright as the sun was shown.
His clothes were as white as the light. Two
more appeared unto them Elias and Moses
were seen with Him.
As they talked He shined as a gem. then
Peter said to Jesus,
"Is it good for us to be here? If
thou wilt, we will make three
tabernacles if you make it clear.
One for each of thee." Then a
bright cloud appeared. A voice came
from the cloud. They must have
been afeared. Saying, "this is my
beloved Son;
in whom I am well pleased."
The disciples heard it and in fear fell
right to their knees.
Jesus came to them
and touched them, every one.
Saying, "Arise. Be not afraid. for I
am God's only Son."
When they had lifted up their eyes they
saw he was alone.
"Tell no one what you've seen until
I've rolled away the stone." The
disciples asked Him saying,
Why do scribes say Elias must come?
Jesus said, It shall happen.
He'll restore all not just some.
I say to you that he's already come.
People knew him not, you see.
When the Son of Man returns
likewise it will be.
Then the disciples understood of
John the Baptist he had spoken. When
they came to the multitude there was
one who was broken.
He kneeled in front of Jesus Saying,
"Have mercy on your son, a lunatic
who falls into the fire
or into water is what he's done. I
brought him to your disciples.
They could not work a cure but I
know you can, Lord Jesus.
Of that I'm very sure."
He said, "Faithless generation How
long shall I be with you?
Bring this man to me. I'll
show you what to do. Jesus
rebuked the devil He left the
child that hour.
The disciples asked Jesus why
their efforts went sour.
Jesus said unto them.
"Its because of unbelief for verily I say unto
you its enough to cause me grief.
If you had faith as a mustard seed you
could say to that mountain there, move
out of the way
and the spot would be quite bare.
Nothing would be impossible if
faith you only had.
Prayer and fasting would help The
results would not be bad. While in
Galilee, Jesus said, "The Son shall
one man betray. They shall kill the
Son of Man, but he'll rise on the
third day.
When they arrived in Capernaum the tax
collector had this to say, We're collecting
the temple tax. Does your master wish to
pay?
Peter said, Of course He does and

started to go right in
but Jesus stopped him asking, Who
pays? A stranger or a citizen? Peter
answered, Strangers pay.
Jesus asked if citizens then went free.
We'd not offend them, Peter so
go down to the sea.
Cast out a hook and catch a fish. In
its mouth you'll find a coin.
Give it to them as tribute then come and
with me join.

Chapter XVIII

The disciples came to Jesus.
They'd been discussing their fate. They
said, "We'd like to know in Heaven who
will be great?"
Jesus called a child to him and sat
him in their midst.
"Except ye become as a little child ye
shall not in Heaven exist.
Whosoever shall humble himself and
become as a little child.
He shall be considered great. Upon
him riches will be piled. whoever
receives one little child in my name
receiveth Me,
but whoever offends a child an
offense to Me he'll be.
It would be better if a millstone were
hanged about his neck and he was
thrown into the sea from a large
ship's deck.
Woe to the world for offenses! Offenses
indeed must come,
but woe to the man who offends.
He shall be known as dumb. If
your hand or foot offends then

sever them as well.
It is better to be maimed than be
whole and burned in Hell.
If your eye offends you pluck
it out for its desire.
It is better to be missing an eye than
to be cast into Hell's fire. Don't
despise these little ones for this I say
to you,
They'll see my Father in Heaven and
you should want to too.
In the morning you say it will be foul if
red is found up there.
Oh! Ye hypocrites! Ye hypocrites!
You can discern the sky.
Why not the signs of the times? I
ask you why? Oh why? Wicked,
adulterous generation
seeketh after a sign
You've the sign of Jonas.
You won't see another of mine. They
went to the other side.
They took no bread if you please.
Jesus said, "Beware of the leaven of the
Pharisees and Sadducees."
They reasoned to themselves saying, "Its
because we have no bread."
Jesus perceived this and said to
them, "Ye of little faith.
Ye shall all be fed.
Don't you understand or remember the
five thousand and five loaves? How
many baskets did we take up even
though we had no stoves? "Don't you
remember the
seven loaves and the
four thousand which were fed?
Remember the baskets of leftovers
when, by the Master,

you were led Now, Why
do you not understand of
bread I don't now speak.
Beware Pharisees and Sadducees for
their doctrine is bleak.
When He came to Caesarea Philippi they
followed God's chosen lamb.
He asked the disciples saying, "Who
do men say that I am?" "Some John
the Baptist, some Elias,
other Jeremias or one of the prophets." He
said, "But who saith thee I am?
Just where are your thoughts set? Simon
Peter answered and said, "Thou art
Christ, Son of
the Living God." He said,
"Blessed is Simon Barjona.
You've received my Father's nod.
Flesh and blood did not show this.
God made you leader of the flock.
I say that you are Peter and
shall be called "The Rock."
Upon this rock I'll build my church. It
will withstand the gates of Hell.
I give you the keys to Heaven for I
know you have done well.
Whatever you bind on earth shall in
Heaven also be bound.
Whatever things you loose, loose
they will be found.
He said the fact that He was the Christ
should be whispered to no one.
From that time on he showed them what
He must suffer as God's Son; how He
must suffer and be killed and raised on
the third day.
Peter took Him and rebuked Him,
saying things shall not be that way.
Jesus said, "Get behind Me. Satan!"

Thou art an offense to Me.
Thou savorest not the things of God but
only what pleases thee.
If any man will come after Me he
must himself deny.
He must take his cross and follow Me.
Never asking Why? Whosoever shall save
his life. It shall be his loss.
Whoever loses his life for my sake shall
gain by the way of the cross.
What is a man profited if he
shall gain the world if on
judgment day
his soul into Hell is hurled? With
angels and God's glory the Son of
Man shall come. He'll judge each
by his works. Every person not
just some.
If the scales of justice warrant You'll
be cast into Hell.
The Son of Man shall come before
some shall hear death's bell.

Chapter XIX

When Jesus finished these sayings He
went to Galilee.
Multitudes followed to Judea.
He said, "From sickness you are free."
The Pharisees came unto Him
trying to tempt Him there.
Can you lawfully put away a wife
for any cause you bear?" He asked,
"Have you not read they
were made female and male.
Marriage makes them one flesh.
This marriage should never fail.
"Why did Moses allow divorce
by a written letter?"
Moses knew your wicked hearts so
he let you break this fetter."
In the beginning it was disallowed.
Now I say unto you "Except for
fornication divorce is strictly taboo.
If you shall be divorced and then
marry again you've committed
adultery and are living then in sin.
Whoever marries a divorcee
commits adultery as if it were
forced."
That person is "one flesh." Divorce
is not endorsed.
His disciples said, "In that case it is
not good to marry."
He said there are some
who could not this message carry.
There are some eunuchs which to
this position were born.
Some were made eunuchs because
others tooted their horn.

Some made themselves eunuchs for
the Kingdom's sake.
He will receive this message for the
kingdom's value he'll take.
People brought children to Him to
lay hands on and pray.
The disciples rebuked them. Jesus
said, "Let them stay.
For of such is Heaven's kingdom.
laid hands on and departed. There came one to
Him just after he had started.
The man called him "Good Master." Jesus
asked, "Why call me good? There is none good
but God. Keep commandments as you should."
He asked to which Jesus referred.
Jesus said, Thou shalt not steal Thou
shalt not bear false witness but tell only
what is real.
Thou shalt not kill or commit adultery.
Honor thy father and mother; love
thy neighbor as thyself; always treat
him as a brother." The young man
said to Him,

,"All these I've done since youth."
Jesus said, "Sell all. Give it to the
poor."
The man thought this uncouth. He
heard and left sorrowfully, for his
possessions were great.
Jesus said, "Its hard for rich to enter.
Riches keep them from the gate.
Its easier for a camel
to pass through a needle's eye
than for rich to enter Heaven.
The disciples asked Him why.
They were amazed and asked,
"Who can enter then?
25 They asked who could be saved?
They asked again and again.
Jesus looked at them and said,
With man it can not be
With God all things are possible.
He'll set the captive free."
Then Peter answered saying, "We
have forsaken all.
What shall we receive therefore for
answering your call?" Jesus said,
"I say to you
Because you've followed Me when the
Son sits on his throne they'll
be twelve thrones for thee.
You'll judge Israel's twelve tribes.

Those forsaking riches for my sake
shall receive a hundredfold.
Eternal life shall be their take.
They'll enter into my kingdom
where they shall never thirst.
The first shall be last and
the last shall be the first.

Chapter XX

The kingdom's like a householder Hiring
laborers for a day.
He sent them to his vineyard. A
penny was to be their pay. There
were some standing idle in the
market at hour three.
He sent them out to work saying
I'll pay a proper fee. At the sixth
and ninth hours he also did the
same.
The seventh hour he asked You idle.
Who's to blame?
They said no man hired us. He
said to my vineyard go.
I'll pay you what's right for
harvesting what I grow.
He commanded his steward when
work for the day was done to call the
laborers in and pay them every one.
The last hired came first
and each received a penny.
The first hired expected more.
They thought they'd get many.

They received a penny also.
When this had been done they
grumbled and complained
about when they had begun.
They said some only worked for
a single hour.
They got paid the same.
Their faces turned quite sour.
They said those who worked during
the heat of the day did the most work of all
and should get more pay.
The householder answered, "I
have not done wrong.
You agreed to work for that and
you agreed to work that long. I'll do
what I want with my money.
Isn't it my own?
I haven't wronged thee so
why do you now groan?
Jesus was going to Jerusalem.
He took the twelve apart and stayed. He
said, "We now go to that city where God's
Son will be betrayed.
The chief priests and scribes the
Son of Man will condemn. They'll
deliver him to Gentiles. They'll
scourge and crucify Him.
Do not be discouraged. Don't
wear a sad disguise. He'll be
placed in a tomb.
On the third day He shall rise."
Zebedee's children's mother came to
Jesus on the run
she asked if in His kingdom
the best places could be for her sons.
Jesus answered saying. "Ye
know not what ye ask
to drink the cup that I must drink for
you is an impossible task.

To be baptized with my baptism I
am sure you are unable." They
said, "We'll follow you.
We're sure that we are able." Jesus
said, "You shall be baptized with the
baptism which I am.
You shall indeed drink of the cup of God's
very precious lamb.
To sit at my right hand and on my left that
day I cannot give to you.
It's my Father's right to say." When
the others were told about what had
transpired indignation was ignited.
Against these it had been fired.
Jesus said, "Gentile princes
exercise dominion over them.
The great exercise authority. This
won't be among my men.
Whoever is great among you let
him minister to the others.
Whoever is chief among you
let him be a servant to his brothers.
Even so the Son of Man came
not to be ministered to but to
minister to those in need
and to give His life for you.
As they departed from Jericho a
great multitude trailed behind.
Two men cried out to them "Have
mercy because we're blind."
The multitudes rebuked them.
saying to hold their peace but
they cried out louder.
Their shouting did increase.
Jesus stood still and called them, saying,
"What do you want me to do?"
They said, "We would like to see so
we can follow You." Jesus had
compassion.

He bent and their eyes He touched.
They received sight immediately.
They followed and thanked Him much.

Chapter XXI

Nearing Jerusalem at Bethphage to
the Mount of Olives they came.
He sent two disciples into the village
saying, "Go. In my Father's name. When
you enter into the village,
as soon as the gates you pass you will find a
colt tied up together with an ass.
Untie and bring them here. Bring
them to me please.
If any man asks what you do say, "My
Master has need of these." Straightway
he will send them.
All this will be done
that prophesy might be fulfilled. The
prophets I shall not shun.
He said, "Tell ye daughter Sion my
King cometh to the meek sitting
upon an ass and her foal."
They did as he did speak.
They brought the ass and colt and
placed on them their clothes.
They put Jesus upon them as
great multitudes arose.
They threw clothes and branches down
upon which they could walk. They cried,
"Hasannah in the highest." The people
began to talk.
They asked, "Who is this man?
Why is He coming here?
The multitudes answered, "He's Jesus.
You don't need to fear.
Jesus went to the temple where

the money changers were.
He cast out all who bought and sold as
they began to stir.
He overturned their tables and
the dove seller's seats.
He said, "My house is one of prayer.
You've filled it with deceit."
14 The blind and lame came to Him.
They were all quickly healed.
When Priests and Scribes saw Him
their true motives were revealed. They
saw the great things done and children
in the temple saying, "Hasannah to the
Son of David."
The priests knew they weren't playing.
They came to Jesus asking. "Do
you hear and see their ways?"
Jesus said, From the mouths of babes
Thou has perfected praise.
Jesus left for Bethany.
He lodged there for the night. In
the morning He was hungry. He
went to the city for a bite.
19 He saw a fig tree on the way but He
found no fruit thereon.
It had plenty of leaves but
of fruit it had none.
He said, "You'll henceforth bear no fruit.
Its leaves grew brown and dried.
Soon the tree began to droop. It
wasn't long until it died.
The disciples saw it and marveled.
They remarked about its demise.
Jesus said, If you have faith this would
come as no surprise.
If ye have faith and do not doubt you'll do
more than you've seen.
If believing you tell a mountain to move
the earth shall be swept clean.

22 All things whatever you ask
believing ye shall receive.
The important thing to remember is
when you pray you must believe.
23 He was teaching in the temple the
chief priests and elders came Saying,
"How do you these miracles?
You are doing them in whose name?" 24
Jesus answered and said to them, "If you
answer this question of mine I'll give you
an answer to yours.
If not, my refusal is by design.

25 The baptism of John.
From whom did it come?
Did it come from men or Heaven?" The
men remained quite dumb. They
thought if we say Heaven He'll ask why
we didn't go near
26 but if we say from men His
followers we must fear.
27 They answered Jesus saying, "We
cannot thus tell you." He said,
"Neither will I reveal to you by whose
authority these things I do.
29 I ask this question about a man who
said, son, work in my vineyard. 29 The
son said he would not go then repented
and worked real hard.
30 The man came to the second son and
likewise sent him to work.
He answered and said, "I'll go but his
duty he did shirk.
31 They said the first did His will
when Jesus asked them who?
He said, "Publicans and harlots will enter
Heaven before the likes of you.
32 for John came unto you and
you believed him not.
They who believed in him were the publican

and harlot.
33 Hear this parable, a man's vineyard was
hedged round about.
He had a wine press and a tower. He
journeyed and rented it out.
34 When time of the fruit drew near he
sent servants to receive his pay. 35 They
beat one and killed another and stoned
another in the way.
36 He sent other servants more
than at first he did. They treated
them the same.
The bodies were all hid.
37 At last he sent his only son saying,
"They'll honor my son."
38 They said he is heir to this.
Lets kill him just for fun. 39
They threw him out
of the vineyard. Then him they
took and slew.
40 When the overseer came with the
renters what will he do? 41 They said,
Destroy those wicked
men then rent it to another.
One who will pay his share and
who won't cheat his brother.
42 Jesus asked, "Have ye not read
how the stone which was rejected
became the head of the corner
in that which the Lord erected?" 43
Therefore I say unto you,
"the kingdom from you shall be taken.
This might come as a shock to you.
You might be visibly shaken.
It shall be given to a nation who
won't kill the Master's Son.
One who will pay its rightful share of
the fruit which it has won.
44 Whoever stumbles on the corner

233

Shall be broke and shout louder
but he on whom it shall fall will
be ground up into powder.
45 The chief priests and Pharisees heard
what Jesus said
They perceived He spoke of them and
wouldn't rest till He was dead.
46 When they tried to lay hands on
Him The multitudes they feared for
they knew Him as a prophet.
To them He was endeared.

Chapter XXII

Jesus, speaking in parables said, "I
say to you this thing.
The Kingdom of Heaven is like a
wedding for the son of the king. His
servants went to all the guests but they
refused to come.
They said, "The best food is there come
and partake of some.
The guest just made fun of them.
Some went their own way.
The others took the servants slaying them
that very day.
When the king heard this he
sent out his armed men.
They killed all involved and burned the
cities where they'd been.
Then he said to his servants the
wedding is prepared.
The invited guests aren't coming.
At the banquet he just stared. He
said, "Go into the highways.
Invite all that you find
so they invited all they saw.
At the wedding feast they dined. The
king came to see the guests.

He saw one without wedding clothes. He
said, "Friend why have you come?" Then
he quickly arose.
The king said to his servants, "Tie
him tightly with lashings.
Cast him into outer darkness where
there's weeping and teeth gnashing.
For many have been called he
said and arose
but few there are who answer and
few will be chose.
15 The Pharisees took council
trying to entangle Him.
They wouldn't admit to wrong.
Chances of this were slim.
16 They sent followers with Herodians
saying, "Master this we know
You teach the way of God and
carest not for show. 17 Tell
us is it lawful
to pay Caesar tax?
18 Jesus said, "You hypocrites.
Why tempt Me with these acts?
19 Show Me the tribute money.
20 Whose image do you see there?"
21 They said, "It's Caesar's." Jesus said,
"Then it's Caesar's fare."
You benefit from Caesar so he
collects tax from you.
Just like belonging to God means there's
things that you must do."
22 When they had heard His answer they
marveled and went their way.
23 Sadducees who deny the resurrection
came with this to say. 24 Moses said if a
man dies childless his brother shall marry
his wife.
He'll raise up seed unto his brother for the
remainder of his life.

25 There were once seven brothers.
The first one took a wife.
He was still childless when he
lost his life.
26 The second brother married her.
He also died childless.
The other five did likewise.
Now we ask you this. 27
After the last brother was
taken away in death
the woman died and joined them. She
was deserted by her breath.
28 She had seven husbands as
Moses said it should be.
Therefore, in the resurrection which
husband will be with she?"

29 He said, "You don't
know God's power.
You err in not knowing His Word.
30 In the resurrection
there's no marriage.
People are as angels of the Lord.
31 Concerning the dead's resurrection.
Have ye not read what God said? 32
I'm God of Abraham, Isaac, and
Jacob. God of the
living not of the dead."
33 When the multitudes heard this they
were filled with astonishment. 34 The
Pharisees gathered together after the
Sadducees had been sent. 35 A
Pharisee who was a lawyer wishing an
argument to start
36 Asked which was the
great commandment 37
Jesus said, Love God
with all your heart.
Not only with all your heart but with all
your soul and mind.

38 This is the great commandment.
All are in it combined.
39 The second is like unto it.
Love thy neighbor as thy self.
40 On these two hang the law covering all
those on the shelf."
41 While the Pharisees were gathered
Jesus said, "I've a question of thee.
42 What think ye of this Christ?
I ask whose son is He?" They
said, "The son of David
43 "Why did David call Him Lord?"
44 He made this very statement,
The Lord said unto my Lord Sit on
my right hand.
Of thine enemies a footstool I'll make. 45
David called Him Lord, not son. What
think you? What's your take?" 46 No man
was able to answer him.
Their tongues He had ensnared, From
that day on they asked no more for not
one of them dared.

Chapter XXIII

Jesus spoke to the multitude; and to
His disciples too.
"Scribes and Pharisees fill Moses seat.
What they bid, observe and do.
Do not follow after them
for they don't do what they say. They
make strict rules and laws and they
make the people pay. They make these
laws for men and don't want them to
linger.
As for obeying these themselves; they
don't even lift a finger.
All the works they do they do
so men will know.
Their phylacteries and hems are enlarged.

They do this just for show. 6 They seek out the showiest room; in the synagogue the best seat.

In the market they make greetings. The name Rabbi they repeat. They should not be called Rabbi for Christ is head of all.

You should call no man Father. He's not in this earthly hall.

9 Call no one on earth Father because He's up above.

10 Let nobody call you master. The Master's shown His love. 11 Whoever is great among you shall be a servant to all. 12 Whoever exalteth himself shall be humbled by his fall.

13 Woe unto Scribes and Pharisees. Hypocrites are what you are. You lock up Heaven yet won't go in. You cause to stumble who'd go far. 14 Your damnation will be greater because you make long prayer while devouring widow's houses and hindering any there.

15 Woe to Scribes and Pharisees. Hypocrites are what you are. To win one convert you cross the sea traveling very far. When you have found that convert of your ways you tell. You make him twice as deserving as you to burn in Hell.

16 Woe unto you blind guides saying it's nothing by the temple to swear but if you swear by the gold of the temple you are bound by the words you bear. 17 You are fools and are blind for which is greater to behold

The gold which is in the temple or that which sanctifieth the gold?

18 And whosoever shall swear by the altar is bound by nothing at all but if you swear by the gift you are bound though it were small. 19 You are fools and you are blind for is the gift greater or the altar which sanctifies the gift? It is to the gift you cater.

20 When a man swears by the altar by what's on it he'll also swear 21 and if a man swears by the temple he swears by the dweller there.

22 He that shall swear by Heaven swears also by God's throne and not only by the throne of God but by the one who sits thereon. 23 Woe unto you, scribes and Pharisees concerning mint, cumin, and anise; Of these small things you are sure to come in and pay your tithes. Of judgment, mercy, and faith; the weightier matters of law You have overlooked these things. This is a grievous flaw.

24 These weightier things of the law you'd have seen if you'd not been blind. You strain at a gnat and swallow a camel yet you don't seem to mind.

25 Woe to you Scribes and Pharisees. On the outside you stress cleanliness but inside you don't mind the dirt. You're full of extortion and excess. 26 Clean first that which is within then clean the outside also.

Because you do things backwards this will add to your woe.

27 Woe to you Scribes and
Pharisees. you are like
whitewashed statues of stone.
The outside appears clean and pretty but
you are full of dead men's bones.
28 Outwardly you're righteous but
it is truly a pity.
Inwardly you're filled with hypocrisy and
also iniquity.
29 Woe to you Scribes and Pharisees
because tombs for the prophets ye build.
You celebrate righteousness and act like
you're sorrow filled.
30 You say if we had lived then we
would not the prophets have slain.
31 You admit that you're
their children.
This fact should cause you pain. 32
Go then and finish what they
started. You'll do the job quite well. 33
You serpents. You generation of
vipers. How can you escape from Hell?
34 I'll send prophets, wise,
and teachers. You'll kill and nail some to
the cross. You'll whip others in your
Synagogues but it shall be your loss. 35
The punishment for all the murders Will fall
on all of you
from the murder of Abel
to Zacharias who between the altar
and temple ye slew.
36 The punishment for all these will
fall on the people of this day for your
unfaithfulness
though you've been shown the way.
37 Oh Jerusalem, Thou killest the
prophets and stonest those I've sent to
you. How often would
I have gathered thee just

like a hen would do.
Behold, your house is desolate.
Ye shall not again see Me till ye say, In
the name of the Lord
Blessed now is He."

Chapter XXIV

1 Jesus left the temple. His
disciples came to Him.
They showed Him temple buildings 2
and Jesus said to them,
"See you not these things," He
said with a frown. "Verily I say
unto you
every stone will be thrown down." 3 He
sat on the Mount of Olives. The
disciples came to Him saying. "Tell us
when these things shall be.
When these buildings will start decaying.
Tell us the signs of Thy coming and when
the world shall end." 4 Jesus said, "Don't be
deceived.
Don't let others your mind bend.
5 Many shall come claiming to be me.
They shall deceive many.
With you don't let that be. 6
Ye shall hear of wars and
rumors of war.
Don't let this trouble you for
the end is not in store.
7 Nation shall rise against nation.
Kingdoms will show war-like faces.
There shall be famines and pestilence and
earthquakes in various places.
All these are just the beginnings of
sorrows which are to come.
9 You'll be hated for my sake.
They shall kill you just for fun.
10 Many shall be offended

and shall hate one another.
11 Many false prophets shall arise and
shall deliver up their brother. 12
Because iniquity shall abound the
love of many will grow cold.
13 All that endure to the end shall be
welcomed to God's fold. 14 In this
whole world of ours the
Gospel will be preached as a witness to all
nations before the end is reached.
15 When you see abomination
spoken of by the prophet Dan stand
in the Holy place.
You shall understand His plan. 16
Let those who are in Judea flee to
the mountain top.
17 Let him who is on the house top go
quickly. He should not stop;
not taking a things from the house; 18
nor he who is in the field
don't return for clothes.
He's forbidden thus to yield. 19
Woe unto those with child and
for those nursing, Pray.
20 Pray that your flight's not in winter or on
the Sabbath day.
21 For then shall be great tribulation like
the world has never known.
22 Except that the days be shortened no
flesh would remain on bone.
23 Don't believe any who say,
"Behold the Christ is here." 24
False prophets shall come.
They'll make it their career.
They'll show signs and wonders.
The best ones they'll select. If it
were possible they'd deceive
God's very elect.
25 Behold, I have said before

26 If they say, "in the desert you'll find
him." or even, "He's in the chambers."
Don't satisfy their whim.
27 Lightening flashes from east to
west, so shall His coming be.
28 Wherever the carcass is the
eagle's you'll also see.
29 Immediately after the tribulation the
sun shall become dark.
The moon shall not give light.
Stars from Heaven shall disembark.
Powers of Heaven shall be shaken. 30
Signs of God's Son shall appear.
Then shall all the earth's tribes mourn.
God's Son they'll see and hear.

They'll see Him in the clouds
with power and great glory. 31
He shall send His angels.
Their trumpet shall tell the story. From
one end of heaven to the other His elect
will gather with Him.
32 Learn a parable of the fig tree
when it has a tender limb.
Upon this limb when you see leaves you'll
know summer is at hand.
33 When you see this taking place
know ye summer's in the land.
34 These things will be fulfilled before this
generation shall pass away.
35 Heaven and earth shall pass but My
Word will always stay.
36 The day and hour of my return no
man on earth shall know.
My Father knows the time; none
other above or below. 37 As the
days of Noah were so shall the
last days be.
38 As the days were before the flood the

same actions you'll see.
Men were eating and drinking and
giving in marriage that day.
You'll see these at the end of time to
escape you know the way.
39 They knew not until the flood came and
had destroyed them all.
So shall God's Son's coming be
surprising the great and small. 40
Then shall two be in the field. One
shall be left the other taken.
41 Two shall be grinding in the mill. One
shall be saved and one forsaken. 42 Be
ready always for you don't know when the
Lord shall appear.
43 If the owner knew the thief's plans he'd
have ended his career.
44 Therefore be always ready. He'll
come when defense is down. 45 The
faithful and wise servant from the
Lord will get a crown.
He'll be ruler of his household. In
due season he'll get meat. 46
Blessed is that servant
who is ready the Lord to greet. 47
Verily, I say the Lord will make
him ruler in that day.
48 The evil servant says to himself, The
Lord's coming is in delay.

49 He'll smite his fellow servants and
eat and drink in excess.
50 The Lord shall surprise him
putting an end to his success. 51
They shall put him asunder.
His place shall be beneath.
He'll be placed with the hypocrites with
weeping and gnashing teeth.

Chapter XXV

1 Heaven is like ten virgins. Each
went forth with a light.
They went to meet the bridegroom wanting
things to be just right.
2 Five of them were wise. The
other five were not.
3 The foolish took no extra oil.
4 The wise took an extra pot.
5 They all slept for a while for the
bridegroom was delayed.
6 At midnight he finally came and
then the cry was made. They said,
Go out to meet Him 7 so everyone
arose;
trimmed their lamps but then 8 They
found foolishness shows.
They demanded of the wise; Give
us some of your oil.
Our lamps have gone out. Their
tempers began to boil. 9 The wise
answered saying. If so we might
all run out.
Go buy some for yourselves so they
retraced their route.
10 He came while they were gone.
They thought things were all right.
The wise went with Him and the
door was locked tight.
11 When the other virgins returned they
cried, "Open for oil we've got." He
answered and said to them, 'Depart for I
know thee not.'
13 Watch carefully for you don't
know the day nor the hour
when the Son shall come in
glory and great power.
14 The Kingdom of Heaven is like a man

preparing for a trip he'd take.

He called his servants together saying,
'Investors of you I'll make.'
15 Unto one he gave five talents
another two and a third but one. Each
according to ability received.
Then his journey was begun.

16 He that received five talents
traded them for more.
He increased by five his talents.
He now had ten in store.
17 The one who was given two
doubled his also making four. 18
The third man dug a hole hiding his
in the earth's floor. 19 When their
Lord returned the servants all
appeared.
20 The first said, "I had five talents.
I added five for you I feared. 21
His Lord said, "Well done. You've
been faithful and good. I'll make
you a ruler over much.
You acted like you should.
22 The man who was given two said, "My
Lord, I now have four.
I knew you would be back so I
made you two more.
23 His Lord said, "Well done.
You've been faithful with these things.
I'll make you ruler over much.
Your joy will fly as if it had wings." 24
The man who received
one talent said. "I knew you as a hard man
collecting money
you hadn't worked for from
each operation you ran.
25 I was afraid and hid it in the earth.
I now return the same to you. 26

His Lord said, "Thou wicked
servant. My kind of man you knew.

27You should have invested my
money. so the interest I would receive.

28 Take therefore the talent from him.
I don't wish to be deceived.
Give it to the others.
29 To him who has it shall be given and
taken from he who has little.
30 From my presence he
shall be driven.
31 When the Son of Man shall come
with angels in all His glory
He shall set up his throne as
told in the Bible story.
32 All nations shall be gathered.
They'll be separated by God's Son.
As the shepherd divides
sheep from goats
33 He'll separate them one by one.
34 The King will say to those on His right
Ye blessed of my Father, come in. Inherit
the kingdom prepared for you since the
world's foundation did begin.

35 I was without food and hungry.
You came and gave me meat.
I thirsted and you gave me drink; 36
naked and ye clothed me neat.
I was sick and felt terrible.
You came over and visited me. I
was in prison and you came until
they set me free.
37-39 The righteous shall
answer saying. "When did we
do these things?"
40 "When you did them to a brother you
did them to me, your King." 41 He'll
say to those on his left.

240

"Depart to eternal fire.
to the place prepared for the devil for
you lived for your own desire. 42 I
hungered and you gave not.
I thirsted and was denied.
43 I was a stranger and you left me; naked
and you denied a hide.
I was sick, in prison and lonely. You
failed to give of your time.
44 Then shall they answer saying.
"When did we do this crime?" 45
Then shall he answer them,
"Verily I say to thee
if you did it not to your brothers then
ye did it not to me.
46 These shall then go away into everlasting
fire.
The righteous to eternal life.
There's nothing they'll desire.

The Gospel According to
Mark
Chapter I

1 The beginning of the gospel of
Jesus Christ, the Son of God.
2 As written by Isaiah the prophet
who lies beneath the sod.
Behold, I send my messenger before
your face today
This messenger is the one
who shall prepare the way.
3 This voice is from the wilderness.
He will to people state: Make
ready the way of the Lord.
Make his pathways straight. 4
John came, who preached the
remission of sin.

Baptizing in the wilderness all
those who were clean within.

5 All people from in and around
Judea to the baptizer went.
All those who came from Jerusalem;
those whom God had sent; Went to
him to be baptized.
Into the Jordan they stepped in. They
went to him and to God each one
confessing sin.
6 John wore a leather girdle and
was clothed with camel's hair.
He ate locusts and wild honey.
This was his daily fare.
7 He preached that one was coming who
was mightier than he
That to tie or untie his shoes he,
John, was unworthy.
8 He said, I baptized with water.
That's all. I do not boast.
He that comes after me shall
baptize with the Holy Ghost.
9 Then Jesus reached the river
from Nazareth he came.
He was baptized in the river, The
Jordan was its name.
10 Jesus came up from the water and
saw the heavens split apart. A dove
descended from above and straight to him
did dart. 11 A voice from heaven said
when the dove was done: I am well
pleased with you. You are my beloved
Son. 12 Immediately
the Spirit drove Jesus to the wilderness. 13
For forty days and nights Satan tempted
without success He was in the wilderness
where wild beasts did stare. Angels
ministered unto him. Temptations were still

there.

14 After John was delivered up Jesus
preached in Galilee

15 The time is fulfilled. God's kingdom is at
hand so repent, all of thee.

16 Walking by the Sea of Galilee he
saw Simon and Andrew.
Casting nets for they were fishermen
through and through. 17 Jesus said,
Come follow me and I will make you
fishers of men

18 They left their nets and followed him
never to return again.

19 Then he saw James, son of Zebedee
with his brother John.
They were mending their nets
before the day was gone.

20 He called and said follow me.
Immediately they left all.
They left their father with servants and
followed Jesus call.

21 They went straight to Capernaum.
When it was the sabbath day He
entered into the synagogue and
taught people the way.

22 Astonished by his teachings for
he taught with authority not as the
scribes who read
as a matter of formality. 23
There in the synagogue a man
cried out to him.
He was possessed by a spirit which
left him rather grim.

24 The spirit said what do you want,
Jesus thou Nazarene?
I know you're the Holy One who
can make all things clean. 25 Jesus
rebuked him saying. Be quiet.

Come out of him now.

26 The unclean spirit crying loudly
then came out somehow.

27 They were all amazed.
What's this?, they asked each other He
teaches with authority
and the spirit left our brother.

28 All around Galilee the report of him
went out. It was the talk of the town and in
regions round about.

29 He came out of the synagogue
with James and John there too.
They entered the house of Simon
and Andrew.

30 Simon's mother-in-law was sick and
to him they did call.

31 He took her hand and healed her and
ministered to them all.

32 When the sun had set they
brought sick to him there.
All who were possessed by demons were
carried for his care.

33 Everyone in the city came
and gathered at the door.

34 He healed many sick and
cast out demons as before.

He wouldn't let demons speak nor
utter yet a word
Because they knew who he was so they
could not be heard.

35 In the early morning he arose from
where he had stayed.
He went into a desert place and that
is where he prayed. 36 Simon and
those with him followed him way
out there. 37 They found him and
said people look for your care.

38 He said they'd go to the nearby towns
so in them he could preach. This is the

reason that he came.
He had need to others reach. 39 He
went into the synagogues
throughout all of Galilee Preaching and
casting out demons for he loved to set
men free.
40 A leper came to him and
kneeling down was seen.
He said Jesus, if you will you can
make me clean.
41 Being moved with compassion Jesus
stretched forth his hand And touching
him said
be clean and feel just grand.
42 The leprosy left immediately and he
was made clean.
43 Jesus said go your way and
quickly leave this scene.
44 Don't say a word to any man who
might see you as you go. Go straight
and find a priest. To him your
cleanness show.
Offer as a testimony throughout all
the land Those things which are
listed
as sacrifices by Moses' command.
45 He went out and began to
publish it all about.
Too pleased to keep silent he
began to shout.
He said so much that Jesus could no
longer enter the city.
In the desert they came seeking Jesus'
pity.

Chapter 2

1 After a while he entered into
Capemaum once more. The news
was noised about that he was
beyond the door.
2 Many gathered around him,
until there was no room; no
room around the door but
unto them he talked.
3 One man with palsy was carried
by four who with him walked.
4 They could not get near the door
so to the roof they went.
And cut a hole in it
and lowered this helpless gent. 5
Then Jesus, seeing their faith,
which was great, you see
Said to the man on the stretcher,
Thy sins are forgiven thee.
6 Some scribes in the house
reasoned within their heart. 7
Why does he blaspheme?
Only God makes sin depart. 8
Jesus knew their hearts and
asked why did they talk?
9 It easier to forgive sins or say take
up your bed and walk?
10 The Son of man can do both
and just so you shall know
11 I tell this man, Arise, take
thy bed. Now go!
12 The man arose, picked up his bed and
walked out of the door.
All were amazed and praised God
saying. We never saw this before.
13 He went out by the seaside and
the multitudes soon came.
He didn't turn them away but
taught them in his name. 14 As
he passed Alphaeus' son, Levi,
was sitting at his trade.
He said to him, Follow me.

Levi joined the parade.
15 While he and his disciples ate
in Levi's house one day Publicans
and sinners joined in
who had followed him that way.
16 When they saw that with publicans and
sinners Jesus ate
The scribes and pharisees came to
his disciples to start a debate.
They said your master ate with
publicans and sinners. Why?
17 Jesus said a physician is for
the sick or those about to die.
Those who are well have no need
and so they do not seek.
I didn't come to call the righteous, but
to the sinners and the weak
18 John's disciples and pharisees,
fasting, came to him to see
Why his disciples did not fast
while they fasted regularly.
19 Jesus said that they had the bridegroom
with them at last.
While He was with them they
had no need to fast. 20 The day
will come when He shall be
taken away.
They will, then join the fast.
They'll do it on that day.
21 Nobody patches an old garment with
new cloth to fit the hole.
It would shrink and tear loose.
They would not have reached
their goal
22 or puts new wine into old wineskins. If
they did, you know
as the wine aged the skins would burst and
leak and bring them woe.
Their wine would then be gone and

the old skins wasted too. They put
it into new wineskins so they'll
have some
when they're through.
23 They went on the sabbath through corn
fields which were near.
As they proceeded the disciples
began to pluck and eat an ear. The
pharisees asked Jesus,
Why do you allow them to Do on the
sabbath day what it is unlawful to do? 25
He asked them, What did David do?
Maybe you didn't read. What
he and his men did when
there was a need.
26 He entered the house of God
when Abiather was high priest And
ate the priest's showbread and his
men did also feast.
27 Jesus said the sabbath was made for
man not the other way around. 28 The
Son of man is lord of the sabbath and his
ways are sound.

Chapter 3

1 He went to the synagogue and found a
man with a withered hand.
2 They watched to see if he would heal on
the sabbath in their land.
They wanted him to do it so
they could accuse of wrong.
3 He said to him with the withered
hand, Stand and come along.
4 He asked them, Is it lawful
on the sabbath to do harm or good?
To save a life or kill one?
but they were silent where they stood.
5 Sorry that hearts were so hard his

gaze at them angrily bored He said,
stretch forth your hand and his hand
was restored.
6 The pharisees went straight to the
Herodians with their ploy. They took
counsel and they plotted how this one
they might destroy.
7 Jesus and his disciples left
and went down to the sea.
A great multitude followed them from
Judaea, Jerusalem, and Galilee. 8 They
came from beyond the Jordan and
Idumaea, Sidon, and Tyre.
The multitude heard what he did.
To see him was their desire.
9 He commanded his disciples to get
into a boat and wait because the crowd
might throng him for their numbers
were so great.
10 He had healed many of
plagues, leprosy and such
Others with these diseases
pressed to receive his touch.
11 Unclean spirits who'd entered men
when Jesus they did see
cried out and fell down before him saying
the Son of God art thee.
12 He told them to hold their tongues and
not to make him known.
13 He called some to a mountain and
they went to him alone.
14 He appointed twelve to stay and
learn what he had to teach When
they were ready he'd send them into
the world to preach.
15 He wanted them to have authority over
demons to cast them out.
16 He told Simon he would be Peter, a
rock, without a doubt.

17 Sons of thunder were James and
John, each was Zebedee's son 18 He
took Philip. Andrew,
Bartholomew and he also
called Simon.
James, Matthew, and Thomas went
with him that day
19 Thaddaeus too, and Judas Iscariot
who would Christ betray.

He took them with him and entered a
house to have a seat
20 But the multitudes reassembled so
quickly they couldn't eat
21 When his friends heard of it they
went to drag him inside. They said
he was beside himself. There was
no place he could hide.
22 The scribes from Jerusalem
came saying Beelzebub has he And
by the Prince of demons he casts
others out, you see.
23 He called them unto himself and
taught them, without a doubt.
By parables he asked them, How
could Satan cast Satan out? 24 If a
kingdom should fight itself
that kingdom couldn't stand.
25 If a house is divided against itself how
can that house be grand?
26 If Satan fights against himself and
must against himself defend And is
divided he can't stand and he must
have an end.
27 Nobody can enter
and steal the possessions of the strong
Unless he binds the strong man first taking
things which to him belong.
28 Verily, verily I say to you

forgiveness is the Savior's theme.
Their sins shall be forgiven them and
also when they blaspheme.
29 He who blasphemes the Holy Spirit
shall forever retain this sin.
30 They say the Holy Spirit has an
unclean spirit within.

31 His mother and brothers came,
stood together and for him sent. 32
The multitudes said they were there.
Their message to him went.
33 He answered and asked them this. Who
are my brethren and mother?
34 He looked around him
saying behold you are my
mother and brother.
35 Whoever does the will of God, the
one who sent me here Is the one who is
my brother and sister
and also my mother so dear.

Chapter 4

1 As Jesus began to teach by the lake people
gathered more and more.
He entered a boat and sat down to teach
as they stayed on the shore.
2 He taught them in parables. By
his teachings he did lead. 3 He
told them this parable
that a farmer went to sow seed.
1 Some fell along the path and birds
that seed did swallow.
2 Some fell in rocks and sprang up
but the soil was shallow.
3 The sun came up and killed them
because roots were shallow there.
4 Some fell among the thorns choking
them so they couldn't bear.

5 Other fell on good ground where
it sprouted and grew to be old
multiplying thirty and sixty times, and
some a hundred fold.
6 Jesus said this to all of them,
If any of you has an ear pay attention and
listen so he can do as well as hear.
7 Later after most of the crowd
took their stuff and went
The crowd remaining there asked
what the parable meant. 11 Jesus
said God's kingdom's secret has
been given to you.
It's spoken in parables to those without so
it is hidden from their view. 12 Ever seeing
and never perceiving and ever hearing
they'll be.
They won't understand, however, or
they might turn and hear and see. 13
Jesus said if you don't understand how
can you other parables know?
14 The farmer sows the word.
15 Hearers listen but never grow.
Satan comes before it gets to the heart and
steals the word away.
16 Word in rocky places was received by
all who heard that day.
17 In the rocks they have few roots, but
for a while they're humble.
With tribulation and persecution
because of the word they stumble.
18 Others who hear the word are
those which are sown among the
thorns.
19 They are soon drawn away, however,
by riches and what it adorns.
20 Those that were sown on good
ground were heard by those
who were bold.

They hear the word and bear fruit, some
thirty, sixty, and a hundredfold.

21 He then said to them,
Does any hide a light Under
a basket or a bed and puts it
out of sight?
22 Nothing is hidden now or in the
future will stay that way.
Nothing has been made secret which
won't be revealed that day. 23 If any
has ears pay attention to what is said,
you see.
Take care what your hear.
As you judge your judgment will be.
25 He that has much more
shall be given each day.
He that has little shall have what he
has taken away.
26 So it is with God's kingdom.
He said, Know this, indeed.
As if a man should go on the
earth and cast seed.
27 Then sleep and rise night and
day without a single care And
leaves the seed
alone to grow and bear.
28 The earth bears fruit of itself.
The plants get into gear. First the
blade then the ear and the grain
within the ear.
29 When the fruit is ripe and
the man himself wants some
He comes and cuts the grain.
Harvest time has come.

Mark 4: 1-14

1 As Jesus began to teach by the lake people
gathered once more.

He got into a boat and sat and
they stayed on the shore. 2 He
taught them in parables. By His
teachings did He lead.
3 In parables He told them that a farmer
went to sow seed.
4 Some fell along the path
and the birds the seed did swallow. 5
Some fell in rocks and sprang up. but the
soil was too shallow.
6 The sun came up and killed them
because the roots were shallow there 7
Some fell among the thorns which choked
them ere they could bear.
8 Other seed fell on good ground.
It grew up to be old.
It multiplied thirty and sixty times.
Some a hundred fold.
9 Jesus said to all of them.
If any has an ear.
Let him pay attention now and
listen so he can hear.
10 Later when most of the crowd
took their stuff and went
the twelve and others asked what
the parable meant.
11 Jesus said, Secret of God's Kingdom
has been revealed to you
but in parables to those without to hide
things from their view.
12 Ever seeing and never
perceiving and ever hearing they'll be.
They won't understand, however, or
they might turn and hear and see. 13
Jesus asked, If you don't know this
how can you let others know? 14
The farmer sows the word.
Some, like the seed, are quick to grow.

Psalm 128

In distress I called out to God.
The Lord heard the cry from my lung.
Deliver my soul from lying lips and
from the wicked deceitful tongue. What
shall be given the false tongue?
What shall be done to it?
Arrows of the mighty with hot coals of
juniper shall make a hit.
Woe is me while in Mesech
if I stay in Kedar's tents any more. My
soul's with him who hates peace.
I seek peace but they're for war.

Bibliography

Buckmaster, Henrietta, Paul: A Man
Who Changed The World.
New York. Toronto.London:
McGraw-Hill Book Company, 1965

Topical Index

Arbor Day:
Tree A...7C

Christmas:
Angelic Beings..................................62A
Candle, A...65A
Christmas Donkey.............................57A
Christmas Wish to the School A 15D
Elves...12D
Innkeeper, The...................................32A
Jesus, The Promised One...................61A
Jesus Tomb...64A
Joseph and Mary................................65A
Journey of the Wise Men....................42A
Mistletoe..14D
My Savior and Christmas.....................8A
No Room at the Inn............................34A
Outlooks on Christmas.......................64A
Real Santa, The...................................7A
Reindeer...13D
Rudolph...2D
Santa and His Gifts..............................8C
Santa Claus...13D

Mother's Day:
Mother's Day......................................1D

Prayers:
Prayer-Dedication..............................33A
Prayer for Guidance............................66A

Santa Filing the Stockings..................14D
Sheep...65A
Snowman, A.......................................12D

Shepherds...66A
Stable, The...64A
Straw..13D
Star of Bethlehem...............................65A
Wise Men Watched.............................62A
Wreath, The.......................................12D
"Xmas"..7A

Easter:
Easter Message-An.............................42A
Empty Tomb.......................................44A
Jesus Tomb...64A

Fall:
Fall Leaves...18D
Leaves..3D
One Day Too Long.............................19D
Season Changes.................................20D

Father's Day:
Father's Day..2D

Halloween:
Halloween Night..................................9D

Heaven:
Streets of Gold....................................66A
Heaven...11A

Prayer to be Worthy............................33A
Prayer to keep Satan Away................10A
Take Us Home....................................66A

Salvation:
Joy of Salvation.................................41A

249

One Day Too Long.............................19D
Plan of Salvation..............................37A
Salvation and Sharing........................ 37A

Songs: Paraphrased:
Thy Boundless Love to Me (Paraphrased)
....69A

Sorrow & Death:
A Christian's View of Death................ 6A
Comfort verse.. 9A
Death..7A
Death of a Christian........................... 11A
Grief that Overwhelms........................36A
Looking Forward To Death.................. 9A
A Loved One's Death......................... 43A
Loss of A Loved One........................... 2A
Sorrow and Death..............................33A
A Time for Everything........................34A
Sorrow's Depth..................................34A
A Spot in the Cemetery.....................70A
When Death Overtakes
Why Me?... 67A

Thanksgiving:
Thanksgiving....................................... 1D
Turkey Day...5D

Valentine:
Daughter.. 11D

Weather:
Lightning..9D
Seasonal Changes...............................20D
Snow Showers....................................20D
Snowflake, A......................................20D
Snow Outside My Window.................. 7D
Thunderstorm...................................... 4D

INDEX

Abraham..............................29A

Absent From the Body (See: Loss of a Loves one)..........................2A

Acts.................................... 1E

The Adventure of Gaw..................... 17D

Airplanes.............................4D

Alligator, An.........................3B

Alligator, The........................ 1B

America, Mission.....................59A

American, A Proud.....................43A

American, Resort Missions.............. 59A

Angelic Beings.......................62A

Angels Unaware...............................58A

Anger............................... 4D

Anhinga...............................4B

Ant..................................3B

Atheism..............................71A

Athletes, Fellowship of Christian
.... 40A

Attitudes............................. 1D

Baby, A New..........................5D

Back, Mountains to Valleys &.............17A

Bald Eagle, The........................1C

Be Troubled Not, Heart..................... 23A

Bear, A grizzly.........................3B

Bear Grizzly...........................3B

Bears, Denning........................ 4B

Bears, Three..........................14D

Best, My.............................. 33A

Big Fish, The..........................18A

Big Fisherman, Peter: The................. 19A

Birds, A Flock of................................ 55A

Bi-vocational Pastor.....................36A

Black Skimmer, The.....................3B

Blessed are They.....................34A

Blood............................... 7A

Book.................................7D

Boundless Love to Me, Thy............... 69A

Brother Of The Prodigal Son, The
.... 5A

Brown Pelican, The............................ 1B

Bubble Bursts, When The..................17A

Bursts, When The Bubble...................17A

Bus Ministry............................ 13A

Bus Ministry, Starting a..................... 69A

Candle, A.............................65A

Cemetery, A Spot in the..................... 70A

Changes, Seasonal...........................20D

Child, Once I Was a.......................... 18D

Christian, The.......................................10A

Christianity & Discouragement 16A

Christian Athletes, Fellowship of
.... 40A

Christian Pathway...............................15A

Christian Service................................15A

Christian Students..............................44A

Christian's View of Death, A............... 6A

Christian Witness, The........................14A

Christian Donkey.................................57A

Christmas Tree.................................... 2C

Christian Wish to the School, A 15D

Church Attendance........................... 12A

Citizens, Senior................................. 15D

Clouds Of life, The............................18A

Conversion...................................... 12A

Comfort Verse...................................9A

Communication...................................16D

Commitment, Total............................ 55A

Corinthians 13; Love, First.................. 1E

Courage of Jesus, The........................ 67A

Crawfish....................................... 6C

Samaritan Story, The Good............. 35A

Santa.................................3D

Santa and His Gifts.............................8C

Crises in the Everglades (See: Everglades: Piney Woods)......................................1C

Crow, The...3B
Cure.. 56A
Daily Prayer...2A
Dangerous Wastes............................... 7C
Date (See "Victim").......................... 10D
Daughter.. 11D
Death...7A
Death, A loved One's.........................43A
Death, Looking Forward To............... 9A
Death of a Christian........................... 11A
Death Overtakes Me, When............... 18A
Death, Sorrow and............................33A
Decision, Jonah's.............................. 63A
Dedication Prayer.............................33A
Denning Bears.....................................4B
Depth, Sorrow's................................ 34A
Deep Sorrows.....................................58A
Devil At Work, The........................... 17A
Devil, Face to Face with the.............. 35A
Devil's Tool, The................................16A
Difference Between, Toad of Frog- The
.... 1
B
Disappearing Pencil............................. 9B
Discouragement..(See   "Devil's
      Tool")..................................... 16A
Discouragement-Christianity &..........16A
Discipleship....................................... 12A
Dive, Wrong....................................... 3D
Doctors, No Use for........................... 61A
Dog..9D
Dogging Our Footsteps......................37A
Donkey, Christmas............................ 57A
Dorothy..14D
Drug, A..15D
Eagle, The Bald....................................1C
Easter Message, An............................ 42A
Easy-He Never Said life Would be
....41A

Egret, The Greater..............................2B
Egret, The Snowy................................1B
Elves.. 12D
Embryo..4D
Empty Tomb......................................44A
Endangered Land, Everglades..............2C
Entry, Triumphal..............................41C
Ethic (Ideal), Work............................18D
Evaluation Day....................................8D
Everglades, Florida's Treasure............. 4C
Everglades, Endangered Land...............2C
Everglades: Piney Woods, The............ 1C
Everglades Story..................................2C
Everglades, A Time for...................... 34A
Evolution...2D
Face to Face with the Devil................ 35A
Fall Leaves..18D
Falling Star, A.....................................7D
Fall, One Day Too Long................... 19D
Family and Friends.................69A & 11D
Father's Day..1D
Fellowship of Christian Athletes 40A
Fellowship...6D
Ferocity.. 4D
First Corinthians 13-Love....................1E
Fish..4D
Fish, The Big......................................18A
Fisherman, Peter: The Big................. 19A
Flock of Birds, A............................... 55A
Florida's Treasure, Everglades............. 4C
Footsteps, Dogging Our.................... 37A
Forest.. 3D
Fragile: Human Being........................43A
Friend, A..19D
Friends, Family and...............69A & 11D
Friend or Foe.....................................20D
Friends and Family.................69A & 11D
Friendship..19D
Frog; The Difference Between

Everglades, North Protecting.................121
    Toad or...102
Gallinule, The.......................................109
Gates of Pearls (See: Seeking
    Entrance to Heaven.....................248
Gar, The...108
Genesis 1-15...198
Getting Older, Thoughts About............132
Gifts for a Promotion...........................131
Girl, It's a...135
God, Leaning On.....................................67
God's Call...21
God's Handiwork..................................116
God's Unfailing Plan.............................19
Good Samaritan Story, The.................55 G
ossip, A......................................130,138Go
ssip..130,138Gos
siping, (See also - The Adventures
    of Gaw).......................................148
Great Commission, The..................25,26
Great Commission, (see Savior's

    Love).......................................25,26
Greater Egret, The...............................108
Grebe, The Pied Billed...................... 109
Geen Heron..111
Grief that Overwhelms...........................56
Grizzlies, Step Poem............................116
Grizzly, A................................110,111,116
Grizzly Bear............................110,111,116
Grizzly Looking for a Meal...110,111,116
Gull, The Sea..108
Guppy, A...110
Halloween Night....................................136
Handiwork, God's.................................116
Handwriting...128
Hard to Say...18
Hawk, The Red-Shouldered..................109
Heart Be Troubled Not.....................39,61
Heaven, Seeking Entrance to.............248
Heaven's Scene..17

He Never Said Life Would
    be Easy...63
Heron, Green..111
Home Missions..88
Hospital Remembrance.........................123
How Much Love?.....................................91
Hershey, Land of..................................146
Human Being, Fragile.............................66
Hungry Sparrow....................................133
If My People..53
I Love to Tell Christ's Story..............97
Improving Ourselves..............................60
Individuals, Unique................................66
Influence...60
Inn, No Room at the...............................53
Innkeeper, The..51
Inspector..135
It's a Girl...135
Jesus..39
Jesus Came to Set Men Free.................84
Jesus Do? What Would.........................104
Jesus – The Courage of..........................98
Jesus Heals...85
Jesus' Love..25
Jesus, The Promised

    One..90
Jesus Tomb..94
Jesus, Treatment of.................................69
John 1: 1-2:24.......................................206
John the Baptist.......................................20
John the Baptist
    (Mattew 3) 20,155
Jonah...15
Jonah's Decision......................................93
Joseph and Mary.....................................96
Journey of the Wise Men.........................64
Joy of Salvation......................................62
Juice Lab..131
Seeking Entrance to Heaven................248

Just An Ordinary Tree...........................11
Kangaroo, The.......................................109
Kissimmee..120
Kite, The Swallow-Tailed...................110
Lab, Life in the...............................131,139
Lab Student....................................128,131
Land of Hershey..................................146
Lazarus, The Rich Man &....................16
Leader, Spiritual...................................56
Leaning On God....................................67
Leaves...127
Leaves, Fall...150
Let Not You Heart be Troubled 61
Liar, A Notorious............................. 147
Life in the Lab....................................139
Life, The Clouds Of..............................31
Life, Purpose of....................................83
Life Would be Easy-He Never
      Said..63
Lightning...137
Lion, A...110
Loneliness...129
Looking Forward To Death.................20
Lord's Temple of the...........................59
Loss of A Loved One...........................11
Love, I Corinthians 13........................153
Love? ,How Much.................................91
Loved One's Death, A..........................65
Love, Savior's...............................84,101
Love to Me, Thy Boundless.............101
Luke   1:1-55.......................................222
Manger, A...92
Mankind in the Web of Life................111
Man's Plan Foiled................................23
Mark 1:1-4:29.......................................241
Mark 4:1-14....................................246,247
Matthew- The Book Of.......................155
Matthew 3..205
Matthew 26:1-51..................................193

(Alternate reading).........................……
Matthew 16:1-25:46............................224
Me, When Death Overtakes.................52
Meeting Needs.......................................60
Men Watched, Wise...............................91
Metamorphosis.....................................128
Message, An Easter...............................64
Miracles...32
Miracles (John 2:1-10).......................222
Mission America..............................87,88
Missions America, Resort................87,88
Missions, Home...............................87,88
Mistletoe..144
Molecules..129
Monkey..112
Moon And Sun.....................................129
Mother's Day.......................................124
Motivation, Inner.................................139
Mountains......................................31,129
Mountains to Valley and Black............31
My Best..52
My Country and Christmas.................116
Needs, Meeting.....................................60
New Baby, A...131
Nobody Special...................................135
No God?..53
No Room at the Inn...............................53
No Use for Doctors...............................90
Notorious Liar-A.................................147
Ocean's Edge.......................................130
Oh ugliness of Garbage Piles.............117
Once I Was a Child.............................149
One Day Too long...............................150
Others, Treatment of...........................104
Our Samaria...101
Ourselves, Improving...........................60
Outlooks on Christmas..........................94
Over Sin, Victory..................................62
Overtakes Me, When Death.................32

Overwhelms-Grief that......................36A
Paperback..4D
Pastor, Bi-vocational.........................36A
Paul...44A
Pathway, Christian.............................15A
Pelican, The Brown..............................1B
Pelican, The White...............................1C
Pencil-Disappearing
   (Use with trick).........................9D
Pentecost...35A
People, If My......................................33A
Peter: The Big Fisherman...................19A
Peter's Testimony (See "Three
   Thousand Came and
   "Pentecost").........................10A
Philippians 4:4-9................................39E
Philippians 4:8 (two versions)............39E
Philippians 4:9...................................39E
Plan of Salvation...............................37E
Pied Billed Grebe, The........................2B
Piney Woods, The Everglades..............1C
Place to Come Back To-A....................4A
Plan of Salvation...............................37A
Pothole Power.......................................6C
Prayer, Dedication..............................33A
Prayer, Rededication.......................... 68A
Prayer for Guidance........................... 66A
Prayer to be Worthy........................... 33A
Prayer to keep Satan Away................. 10A
Proof of God.......................................10A
Promised One-Jesus, The....................61A
Promises..9D
Proud American, A.............................. 43A
Purpose of Life...................................56A
Psalm 104..2E
Rainbow...59A
Rainbow Rope (Use with
   magic trick)........................... 9D
Real Santa, The.................................... 7A
Recycle... 7C
Red Shoulder Hawk-The...................... 2B
Rededication Prayer............................68A

Red Wolf...4B
Reefer-A.. 3D
Reindeer.. 13D
Rely on God's Word........................... 18A
Requirements of a Writer.....................2D
Resort Missions America................... 59A
Retire, Time to..................................... 8D
Retirement Activities.......................... 10D
Retirement..5D
Rich Man & Lazarus-The.....................1A
Romans 1:1-13...................................42E
Romans 1:10-2:13..............................43E
Room, No at the inn............................34A
Rope, Rainbow (Use with
   magic trick)........................ 9D
Rudolph..2D
Rumor...10D
School, A Christmas Wish to............. 15D
Spawning Salmon.................................4B
Salvation and Sharing........................ 37A
Salvation, Joy of.................................41A
Samaria, Our.......................................68A
Seeking Entrance to Heaven...............11A
Senior Citizens................................... 15D
Serpent, The..71A
Samaritan Story, The Good................ 35A
Santa.. 3D
Santa and His Gifts.............................. 8C
Santa Filing the Stockings..................14D
Santa, The Real.................................... 7A
Satan, Alive and Well.......................... 8A
Savior's Love.......................................57A
School, A Christmas Wish to the 15D
Science Student, A............................... 3D
Sea Gull, The....................................... 2B
Seasonal Changes...............................20D
Set Men Free, Jesus Came To............ 56A
Sharing, Salvation and.......................37A
Sheep...65A
Shepherds..66A
Shouldered Hawk, The Red..................2B
Showers, Snow....................................20D
Sin in Our Lives..................................70A

I Love to Tell Christ's.............................97
Sunday School......................................103

Sorrow...125

Sinner, A..
Skunks...149
Sunday School......................................103
Sinner, While I Was Yet a..................49
Sin-Victory Over.....................................62
Skimmer, The Black....................109
Snail, The..108
Snake, A..107
Snowflake..129
Snowflakes......................................129,153
Snowman, A...141
Snow Outside My Window.................133
Snow Showers....................................133,153
Snow Egret, The..................................108
Solution, The...18
Sorrows, Deep.......................................86
Sorrow and Death..................................52
Sorrow's Depth......................................54
Sparrow, Hungry...................................133
Spawning Salmon.................................116
Special, A Tree.......................................81
Spider, The..110
Spiritual Leader......................................56
Spoonbill, The.......................................109
Spot in the Cemetery-A.......................103
Stable, The..95
Star, A Falling..134
Star of Bethlehem..................................95
Starting a Bus Ministry........................102
Straw...142
Step Poem, Grizzlies.............................116
Storm, The...127

Story, The good Samaritan...................53
Streets of Gold..97
Stress, Treatment for..............................32
Student, Lab...128
Student, A Science...........................128,145
Students...128,145
Students, Christian............................67,145

Student Success.....................................145

Summer and Winter...............................127
Success, Student....................................145

Sun, The...127
Sun-Moon And.....................................129
Swallow-Tailed Kite, The....................110
Take Us Home...98
Teachers...129
Teacher's Prayer...............................93,129
Teenager...128
Temple of the Lord's...............................59
Tenth Anniversary................................136
Thanksgiving...124
There, You Were......................................60
They, Blessed Are...................................54
Things Go Wrong, When........................30
This Land Was Ruined by
    You and Me......................................116
Thoughts About Getting Older............132
Treatment of Others.............................104
Threat to Tiger Creek...........................118
Three Bears...144
Thunderstorm..130
Thy Boundless Love to Me..................101
Tiger Creek, Threat to..........................118
Time for Everything, A...........................53
Time to Retire..134
Timothy-
    I Timothy 1:1-6:21...........................212
    II Timothy 1-4..................................218
Toad of Frog; The Difference
    Between..107
Tool, The Devil's.....................................30
Tomb, Empty..66
Total Commitment...................................82
Treasure, Everglades; Florida's...........117
Treatment for Stress................................32
Treatment of Jesus..................................69
Tree, A...121,133,134
Tree, A Special.................................81,121,133
Tree in my Yard, The.........................133,134
Tree, Christmas.....................................114
Triumphal Entry......................................63
Troubled, Heart Be Not.....................39,61
Troubled Waters....................................107
Turkey Day..131

Turtle, the...107
Unique Individuals..................................66
Unequally Yoked..................................102
Unkind Word, An................................138
Valleys, Mountains to and back........31
Verse for a Wedding Card.................131
Victim.. 139
Victory Over Sin..................................62
Vocational Pastor, Bi..........................57
Water..138
Waters, Troubled.................................107
Wastes, Dangerous..............................121
Web of Life, Mankind in the...............111
Wedding Card, Verse for a..................131
Wetland Heritage........................119,120
Wetlands......................................119,120
What Would Jesus Do?.......................104
When Death Overtakes Me...................32
When My Eyes Shall Close (See:
Forward to Death)...............................20
When The Bubble Bursts.......................30
When Things Go Wrong........................30
When You Feel Discouraged...............101
When You Look in the Mirror............134
While I Was Yet a Sinner......................99
Why Me?..99
Winter, Summer and............................127
White Pelican, The..............................113
Witness, Christian................................26
Wind Through the Trees......................134
Wise Man, A.................................64,91,98
Wise Men, Journey of the..............64,91
Wise Men Watched..............................91
Wish to the School, A Christmas 145
Why Worry...31
Wolves, Red...112
Woods, The Everglades: Piney............113
Word, An Unkind.................................118
Word, Rely on God's.............................32
Work...148,150
Work Ethic.................................148,150

Work Ethic (Ideal)...............................150
Working For the Lord............................98
Work, The Devil At...............................31
Worry, Why...31
Worthy, Prayer to Be.............................52
Wreath, The..141
Writer, Requirements of a............125,126
Writer's Life, A.............................125,126
Wrong Dive..127
rong, When Things Go...........................30
Xmas"..18
A Yoked, Unequally.............................102
A You're a Grand Old Earth.................122
7C You Were There................................60

258

www.ingramcontent.com/pod-product-compliance
Lightning Source LLC
Chambersburg PA
CBHW051301120626
46547CB00015B/2046